The Italians of New York

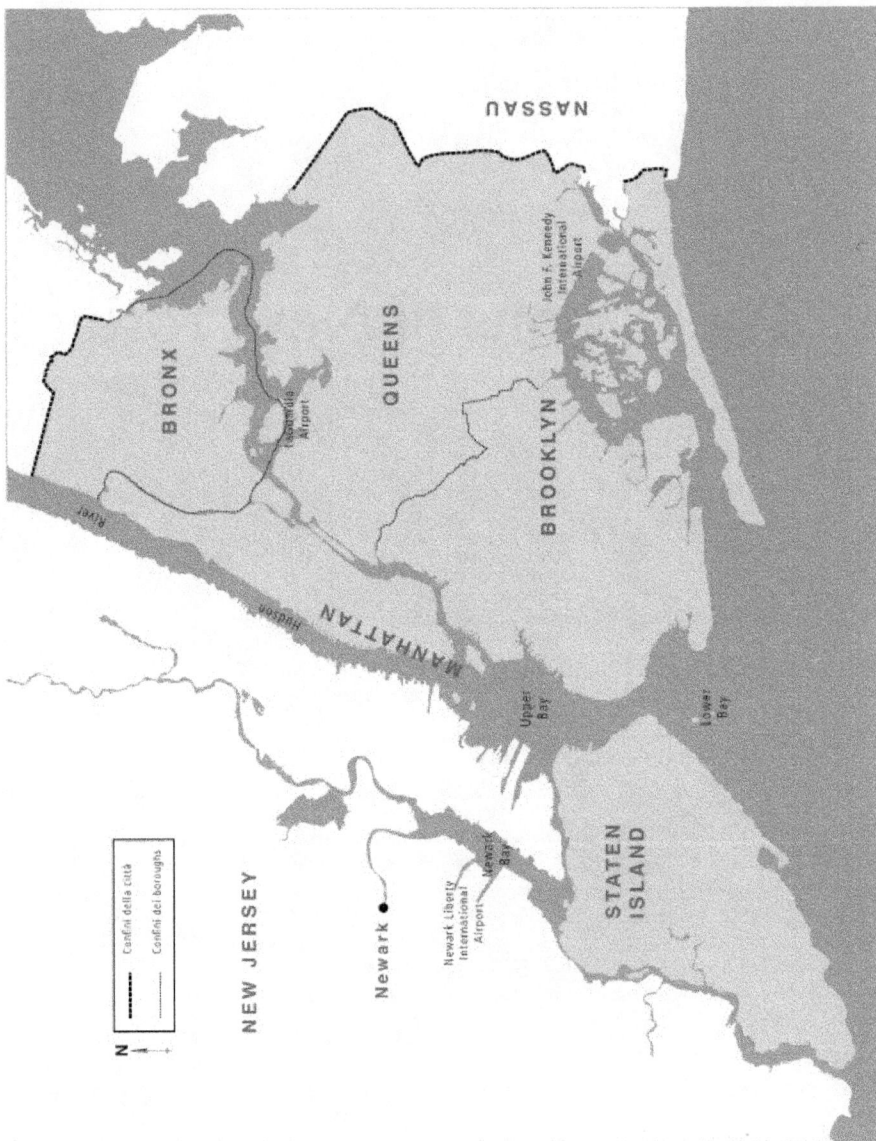

NEW JERSEY

Newark

Newark Liberty
International
Airport

Newark
Bay

STATEN
ISLAND

Lower
Bay

Upper
Bay

MANHATTAN

Hudson

River

BRONX

LaGuardia
Airport

QUEENS

BROOKLYN

John F. Kennedy
International
Airport

NASSAU

N

Confini della città
Confini dei boroughs

The Italians of New York

Maurizio Molinari

Translated by Louise Hipwell

VELLUM NAP NEW ACADEMIA
PUBLISHING

Washington, DC

English edition, © 2012 New Academia Publishing

Translated from *Gli Italiani di New York,* © 2011, Gius. Laterza & Figli

Translator, Louise Hipwell

Printed in the United States of America

Library of Congress Control Number: 2012944759
ISBN 978-0-9855698-0-8 paperback (alk. paper)

VELLUM   An imprint of New Academia Publishing

New Academia Publishing, LLC
P.O. Box 27420, Washington, DC 20038-7420
NEW ACADEMIA
PUBLISHING   www.newacademia.com - info@newacademia.com

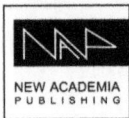

All photos by the author if not otherwise indicated.

To Eli, Chana, Dan, Naomi and their grandparents

Contents

Introduction

If you want to learn something about Italian creativity, come to New York. Here you'll find Italian pride at the Fifth Avenue Columbus Day Parade, the American patriotism of those who lost their lives at Ground Zero, the courage of firefighters and marines on the frontlines of the war against terrorism, a babel of dialects at the Arthur Avenue market, portrayals of social change in the writings of Gay Talese, stories of successful business ventures on the TV shows of Maria Bartiromo and Charles Gasparino, political passion in the battles of Mario Cuomo and Rudy Giuliani, creative imagination in the works of Gaetano Pesce, Renzo Piano and Matteo Pericoli, and provocation in the attire of Lady Gaga. You'll find the enthusiasm of the younger generations on the stages of Broadway, on the trading floors of Wall Street, in the classrooms of the Columbia University Business School, and also among the illegal immigrants who live precariously, surviving with the help of charitable priests and missionaries who run frontier churches, in those places where the mafia has not yet been defeated.

New York melds and amasses Italian identities from both the past and the present; not all of the more than 3.3 million Italians who live in New York share the same background and cultural perspectives. The top managers of the Midtown banks who arrived in the last twenty years are oriented towards XXI century life whilst, on Fresh Pond Road in Ridgewood, Sicilian style *panelle* are made following recipes that have been passed down for generations. In

Larry Gagosian's gallery, a temple of contemporary art on the very exclusive Madison Avenue, a forty year old Turinese woman works tirelessly to reinvent Pablo Picasso. In the laboratories of New York University, it is a female Italian doctor who is at the fore in the fight against cancer. In the classrooms of Rutgers University, twenty year old grandchildren and great grandchildren of immigrants who came through Ellis Island dedicate themselves to their textbooks to learn the language of Dante that wasn't taught to them at home.

What sets the Italians of New York apart is the energy with which they debate their Italian identity. An eighty year old reporter for *America Oggi* talks about the "Italian Americans" who meet up at countless religious holiday celebrations, clubs and associations. Each one of them defines him/herself in reference to a specific geographical place of origin, not a region but a city, town, village or even small suburban area. Researchers at the Calandra Institute prefer the term "American-Italians" because the characteristics they have acquired in their new homeland prevail over the heritage of the Old Country. On Mulberry Street, the last street of Little Italy on the Lower East Side, the use of the term "Italians" has declined and has been replaced with terms such as "Calabrian," "Sicilian," "Neapolitan," and "Apulian." US Navy Admiral Edmund Giambastiani considers himself "an American of Italian descent" as do police officers, firefighters and soldiers who safeguard national security. Top pharmaceutical manager Lamberto Andreotti and UN veteran Giandomenico Picco speak of having "a global identity with an Italian component." An ex-paparazzo who moved to Harlem from Rome points to the photographs on the wall of his restaurant, the sculptor Arturo Di Modica cites "the freedom to create what comes naturally to me without having to submit to the diktat of the galleries," for Lady Gaga it suffices to recall her grandfather.

It all culminates in a universe of voices and values where contradictions abound. In some families, parents forbid their children to see *The Godfather* because they consider it an expression of a very dangerous anti-Italian prejudice. This sentiment is in tune with the complaints expressed by the resolute activists of the NIAF (National Italian American Foundation) and the Italian Citizens Foundation against the TV series *The Sopranos* and the reality TV show *Jer-*

sey Shore which are accused of presenting an image of mobsters and tacky youths. For Anthony J. Tamburri, the director of the Calandra Institute, *Jersey Shore*, instead, helps to better understand what is occurring within the American "working class" and the American-ist Franco Zerlenga goes even further, explaining that "one of the distinguishing characteristics of the Italians of New York is that they don't lament their lot like others do." In the Bronx there are vendors who sell car tags displaying the words "Cosa Nostra." In the classrooms at Rutgers University there are people who willing to fight anyone who flings the insult "Mafioso" at a third genera-tion Italian, with their bare hands. As for politics, the elections for governor in New York put the spotlight on the duel between the Democrat Andrew Cuomo and the Republican Carl Paladino. As a result of their very different experiences of integration, Cuomo emphasized his complete integration into the American way and Paladino, instead, exalted his ethnic background. Beyond this, in some churches in Brooklyn mass is said in Italian for the older gen-erations and in English for the younger church-goers. But it could be said perhaps that food is the common ground that best summa-rizes the Italian cultural mosaic. Thousands of restaurants, super-markets, delis, butchers, bakeries, pizzerias, bars, coffeehouses and stands offer dishes and foods that describe the parabola of flavors that echo those of the immigrants themselves. It all began with the flavors of the original Italian dishes which were then modified by the impact of the ingredients that were actually accessible. Little by little restaurants went back to serving authentic Italian cuisine, or as in the case of Del Posto, the only Italian restaurant that can boast four stars from the New York Times, they moved a step further to include the best of American products and flavors.

From the church-goers on Saint Padre Pio Way in Williamsburg, to the customers at the "Festa di San Gennaro" in Little Italy, to the patrons of the rooftop bars of Manhattan, there is always an ele-ment that distinguishes the Italians of the Big Apple: the belief that if you give it your all, anything is possible. These days, the twenty year olds coming to study at the best universities or choosing to face the risks of life as illegal immigrants share an expression with the immigrants of the past: "we are hardworking people."

* * *

These pages are a real life snapshot of the Italians of New York that welcomes any traveler who arrives in 2011. The journey through faith, politics, people, the relationship with Italy, businesses and artistic endeavors, unravels describing the characters and the places that belong to them. We are delving into a world that, even though it is 6916 km from the Old Country, it belongs to us. It is part of every Italian, no matter where he/she is born or lives. It therefore challenges us because the stories that are told raise questions that Italy must confront. In a club in Brooklyn that takes its name from Partanna in Sicily, a group of patrons, all over age 60, say they are "saddened" every time they hear about "quarrels between national political leaders on Italian TV news" because they would like to see a "united" Italy where "there are shared interests and respect for state institutions." In Bensonhurst, Father Ronald Marino speaks about the young Italians who have chosen to live as illegal immigrants, risking deportation just to stay in America. In Flushing, the missionary Al Barozzi believes that the ministry of women is the way to revitalize the church, whilst the Bishop of Brooklyn and Queens Nicholas DiMarzio speaks of "anticlerical believers." The top manager of an important financial company on Madison Avenue reproaches the big Italian banks for having "abandoned Wall Street," leaving the playing field open to competing German and French banks. A young entrepreneur in the Luxury Goods sector attributes the lack of Italian investments in America to "a business culture that favors family members over managers" and "undervalues attention to the customer." A professor of Cinema at New York University blames the difficulties we have with winning Oscars on the structural weaknesses of our cinema. As for why Italy doesn't attract American investments? The response of many voices on the topic of the economy is unambiguous: "there is no certainty in the laws, labor laws penalize businesses and the divide between North and South is such that it makes development projects on a national scale very challenging." We must also mention the Italian passport holders who don't take advantage of the right to vote that is guaranteed to residents abroad and who instead express a lack of confidence in a nation whose political system is "too chaotic." Set on this backdrop of questions that beg answers, the two most frequent topics that come up in the reflections of those interviewed are: memory and language. Memory concerns the fact that during a period that lasted roughly a century, from 1870 to the end of the Seventies, Italy turned its back on millions of emigrant families and this was a factor that contributed to creating a rift filled with resentment, misunderstandings and the need to really know one another that must still mended. Language can be the key to putting things right but to do this, second, third and fourth generation immigrants must learn the language that wasn't taught to them at home because in their families dialect was often spoken. An enormous commitment must be made to teaching Italian in American schools.

* * *

As this is a snapshot of a vibrant and vivacious present-day community, difficult choices were inevitable and the selection of examples was guided by the desire to highlight novel elements. I know that if I were to write this book again, considering the pace at which New York changes, the story would probably be quite different. What comes out of this endeavor is a portrait of the largest Italian city in the United States: 3,372,512 residents who represent 16% of the 21.2 million inhabitants of the Greater New York area, or, in other words, the first ethno-linguistic group in the urban area that includes New York, Northern New Jersey and Long Island, which illustrates the sacrifices, challenges and successes of the more than 15.6 million Americans (the fifth largest national ethnic group) who in the year 2000 census wrote that they are originally from our country.

This book is the product of the encouragement of my editor who after the publication of the *Jews of New York* suggested I explore the Italian soul of the Big Apple, of the choice of *La Stampa* to have me as a correspondent in the USA and of three years of interviews, meetings with the people cited and visits to the places indicated. It was all made possible by the constant support of a small team of people whose diverse sense of "Italianness" reflects the reality of the city. I thank them for their time, passion and resources. Vincenzo Pascale, an Italianist at Rutgers University supported me in multiple ways, setting his wealth of valuable historical and human knowledge at my disposal. This complemented the very intimate

familiarity with the territory of the indefatigable Rita Bonura and
Antonio Barbera. The help of the young diplomats Maurizio Antonini and Giuseppe Favilli as well as the veterans of the Columbia
University Business School Marco Magnani and Carlo Mantica was
indispensable as I examined one of the capitals of the business community. A particular acknowledgement goes to Enzo Viscusi, the
New Yorker on whom Enrico Mattei chanced a bet, for helping me
overcome the most difficult obstacles. But without my wife Micol,
a constant source of discerning curiosity about the city in which we
reside, this book would never have been written.

Maurizio Molinari

New York, May 1, 2011

The Italians of New York

Note

Most of the accounts cited in this volume were documented by the author during personal interviews and conversations. In all other cases sources have been precisely indicated.

The People

The heroes of Ground Zero

The attack against America on September 11th 2011 left 2976 victims. 2752 of the victims perished at Ground Zero and 302 of them had Italian last names. Among these names were Esposito (4), Mauro (4), Giordano (3), Marino (3), Virgilio (2) and also others such as Abate, Acquaviva, Amato, Angelini, Benedetti, Calcagno, Cannizzaro, Colasanti, Difazio, Firoi, Galla, Ingrassia, Peroncino, Pugliese, Ragusa, Vitale and many many more. We must also add the Italian Americans with American last names to this list. After white Americans and Hispanics, Italians were the ethnic group that suffered the most losses during the assault on America by Bin Laden's 19 kamikaze terrorists aboard four commercial planes turned rudimental missiles. Among the 302 Italian victims left beneath the Twin Towers was Peter Ganci, the highest ranking firefighter and 33 years veteran of the New York Fire Department. That morning, at the age of 54, he was on the seventh floor of Fire Department headquarters in Brooklyn. At 8:46, from the window of his office, he saw American Airlines Flight 11 crash into the North Tower and he instinctively turned to Dan Nigro, chief of operations and said: "Look, an airplane just hit the World Trade Center." A few minutes later they were both on board a speeding car whisking them over the Brooklyn Bridge and bringing them close to the Towers. They decided to drive around the Towers looking up to establish what the real damage was. The most heavily damaged part of the North Tower was on its northern side where the impact occurred. Ganci set up a command post at the base of the South Tower and from there he gave orders by radio to the firefighters entering the North Tower. At 9:03 AM, the second blast occurred. United Airlines Flight 175 hit the South Tower. Ganci and Nigro were covered in dust, the radio transmitters were barely working, they got separated. "Chief Ganci," as everybody called him, knew that the South Tower was in worse condition than the North Tower. He started to direct traffic in front of World Trade Center 1 in an effort to divert as many people away as possible. At 9:59 AM the South Tower collapsed and he was almost buried, but when the dust settled he managed to get out with his team and get back to work. He told his men to "go north" while he did the opposite and went back south to the site of the collapse to create a command post from where he could find the survivors. The reports of the last minutes of his life describe him as "heading right back into the chaos." At 10:28 AM the North Tower collapsed and "Chief Ganci" died after having contributed to, along with his firefighters, the rescue of almost twenty thousand people. 343 firefighters lost their lives at Ground Zero, at least 64 of them came from Italian families. Among the survivors was Daniel Tardio, Capitan of Engine 7 out of Duane Street, who got to the base of the North Tower with his men where he saw "people jumping to their deaths." He wasn't able to sleep for the next three days.

There were thousands of people inside the Towers at the time of the impact and among them was Lucio Caputo, president of the Italian Wine and Food Institute. As on every other day he arrived at his office on the 78th floor of Tower 1 (North) at 8:00, he went up to the 107th floor to have breakfast at Club Windows on the World, and then came back down at 8:30. He was on a call to Italy when a blast caused him to drop the telephone receiver. The antique mirror that covered the whole wall in front of him moved a meter, the power went out, doors slammed, sirens screeched, so much dust fell from the ceiling that his green couch turned white. He thought it must have been a bomb just like in 1993. He tried to make a phone call but the lines were down. He went out into the corridor enveloped in a thick fog. There were pieces of marble on the ground, people crying and screaming. He learned of the impact of the plane. He waited for instructions from the Tower loudspeakers as always happened during a drill but no announcements came. He grabbed a torch, a bottle of water and a wet towel and began to run down the stairs. He had 78 floors in front of him. On the 40th floor he met firefighters coming towards him weighted down by masks, tubes and protective gear. He asked "what happened?" and the reply was "I don't know." He ran into a naked woman, her skin burned away, and into a blind man accompanied by his dog. All this occurred in a surreal stillness. On the way down the stairs there was fair play, no pushing, everybody let the injured get by. After an hour he got to the 23rd floor where two people in plain clothes pushed everyone into an air-conditioned room. Caputo, however, fearing the worst, in search of the emergency stairs he ran to the hall which was now unrecognizable strewn with broken glass, debris, marble and broken light fixtures, countless sheets of paper were drifting in the air. He got out and ran towards Broadway in time before the wave of smoke containing objects and human remains erupted after the collapse. "It's a memory that I will take with me for the rest of my life", he said, considering himself "lucky." Also among the survivors was Andrea Fiano, a correspondent for "Milano Finanza" with an office inside the Dow Jones headquarters: the ashes of human remains reminded him of what his father, a survivor of Auschwitz, had endured more than 50 years earlier.

In the days after the collapse the dead were counted. Among the dead there were 58 officers of the Police Department and the Port Authority and 9 of them had Italian last names: Amoroso, Cirri, D'Allara, Infante, Langone, Mazza, Morrone, Pezzulo and Vigiano. At each funeral the whole police department gathered. Sergeant Giovanni Porcelli from Raito in Campania, president of the Columbia Association, was there to lend a hand to the families of the victims. He brought the New York police officers of Italian descent together in the name of Joseph Petrosino whose brother lost a brother-in-law, a firefighter at Ground Zero. "On September 11 there were many Italian victims and the impact on their families was indeed great, the deaths brought suffering, financial disputes and the loss of homes. The impact of the tragedy continues still today" Porcelli explains, lingering on the fact that "groups of Italian Carabinieri and Police officers offered to help, but no one from the

Italian government did." The gesture of solidarity most profoundly felt by the officers of the Colombia Association was the initiative of their Californian "colleagues and compatriots" on Columbus Day that was celebrated about one month after the collapse of the Towers. That year the New York Police Officers were not able to march along Fifth Avenue in the customary parade that celebrates Italian heritage, and instead their banner was raised during the parade that took place in San Francisco.

In the case of the Fire Department, the tally of victims was so great that the new mayor Michael Bloomberg decided on January 1st 2002 to completely reshuffle it. The task fell to Nicholas Scoppetta, born in 1932, father from Amalfi and mother from Naples, who grew up in an orphanage in New York and became the Assistant District Attorney. He remembers his first days as Fire Commissioner as follows: "343 victims and only a few bodies found, there were funerals without remains, there was nothing inside the coffins, we supported each other like a big family, it was terrible, we had to rebuild everything." As a result, many of the survivors chose retirement, leaving their posts to the new recruits for whom Scoppetta revised duties and updated technology "to confront every eventuality, even the most terrible." Scoppetta too was at Ground Zero on Settember 11: "the firefighters were itching to get their assignments, in every base there were overlapping shifts, everyone we called answered, they all came, nobody hung back and many died because of it, like Chief Ganci."

September 11 continues to kill. 33 year old Joseph Graffagnino from Brooklyn, died on August 23rd 2007 along with 55 year old Robert Beddia from Staten Island. Almost six years after the attacks, they died in a fire that engulfed the Deutsche Bank. The bank was still standing but was about to be demolished after the necessary care to uncover any human remains had been taken. John Botte, instead, risked death. He was the officer to whom Commander Bernard Kerik delegated the task of taking thousands of photographs of what remained of the Towers. He worked tirelessly around the smoking rubble from September 12 until December 31 2001, inhaling toxic fumes that destroyed his lungs. "I felt like I was walking in hell, I was inhaling vapors that consumed me and the air was heavy, dense with ash, but I went to the very depths to document what had happened," he remembers showing a pride that has not been attenuated by his serious disease. In remembrance of the victims and heroes of Ground Zero both "Italian and of Italian descent" there is a stone plaque at the entrance to the Consulate on Park Avenue, positioned so that it can be seen by all who enter.

Police Plaza

The upturned red brick pyramid, 12 floors high, at number 1 Police Plaza, the headquarters of the New York Police Department, where George Grasso lived until 2009 when he served as the First Deputy Commissioner of the Department or Officer No. 2 of the city. New Yorkers know his name because after September 11 the head of police, Ray Kelly, assigned him the coordination of activities with the FBI. This meant having access to the keys of city-wide security beginning with the futuristic mega computers of the Real Time Crime Center on the eighth floor of Headquarters. In May of 2010 these computers led to the identification, within 53 hours, of the Pakistani-American terrorist Faisal Shahzad who had left a car bomb in front of the Miskoff Theatre in Times Square with the intent of massacring a group of children. George Grasso comes from a family originally from Basilicata and his Italian identity is linked especially to his grandfather Angelo born in 1897 on the outskirts of Melfi, who after having seen the horrors of World War 1 combat in the Alps, decided to leave everything behind to go to America. After two weeks at sea, he arrived at Ellis Island on March 16 1921 with 20 dollars in his pocket. He told the officials that interrogated him that he was "neither a criminal nor a polygamist" and when they allowed him to disembark he went to find a stepsister who lived at 2355 Atlantic Avenue in Brooklyn where he settled down. The first thing he did was search for a wife from Basilicata who shared his values. Maria Fabrizio was the one who impressed him. She was 9 years younger than him and he saw her on the street carrying a large bag of garbage and from that point he decided that a woman with such physical strength was the one for him. They married in 1922, had six children – four boys and two girls – and Angelo worked first as a brick-maker and then became a chef. He had a passion for wine and, just like they did in Melfi, he started to make wine, red wine, in the basement of his home on Rockaway Avenue. The aroma permeated the building, day and night. He was proud of it. He taught his children the value of loyalty, hard work and an appreciation for good food. He never went to a restaurant because he was convinced that better food was prepared at home. When his children grew up, got married and grandchildren were born, it was his red wine as well as his ravioli and linguine that became the backbone of family cohesion. His son George, father of the First Deputy Commissioner also named George, was a printer who came home every day at 5:00 PM on the dot to share a meal with his wife and children, all gathered around the table. For the young George the most anticipated moment of the week was Sunday morning, when all the men of the family got together, about 15 of them, to play "bocce" for the prize of a turkey and then they all ran home to eat homemade pasta with tomato sauce. George says, in his English that is peppered with Italian words, "For both my grandfather and my father, family was everything and they had a commitment to hard work because it was essential to support the family, nothing else was important." In 2006 George went to Melfi for the first time, he sought out and found his grandfather's elderly sister Luigina, who greeted him with a very friendly "What took you so long?" That day they shared homemade pasta and wine. But why did the grandson of the cook and the son of the printer choose to become a police officer? He replies, "Because I believe in the ideals of hard work and loyalty that were taught to me." To explain what he means by loyalty he recounts what used to happen on Christmas day: "in the Grasso household, Grandfather Angelo would dress up as Santa Claus and at 7:00 PM sharp he would come down the stairs from the second floor and deliver gifts to his grandchildren who had to be 'loyal to each other' or rather get on line one behind the other from the youngest to the oldest. If one of them cheated by giving the wrong age, Santa Claus would discover it and send the offender to the back of the line." Just like Grasso, Sergeant Porcelli focuses on the concept of "loyalty" to explain why "Italians from generation to generation wear the uniform and carry the badge." Porcelli reiterates that "loyalty means working hard to maintain ones family and to give security to ones relatives, without complaining about the effort that it entails." Having retired from the force Porcelli now works for security at American Express at 200 Vesey Street which is right next to Ground Zero. In his opinion "security can come from being in the police force just as being in the mafia, the difference being that in one it's legitimate and in the other it's not." Many families have been split between the two loyalties, there are police officers with brothers in the mob and vice versa and both share a reciprocal respect as can happen between "feuding relatives." There are "many examples of this, one only has to think of the Italian-American soldiers who landed in Sicily to fight against their brothers who had joined the fascists." Grasso reiterates that "if we count the number of Italians in uniform and those involved in organized crime we realize that there are many more of the first rather than the second." In fact Italians are the largest group within the police force, after the Irish. Both Grasso and Porcelli agree that "jobs in the police force and in the fire services are the most sought after professions by immigrants because they permit rapid integration." Porcelli adds, "The integration of Italians into the fabric of life in New York City owes much to the silver badge." This brings us to the importance of Joe Petrosino, the police officer from Campania who was the first to bring Italians to breach the circle of silence that protected members of the Black Hand, and who today is still the only New York police officer to have perished abroad – he was killed while on assignment in Palermo in 1909. The piazza that bears his name is situated at the point where Lafayette and Spring Streets merge, in the heart of old Little Italy, where before him mafia clans led by Vito Cascio Ferro, the godfather of the time, ruled. "Joe Petrosino is a symbol of pride and dedication for us all" states Porcelli, comparing his assassination by the clans to that of "the labor unionist Marco Biagi carried out by the Red Brigades." Every month about 400 Italian police officers gather in the club named in Petrosino's honor. They are veterans in the fight against Cosa Nostra called "organized crime" today. The roots of Cosa Nostra lie in the phenomenon of immigration itself because when immigrants arrived at the end of the 19th century penniless and in dire straits "the police force, made up mostly of Irishmen, was the enemy and they instead sought out those who could help them, in Sicily or in New York." There are two reasons why Petrosino is held as an example by police officers of Italian descent: in Little Italy he was able to change the image of the force "from foe to friend" and he set up squads of undercover agents that infiltrated the clans as a way of learning about changes occurring within criminal organizations. "Even today the mafia is continuously evolving and now it operates on the financial front," Porcelli concludes, explaining that if Italian organized crime has ceded its place to the Chinese and Russian mob, "in New York it is still on top of the list" thanks to the aggressiveness of the Calabrian *'Ndrangheta.*

Admirals and generals

The commander of NATO submarines, the first marine to guide the entire American armed forces and the officer who commanded the soldiers who caught Saddam Hussein are all generals of Italian descent who share a strong sense of family. To better understand who these men are we must start at Thompson Street in Greenwich Village. It's the street that many New Yorkers know because of Le Poisson Rouge on nearby Bleecker Street, a local hot spot offering burlesque shows and a retreat for the penniless after the financial crash of 2008. But at the beginning of the twentieth century, Thompson Street was a street where Italian was almost exclusively spoken. At 206 Emma Capellino grew up in the Italian Fine Cake Bakery selling fresh baked bread and desserts of the Marche region from where her parents originated. Emma Capellino is the "nonna" of whom Admiral Edmund Giambastiani speaks when explaining his Italian identity. He is the ex-commander of the NATO submarine fleet, one of the most delicate appointments of the Pentagon, who George W. Bush nicknamed "Admiral G." Bush assigned him the position of Vice Chairman of the Joint Chiefs of Staff which he held until 2007. One of the reasons why it was a very great honor for the Italian American community is because Giambastiani was born and raised in Canastota. This village, close to Lake Oneida, north of New York, has a population of only 4425 residents almost all of whom share the same heritage. It's in Madison County in Upstate New York between Syracuse, Milan and Rome, where hordes of immigrants from peasant families settled between the end of the twentieth century and the beginning of the twenty-first. These immigrants came to work in mines, factories and on the banks of Lake Erie. Living there meant growing up on a sort of Italian island embedded within New England. In 2008, Giambastiani was appointed Grand Marshal of the Italian Columbus Day parade on Fifth Avenue and this was the first occasion, donning the tricolor sash, when he publically spoke about his relationship with his grandmother Emma. "When I think about what being Italian means to me, my mind wanders to family, to my parents and grandparents who are no longer with us, and in particular to my mother and most especially to my maternal grandmother who raised me with an extraordinary amount of affection, this is the foundation of what makes me Italian." In truth, the Italian identity of the general who led some of the most top-secret submarine operations in recent years, has roots that extend from many places. His paternal grandparents came from Lucca and his maternal grandparents from Montemarciano in the province of Ancona. His father, a decorative artisan, lived on Staten Island and worked in Manhattan where he participated in the construction of the Chrysler Building before marrying and moving to Canastota. "My grandparents always devoted themselves to this great country and to their children, but they always looked with affection on the country of their ancestors," the Admiral remarks while describing the constant balance lived between the love of two homelands.

Giambastiani spoke of his Italian grandmother on Columbus Day but his direct superior is also of Italian descent and at the most important point of his career he was deeply moved as he remembered his parents. His name is Peter Pace, the first Marine Corps soldier who in 2005 became head of the Joint Chiefs of Staff. He was born in Brooklyn into a family that was originally from Noci (Bari), he grew up in Teaneck NJ, he was an enthusiastic soccer player and a model student. In 1968 he went to Vietnam to lead a platoon of marines in the recapture the city of Hue during one of the bloodiest battles of the Tet Offensive. Five of his men perished there and he chose the photograph of the first one of them to die, Guido Farinaro, to display on each of his command desks since then. He participated in military operations in Japan, Korea and Thailand and in April of 2003 he was a high ranking official of the marine division that entered Bagdad. On this occasion he showed an exceptional ability to communicate with the press. His abilities struck Bush who called him back to Washington to award him the highest rank of the Armed Forces. He was the first Italian American to attain this coveted position but his nomination had to be ratified by the Senate Armed Forces Committee and he was called to testify before the committee on July 19 2006 in the Chapman Center in Miami. Among the senators who pounded him with questions on the difficulties of the war in Iraq and on his relationship with the Minister for Defense Donald Rumsfeld, were the Capitol Hill heavyweights: Ted Kennedy, John McCain and Lindsey Graham. General Pace responded to each enquiry resolutely and competently exemplifying the perfect blend of military man and communicator, but this composure disappeared in a flash when he began to speak about his Apulian heritage. He spoke of the poverty in which he lived as a child in the house in Brooklyn, his high school in Teaneck, and he lingered on the sacrifices made by his father and the hardships endured by his mother to raise four children, have them graduate college and give them the opportunity to achieve success and prosperity. It was this summary of the American dream that brought the General to tears, to the point where he couldn't speak anymore and the room fell into total silence. "You have greatly moved us", Ted Kennedy said to him, "let's hope that Congress and America listen to you." Republican Senator Lindsey Graham, from South Carolina, added "When one has Italian blood, one has to listen to his heart, only a true Marine knows how to cry." Pace often refers to this effect of "Italian blood." He describes himself in the following way: "I'm obviously an American but I appreciate my roots. When I was young I learned the importance of having Italian blood that makes the heart beat fast when one gets emotional. Being warm-blooded has often served me well and being of Italian descent makes me a better person because it makes me feel like I am a citizen of the world, and it makes me appreciate even more the importance for America to be such a diverse nation."

The US Army General who underwrote the capture of Saddam Hussein is Raymond Odierno who today leads the US Army Joint Forces Command. He is a bald and hefty 6'6" looming figure, known for keeping his adversaries on their toes. When the war in Iraq was in trouble in 2007 because of the Jihadi Uprising, the commander of US troops David Petraeus gave him command of the Sunni Triangle, the Al-Qaeda terrorist stronghold, putting him in charge of the reinforcements who changed the outcome of the conflict. Odierno applied the Petraeus principle, based on creating alliances with the local tribes, in such an efficient way that he became his logical successor to lead Iraqi Freedom in 2009. But the military has taken its toll on Odierno: in 2004 his son Anthony lost an arm when a rocket hit his jeep southwest of Bagdad. In May of 2012, when they both climbed to the stage of the "Sons of Italy" at the Omni Shoreham in Washington to receive Leadership Awards, they both spoke the language of heroes. The general, wearing a decorated tailcoat, remembered Sergeant John Basilone, the only American soldier in World War II to have received the Navy Cross and the Medal of Honor, and characterized him as "a shining example of how much Italian Americans gave to this country." Then it was Tony's turn, his son, who spoke of "courage and patriotism" as "actions of ordinary people in extraordinary situations" to which "enough attention is often not given." Their embrace on the stage set off a long standing ovation by the almost one thousand Italian Americans present, some audience members even began to cry. When the applause stopped, Tony was the one who remembered his Italian roots: "My grandfather, Basilio Odierno, came from Sarno, near Naples, and he went to live on the Lower East Side. My father, instead, grew up in Rockaway, NJ, and my mother is German. For us, being Italian means spending as much time as possible together as a family, and sharing meals together." And to those who asked what advise he would give to young Italian Americans who want to follow in his footsteps he said: "in life we run into many obstacles, one for me was losing an arm, but there's always a way to adapt and overcome difficulties and to get back on track."

The judge of Madison Square Garden

We meet Eugene Nardelli, New York Court of Appeals Judge, at Bella Blu on Lexington Avenue, at the corner of 70th Street. He orders a caprese salad and penne pasta with tomato sauce, the dishes on which he bases his quality assessment of Italian restaurants. He was born in 1934 in Fasano, in Apulia. His mother's family was from New York and they moved back to New York when he was very young. They lived in East Harlem: his father had a little store that Nardelli eventually took over and often went back to visit later. "My father was the *store-man*, he was always in the shop and in an East Harlem that was populated back then by poor people, Italians, Jews and Blacks, he used to sell what he could for a small price." He got a degree from Fordham University and became a lawyer, but what he most cared about was helping the people of his neighborhood overcome a myriad of everyday problems. What pushed him was the belief in giving back to his community at least part of what it had given to him. In this way he helped many individuals and families with few resources, resolve small everyday problems, often working for free. "I was a kind of community organizer." Then he served in the US Army for 13 years. When he returned, East Harlem had changed: Puerto Ricans had taken the place of Italians and many of the old stores had disappeared. But the memory of what he had done for the community remained and in 1962 the neighborhood elected him as their representative. "I went into politics because of the Democrats and I was elected by the Porto Rican base that knew how much I had done for the neighborhood. At the time Italians weren't there anymore and we didn't have a big family." His fight for the democratic cause led him to be a delegate at the convention in 1972 that gave the nomination to George Mc-Govern and then, in 1975, he was elected Judge of the Civil Court of the City of New York where he remained until 1985. He was then nominated to the Appellate Division of the Supreme Court in 1993.

Nardelli is a democrat but his approach to law is conservative. "With regards to the role of judges, I agree with Supreme Court Judge Antonin Scalia who believes that they should judge and not legislate" because "judges are the engineers of society, they help make the industry of humanity work by applying laws." Thus, he doesn't like "judges who say they are in favor of gay marriage" because "they are trying to make laws, forcing the hand of the majority of citizens who are against it. When it comes to values the people must decide and not judges." Behind what he thinks and says lies the idea that "judges represent the law and lawyers represent the people" and "they are both quite separate roles."

Every so often he uses Italian terms, smiles, puts his fingers together making the gesture "but what are you talking about?" His facial expressions, gestures and jokes are in Italian, but his language is English and he is careful to emphasize that "my Country is America." "I made that choice because I am American."

In the last thirty-five years as a judge in New York, he has signed almost twenty thousand Court decisions, including some rulings that have had an impact on life in the city. An example of this is the case of the Peter Cooper Village in Stuyvesanyt Town. In March 2006, the Appellate Division voted unanimously that the real estate giant Tishman Speyers had acted 'improperly' when it raised the rent of thousands of low-income housing tenants after receiving particular tax-exemptions for the construction of the building. His argument was that because the company had already received tax relief it couldn't raise the rent because "two fiscal privileges cannot be summed together." It is one of the principles that changed the law. In other cases it was a matter of affirming that "a gift is a gift" or defending those who act "in good faith." "What counts is that the law must always prevail and when there is space for discretion a decision must be made in a pragmatic way to obtain the desired results based on common sense, the cornerstone of the Anglo-Saxon judicial system." He epitomizes the idea of America as a "nation of laws not a nation of men" where "liberty is under the law" which is "consequence of Benjamin Franklin's ideas as well as of the writings of Gaetano Filangieri, the Italian Illuminist who wrote the Science of Legislation in 1780." "American people respect the law because the principles that they elaborated are deep-rooted, diffused and shared." The comparison with Italy comes to him spontaneously: "the problems stem from the fact that many judges in Italy are corrupt because they are not elected. If you are elected you answer to the people and you must be fair, instead if you are nominated you answer to partisan interests." As for the judges who are also public prosecutors: "It is shameful" he says revealing his anger, "Italy is the nation of Filangieri who inspired Franklin, how can we permit there to be judge-prosecutors or never-ending trials?" Ex-governor Mario Cuomo, who nominated him in 1992 for the Commission on the 500 Years since the Discovery of America, describes Nardelli as a judge "capable of formulating practical solutions to abstract legal problems." Jonathan Lippman, Chief Judge of the State of New York, speaking at the ceremony in honour of Nardelli's thirty-five years in the profession, praised his ability to be "collegial even when in disagreement."

Nardelli who is a protagonist, promoter and ex-president of the Columbus Citizens Foundation and of the Columbus Club that organizes the annual Fifth Avenue Parade, says that New York Italian Americans "were poor but made incredible economic and social progress" and "they vote for the Democrats because here the city is democrat but they have always been Republicans because they loved Lincoln who freed the slaves from poverty and because they believe in the conservative values of the family." He knows the Democratic Party from the inside and he speaks of it with cynicism: "Roosevelt and Kennedy played the ethnic card to get Italian votes, but philanthropists like Rockefeller and mayors like LaGuardia and Giuliani, who were both Republicans, did more for our people. In the aftermath of 9/11 the compelling topic was "the line that must be traced between personal freedom and collective safety." In his opinion "the answer comes from the Constitution, which is not a suicidal contract" as Lincoln believed when he "suspended habeas corpus during the civil war or let's consider when in World War II Japanese and Italians were put in confinement camps to protect the nation." If "today the danger comes from Muslim men between the ages of twenty and fifty, then it is necessary to identity them and that doesn't mean that we are being racist." He talks about this in his office with a view of Madison Square Garden on the second floor of the neoclassical building constructed in 1900, located close to what used to be the house of Winston Churchill's mother. This office has become a sort of second home now for the past seventeen years. Court rulings aside, Nardelli has also had the responsibility of overseeing the renovation of the building, starting with the historical façade with the statues of Strength and Wisdom. He also supervised the reorganization of the cafeteria as a way of improving the judges' quality of life. Employees, advisers and officers greet him by calling him "Judge" with a mixture of both affection and respect. He works at a desk surrounded by photographs of Sophia Loren, Luciano Pavarotti, Senator "Scoop" Jackson, Cardinal John O'Connor, Judge Antonin Scalia, Mayor Dinkins, Joe DiMaggio,

Frank Sinatra, President Sandro Pertini and Governor George Pataki. The picture that he loves the most is on a little table near the doorway. It was taken in the Thirties in Fasano and it shows the young Eugenio standing beside his father Vito, shortly before they left for America.

The defenders of Arthur Avenue

Olive bread, *cantucci* with almonds and lemon cannoli. The over seventy year old Peter Madonia is very particular about his young servers' manners as they sell the same products that his father Mario sold when he opened the bakery in 1918. It's at 2348 Arthur Avenue, on the one block within the entire metropolis of New York that most resembles Italy. In Little Italy, Italian families sold their homes and stores to the Chinese and in Bensonhurst, Brooklyn, the Italian presence has dwindled among Hispanics and Asians, but on Arthur Avenue, in the Bronx, there's still an Italian stronghold that endures. To be aware of this all you have to do is walk down Crescent Avenue to the intersection with East 187th Street. These two blocks come alive with Italian flavors, colors and dialects as a flood of passersby stop, eat, and purchase all kinds of things in the stores that remain unchanged for three generations. Between Mario's restaurant and the Madonia bakery there's the entrance to the Retail Market. This indoor market was inaugurated by Fiorello LaGuardia in 1940 and it sought to recreate the atmosphere of the Italian Piazza, with a series of stalls selling oil, vegetables, meats and pizza, where the owners knew each other and greeted each other by name. The telltale signs that you are in America are the series of little American flags that stand next to the Italian tricolor, the uniforms of firefighters who come here to have a sandwich on their break, and an outdoor cigar lounge with photographs of Al Pacino smoking a Tuscan cigar (just like the guests at every wedding as the party winds down). Next to Madonia's is Biancardi's butcher shop, then another bakery, Addeo Bakery, Cosenza's fish market and, after the intersection with East 186th Street, Teitel, a grocery store and delicatessen with shelves and counters brimming with all types of cheese, vegetables and cold cuts from Italy. The Star of

David adorning the bricks at the entrance indicates the origin of the store owners. A little further down on East 187th Street, opposite the Church of Our Lady of Mount Carmel, third generation retailers own Borgatti's Ravioli and Egg Noodles, where egg pasta is sold and Frank Sinatra plays in the background. It's just like at Randazzo's where fish is laid out on long counters and Neapolitan melodies like *Luna caprese* endlessly play. To understand the connection the families here have to this neighborhood in the Bronx called Belmont, in honor of the family that was first to buy land there in the Eighteenth century, it doesn't suffice to just stop at parish rec centers or churches that proudly remember Joseph Maria Pernicone who was the first Italian American to be appointed bishop in 1954. You must go back to the Sixties when racial tensions between the Italians who were living here and the blacks (mostly Port Ricans) who resided in the bordering neighborhoods were very high. There were clashes in the streets both day and night. At the time there was a city bus that passed through Belmont and it became the target of these attacks. On one occasion a group of young Italians overturned the bus so that the blacks couldn't launch objects as well as insults from the windows. The city chose to terminate the bus route, and it hasn't been restored since, and that helped to ease the tensions until the night of July 13th 1977 when New York went dark due to a blackout that sparked city-wide violence and looting. The Bronx, Queens and Brooklyn were the areas most affected by looters. With smoke and flames billowing, the families of the Italian shop owners along Arthur Avenue feared they would lose everything that they had built with decades of hard work and sacrifice. So they chose to defend their stores. Fathers and sons (many of whom were still not of age) stood outside their stores holding baseball bats ready to fight anyone who dared approach. The bands of vandals and looters assessed the situation and cautiously retreated without setting foot on the sidewalks. This event convinced the Madonia, Biancardi and Borgatti families, as well as many others, that there was nothing more important that saving Arthur Street, protecting it from every danger.

Fast forward a few years and one of the young boys wielding a baseball bat, Peter Madonia Jr., grandson of Mario, walked into City Hall as a young adviser to the democratic mayor Ed Koch. His task was to reorganize the Fire Department, but soon but he felt obliged to take the opportunity to strengthen the "Arthur Avenue community." This is how the idea of duplicating what the big corporations were successfully doing in Times Square in this Italian-American enclave: create a fiscal mechanism to devote part of the tax revenue to the development of the neighborhood. And so Arthur Avenue became a Business Investment District (Bid) in which each business owner pays 4% more real-estate tax to the city, which in turn deposits these funds into a special account managed by a board elected by the merchants. This means that the families of Arthur Avenue have nearly 400 thousand dollars at their disposal each year to dedicate to improvements of the area that range from street cleaning and night security to garbage collection. Because of this, the blocks surrounding the Retail market have become the jewel of the Bronx, so much so that the Italians refer to it as "Uptown" in reference to the quality of life there. They have vehemently opposed the return of buses and the installation of a subway station in an effort to protect its precious isolation. Nevertheless, customers come from every part of the city and even from Connecticut and New Jersey, thanks to another innovation introduced by Peter Madonia Jr. at the end of the Eighties: TV advertising, the precursor of internet websites today. "Up until then we sold only to the residents of the area, but the business then changed, ethnic food became popular and we discovered that we had customers everywhere." This is why we need more parking lots to accommodate people coming by car to buy cheeses, cold cuts, desserts, oil and sundried tomatoes. The proximity to the Bronx Zoo, Bronx Park, the Botanical Gardens and Fordham University expands the clientele further. The majority of those who come to shop, do so because they are attracted to the image of "the real Little Italy" that Robert De Niro presented on the big screen in the movie *Bronx Tales* inspired by the book of the same name by Chazz Palminteri. The most popular destinations are the *Casa della Mozzarella* deli on East 187th Street, and the restaurant Zero Otto Nove (089 was the original city prefix) recently opened by Robert Paciullo from Salerno. The place is decorated with election posters from the most recent elections in Campania. At the very other end of Arthur Street, at the intersection with Crescent Avenue, there is a garden with a gazebo where people gather for a barbeque on Columbus Day. Here there is a statue of Christopher Columbus by Attilio Piccirilli. He is the marble sculptor who with his five brothers opened their studio on 142nd Street in the Bronx producing works such as the Maine Memorial in Central Park, the lions at the entrance to the New York Public Library, and the commanding statue of the Lincoln Memorial in Washington DC.

Eighty-seven year old Cecilia with her purse and shopping bag in hand complains that this Italian corner of the Big Apple "is overrun by foreigners," she shakes her head disapprovingly as she crosses Hughes Avenue to return home from the market. In the middle of the street there are Mexican children playing soccer, the restaurant La Casita Poblana is full of regulars and a cloud of smoke wafts out of Cuba Cigar. Cecilia came here from Torretta "near Palermo" and she grew up on Arthur Avenue where her children and grandchildren were born. She says grudgingly, "look around: there are almost no Italians left." From the Fifties on, the Italians of Manhattan's Little Italy left for Brooklyn to escape to the suburbs, and a generation later the second and third generation immigrants moved to Staten Island and New Jersey in search of better neighborhoods. Arthur Avenue, near the Retail Market, had resisted these changes but now its Italian identity is challenged by the newcomers due to the exponential growth of two groups that couldn't be more different from each other: Albanians and Mexicans.

Albanian writings adorn the huge mural of Jesus at the entrance to the only parking lot in the area (the metro doesn't come here so this parking lot is vital). The Guro Café, a restaurant with prices that are prohibitive for some, serves Shqiptare specialities to a clientele that then goes home to watch Alb TV, the Albanian station whose name adorns the two-storey building at 2220 Arthur Avenue. It's there because of a thirty year old Albanian American, Leonel Dreshaj, who set up the company Fta Market that sells what he defines as an "ethnic decoder" with which "the people of the area can watch TV stations in their native language." 23 Albanian channels are available. His mother, Nusha, is an ex-refugee from Kosovo who doesn't know much about TV but she offers a drink to anyone who comes in "because we Europeans are very hospitable." The store nextdoor is run by another two Albanians, one from Tirana and the other from Pristina. It is a deli that sells everything:

newspapers in the original language, CDs of singers like Gazi, Leke and Dava, Shqiptare costumes, flags depicting an eagle and combat manuals for the "Dervish warriors" in their struggle against the Serbs. Drina, who is from Tirana, speaks of the Italians of the neighborhoods as "unfamiliar, complete strangers" because "they never come in here" and "on the street they almost never say hello." The Albanians, however, line up at Madonia Brothers Bakery that has been selling fresh bread and *cantuccis* since 1918. The Albanians and the Kosovars make up an aggressive minority group that is determined to make space for itself without apology; the Mexicans instead are already a well-established group. They smile, without much consideration for the tensions with non-Hispanics. "Italians who?" asks Gregorio Castro with a smirk, the 45 year old owner of the sporting goods store Mexico Sports Center who has been here for seven years. "I sell black and green t-shirts of my country's national team, only Mexicans come here, are there really so many... Italians in this neighborhood? They don't come around here much, here everyone keeps to themselves" he says as he strolls back and forth in the patch of grass in front of his store where a marble bust of Christopher Columbus stands, a symbol of the settlement of Italians in New York. But past History doesn't interest the Mexicans who for the most part are young and focused on "working hard to earn a lot." This is what Ramiro says, a thirty-seven year old from Puebla who owns the snack bar El Sureño where the prices are low and "the food is so hot that Italians won't even come close." In 1980 only 35 of the inhabitants of Arthur Avenue were Mexican, about 0.2% of the population, now there are 3,200 which is about 14%, similar to what's going on in the rest of the city. These changes are noticeable in what's happening to places of worship in the neighborhood. In the Catholic Church of Our Saviour about 80% of the congregation is Hispanic and in Our Lady of Mount Carmel, permanently festooned with Italian flags, the Archdiocese of New York has ordered that mass be celebrated in Spanish at least twice a week. A few Hispanic nuns have also been appointed to nurture relationships with the churchgoers who are native speakers of Spanish. "These changes aren't surprising at all," says Salvatore De Cicco, a Neapolitan store owner who sells personalized name tags on Arthur Avenue, "because the Albanians and the Mexicans keep coming, multiplying, but Italians don't come to New York any-more, they're staying at home." Maurizio who is a head waiter in the Salernitan restaurant Zero Otto Nove adds, "It's all true but not very important, here in America the only way to make progress is by working hard and it's a rule that everyone must follow whether they're Italian, Mexican or Albanian." Alessandro Fava, a twenty year old Palermitan-New Yorker admits that "almost everything has changed" and the only constant according to what his parents say, is the boom in sales of Italian food products like what he sells at Orazio Carciotto's Casa Della Mozzarella where when you enter you can see firsthand how the most popular Italian cheeses are made. Whilst Italians seem to have resigned themselves to the fact that they're destined to lose control of Little Italy in the Bronx, the Mexicans who work among the live octopi and fresh halibut at Cosenza's and Randazzo's fish stores rejoice without hesitation at what's happening and see a very rosy future for themselves: "there are more and more people here who speak our language."

The "panelle" of Ridgewood

To hear a conversation about the mafia between bartenders and police officers you need to go to Ridgewood, in Queens. The main thoroughfare with the most Italian-American coffeeshops, restau-rants, clubs and supermarkets is Fresh Pond Road. Moving a few streets away you get to L'Aroma del Caffè located in a small build-ing on the corner. Francesco Aluzzo, who emigrated in 1968 from Castellammare del Golfo, first bought the place and then remod-eled it with his own expert hands as a builder after a fire broke out in the basement. Besides espresso, Aluzzo serves Chinotto, orange soda and pastries, and among the customers there are also some New York police officers. They come in plain clothes with their guns and badges under their shirts or t-shirts, and sipping their favorite drinks they engage in heated discussions with the other customers. They talk about the mafia, murders, tip-offs, arrests and it usually goes that the customers complain or ask questions and the officers explain, almost always in Italian or sometimes also in Sicilian dialect. The topic that fires up the customers most is the topic of "rats," or as they are often called "the infamous," those who commit crimes and once captured plea bargain for lighter sentences and financial benefits by collaborating with investigators. Aluzzo says, "There are things that are difficult to understand," like the "rat" who killed 30-33 people, then chose to collaborate and is now back in the neighborhood where he has become a sort of street boss." The officer who responds is one of the younger ones: "See Francè, you don't understand how America works, this country was founded on the exchange of money, if a criminal goes to prison and then the lawyer asks for a plea-bargain the agreement is made provided that those who hired the murderer are arrested." The most difficult thing for the officers isn't catching the gunmen but finding who hires and pays them. To kill somebody in New York costs on average two thousand dollars, but the gunmen aren't local, they are hired from other cities or from Italy, they do what is asked of them and then they disappear. It's difficult for the police to catch them. They worked really hard to catch the "pole" for example, a ferocious man who required 12 thousand dollars per assassination because he used to offer added guarantees to his employers: when they deed was done he'd send a video that showed rats gnawing at the corpse of the desired victim. The "pole" was arrested and he died of cancer in federal prison, but there are many murderers on the loose and as soon as the officers capture one they are willing to negotiate if the names of those who hired the killers are given, killers usually tell the truth.

In the Fresh Pond Road area, most of the residents are either Italian American or Polish. There were Germans and Irish here before but they moved leaving space for the newcomers from countries in the East, whilst Italians are the only ones from the first wave of immigrants to have stayed. Old and new immigrants meet at Valentino's at 6664 that the owner Filippo Barone and his father opened in 1975. He now runs it with his three sons and thirty employees. He came with his father in 1968 when his town, Santa Margherita, was destroyed by the Belice earthquake. It offers all sorts of Italian products, pasta imported via air, citrus fruits bought at the markets in New England, but what he's most proud of are the foods prepared by the cook, Stella, originally from Alcamo. She makes Sicilian style loaves, made with chickpea flour, and huge rice balls filled with ground beef. Both are on display at the deli counter, near the checkout where Polish and Albanian employees work beneath large family photographs and a giant poster of the truck (with a huge picture of Padre Pio on the door) that Filippo uses to transport his goods. Tony Mulè, originally from Partanna, an entertainer in the local community explains: "Here we are all devoted to Padre Pio, every time we go back to Italy we go visit him." The faith in Padre Pio is manifested in the belief that the Saint has miraculous powers. Faith is also expressed in the decision to have Italian lessons taught to the youngest children in the Church of Our Lady of the Miraculous Medal. There are afternoon courses, and at the end of every year there is a huge party where the families get together and about fifteen Ferraris are put on display by their owners to the delight of the children.

The other celebration that the Fresh Pond Road community is very proud of is the Italian-American parade that is held every year at the beginning of September. The entire neighborhood meets at the Padre Pio Procession that concludes with vendors selling lots of food, the band playing Italian tunes and shows on the stage. "It was a challenge to launch this celebration," Tony Di Piazza, head of the Italian Cultural Association and Vice President of Comites in New York, remembers "because in the Nineties, the Germans and the Irish fiercely opposed it fearing that the celebration would bring an invasion of the mafia." At first it seemed that the opponents would get the upper hand but then Rudolf Giuliani, the Mayor at the time, intervened to allow the Padre Pio procession parade in front of the Italian cafés on Fresh Pond Road. When you go into these places it's like being in Italy. There are large TVs tuned to Italian channels that show soccer games, horseracing, news and popular shows. There's no end to the production of coffees and cappuccinos. Friends sit around little tables chatting. In the back there's a larger room for playing cards. This all happens at any time of day or night, just like back in the home country in towns like Partanna, Santa Margherita del Belice, Polizzi Generosa and Castellammare del Golfo. The round tables seat up to six people and in front of each one there's a little space carved into the wood for money. Then all the regulars have to do is decide which game to play. The most popular games are Briscola played in five, Cinquecento, Tresette, Scopone,

Rummy, Scala Quaranta and Poker which is the most popular because it's the one with the highest stakes. Here almost everybody always plays, and most especially the pensioners who go home to eat at lunch time and then come right back to the tables afterwards. Giuseppe Battaglia is one of them. He arrived in America illegally in 1958 "leaving a nation that was on its knees after the war" and he never went back "because this is a difficult country, but it's a country that gave us what Italy couldn't give us." Mulé, sitting in the headquarters of the Partanna Club surrounded by heirlooms of the Garibaldi epoch adds, "I'm proud to be Italian but God Bless America" because "the Italians who came here did well whilst those who went to Latin America got a bad deal with dictators, coups, violence and economic crises from Argentina and Brazil all the way to Venezuela." The bond to Italy stays strong, nevertheless. "Those who live here love the national anthem, the tricolor and the celebration on June 2nd more than many Italians who live in Italy," Di Piazza says with confidence, "because we miss those things here." This is the generation of emigrants that arrived between the Sixties and the Seventies. They're the last to arrive. "Since then nobody else has come" Mulé states, remembering how "there were weeks when an average of 400 Sicilians came." All that ended when the quality of life increased in Italy and its economic growth reached levels similar to the United States. It's like as if the immigrants who came in the last twenty years are from another planet. "One time I was at a dinner in Manhattan, there were five hundred young Italians, all professionals, " Di Piazza recounts, "we don't know them and they don't know us but this separation weakens both of us."

Italian Ridgewood is also home to Antonino Colombo who owns the fruit and vegetable store Colombo's on Metropolitan Avenue in Middle Village. He was born in Balestrate in the province of Palermo in 1932. He emigrated first to Argentina in 1952 and then, ten years later, to New York where he worked as a builder first and then went into the vegetable business. He is an elderly man and when you meet him for the first time you could take him for a beggar because of what he wears: a tattered old coat, faded red pants, worn-out shoes and a dusty hat. But despite the image, he is a capable businessman who owns houses and pharmacies. He managed to sell and buy back his own supermarket from Koreans who proved themselves to be not quite so capable of selling fava beans and artichokes. He doesn't like to be complimented on his economic success, but when he speaks about Italy he is unfettered: "My homeland has been invaded by non-EU immigrants, they even want to take the crucifixes off the walls, the politicians are all corrupt, the last decent one was Sandro Pertini, poor Italy!" If you ask Antonino Colombo what his favorite coffee in town is he says it's "the one that Joe makes." He's talking about Joe Bonura, an eighty-three year old from Castelvetrano who has been in New York since 1967. He has owned five cafés since then. The first one was in Brooklyn on Knickerbocker Avenue in Bushwick, and now at 917 North Broadwasy in Massapequa, where he continues to serve what his customers most appreciate: cappuccinos with pastries made by the Milanese bakery Bindi and ice-cream in 50 different flavors. The walls of Caffé Gondola are adorned with Sicilian carts, pictures of Venice, little gondolas and a postwar radio that still works. He arrived with a tourist visa for only three weeks and since then he has only visited Italy to see family and friends. "The last time I went, I couldn't wait to get back. The people I used to know in Sicily have died, here in New York I have a café that is my life, there's nothing in the world like America." To understand what he means you need to wait for closing time at Caffé Gondola: every day, just as he starts turning out the lights, a client who's very fond of him arrives, he's a police officer by profession, and he helps him bring in the chairs and umbrellas. "Only in America."

Spaghetti Park

Vincent Barbacci sells Italian ice in William F. Moore Park, or as the Italians from Corona, Queens simply call it, Spaghetti Park. The reason it's called Spaghetti Park isn't so much because when the Barbacci family arrived in 1957 all of the inhabitants were Italian, but because of the topographical characteristics of the little neighborhood. Around William F. Moore Park, small streets and lanes branched off creating hidden corners, alleys and junctions that reminded the newcomers of the places they had left. If you looked at it on the map "it looked like a roll of spaghetti," Barbacci says.

The topography of that time has now all changed. The old wooden houses have been replaced by apartment buildings, the alleys have made way for wider streets with sidewalks and most of the Italians have left. They've moved to better neighborhoods on Long Island or Staten Island. The name "Spaghetti Park," however, remains, as does the store The Lemon Ice King of Corona. This store is identical to the one created by the founder Benfaremo which was inherited by the Barbacci family that comes from Godrano in the province of Palermo. The piazza starts to speak Italian again on Columbus Day at the beginning of October because families come from other neighborhoods to meet up, play bocce and have a barbecue together. "We had to change the flavors that we offer because most of the residents here are Hispanic now." Barbacci explains, "Before we used to offer mostly pistachio, orange, lemon and almond, now we have replaced them with mango, piña colada, coconut and tropical fruits, because this is what South Americans like. "He calls the ice he sells *ice-water*, it's a little mound of colored ice that you suck your favorite flavor from. Using a spoon is "an old way of doing it, for connoisseurs, like my parents used to do." On the opposite side of the park, there's the only other remaining Italian place, Anthony Federici's Parkside Restaurant with lots of photographs on the walls of Luciano Pavarotti eating spaghetti and tomato sauce with a napkin tied around his neck.

Fortunato Bros in Greenpoint

Greenpoint in Williamsburg is one of the areas in New York where up until a century ago ethnic gangs fought each other for control of every little section of street. Now it's a place of delicate cohabitation between Italians (mostly from Campania with some Apulians) and Hispanics. This Little Naples near the East River buzzes around the Fortunato Bros pastry shop at 289 Manhattan Avenue. A long counter with all sorts of Neapolitan pastries on display, covered tables with a view of the street and a Chantilly cream that Frank Sinatra was crazy about, make Fortunato Bros a must-see stop for anyone coming to Brooklyn who wants to meet Italian Americans. The State Police Band has come here many times before playing in the Columbus Day parade. The five Italians who died in August of 2009 when their helicopter crashed into a small plane over the Hudson came to get their last coffee here too. The pastry store is owned by three brothers who are very close to one another yet also very different in personality and in their responsibilities within the business. Michele makes the delicious cream, Mario comes from the construction industry and Salvatore is a professional tailor. They come from Saviano near Naples and they arrived in New York in 1970, opening their business 6 years later. Since then, it's been a continuous production of cannoli, *sfogliatelle*, Chantilly cream, *babà* and an "unfaltering support for the Napoli soccer team" is written on the walls in block letters. Celebrities such as Gianni Morandi, Renzo Arbore, Nino Benvenuti, Nino D'Angelo, Gigi D'Alessio and Giorgio Panariello have come to rest, eat, and sing here. Matilda Cuomo, when her husband Mario was governor, came here and grew so fond of Fortunato's pastries that she often sent her driver to get them, giving into the nostalgia for a taste of Campania where her husband's parents hail from. In 1994, the dream of the Neapolitan brothers of Greenpoint encountered a snag. On St. John's day, Mario was in one of the Italian clubs of the neighborhood and as he was playing cards two assassins stood in front of him and killed one of his poker buddies, out of the blue, right before his eyes. The police suspected his involvement and when in 2002 the FBI found an informer who accused Fortunato of "collusion with the Genovese clan," everything changed. Mario became an outcast, peopled started to talk about him as if he were a murderer and going to eat cannolis at Greenpoint became a matter of choosing sides. Mario was emarginated from the family business, and confined to a prison cell that he described "as a complete hell, where 97% of the prisoners were black or South American." But it all ended in 2010 when the federal court that wanted to convict him as an accomplice in the crime backtracked, acquitting him completely, to the point of even considering the offer of some compensation. For Michele, the pastry chef, it was a victory for the family that topped "long years when we used to bring dozens of pastries and cannolis to the prison guards in an effort to help improve, from the outside, the conditions of his imprisonment on the inside." On his return to Manhattan Avenue, the ex-prisoner celebrated by taking back his rightful place in his neighborhood. He has since sought to celebrate Thanksgiving Day that commemorates the arrival of the first settlers, to pay tribute to the nation "where anything is possible, even being completely cleared of all wrongdoing after eight years of hard time." And to those who, like the blogger and writer Jerry Capeci, continue to accuse him of being a "cloaked Mafioso" and another pawn on the board of Gangland, Mario Fortunato replies, taking his cue from the film Gomorra based on Roberto Saviano's novel, "He has been very wrong about many things but when he describes a mafia that has been defeated in America but that still persists in Italy, he is completely right."

Sunset Park, pizza wars

On Fifth Avenue on Sunset Park in Brooklyn, a fierce pizza war is being fought. The battlefield is the sidewalk between 58th and 59th Streets. This is the central core of the neighborhood because just a few meters away the Church of Our Lady of Perpetual Help stands, the largest Catholic Church in Brooklyn. At 5806 there's the entrance to Johnny's Pizza which was founded in 1968 by John Miniaci and which has been proudly serving dishes since then thanks to his wood burning oven. At 5804 there's Papa John's Pizza (a fast-food place) that opened in 2007 and is run by an Indian. The customers at Miniaci's are for the most part Italian Americans, descendants of those who settled on the Brooklyn Waterfront in the middle of the XIX century. These immigrants helped transform the Waterfront into a commercial port centered around the Army Terminal through which at least 63 million tons of supplies and 80% of the troops passed during World War II, and where today a modern shopping center stands. But the Brooklyn of those days is fading because in place of Italians, Polish, Dutch, Finns and Norwegians, now most of the residents are Hispanics or Asians who started to settle in the Eighties. The Hispanics and Asians frequent Papa John's Pizza because the pizza that they're looking for and live on is simply another variety of the fast-food that they learned to consume as they assimilated into the American way of life. The two pizzerias fulfill the needs of two very different kinds of customers. The first crave Italian flavors and the second, instead, seek a quick meal at a low price. The clash, between both that is first cultural and then culinary, is inevitable. The duel restarts every day on two parallel fronts. As far as pricing is concerned, Papa John's is much more aggressive because it's the franchise of a chain of pizzerias that is based out of Kentucky and so can offer pizzas at bargain prices. It offers home delivery to the entire neighborhood, it has an efficient national toll-free number and it increases its earnings based on the number of clients rather than on the uniqueness of the product, selling food that is Italian only in name. Johnny's Pizza, instead, competes based on the quality of the food. Rocco Coluccio who has worked there since he was sixteen and who after a long court-ship married the daughter of the owner boasts that he, along with his brothers-in-law John and Louie Miniaci, does a quality control check of all of the pizzas that come out of their oven. They know where each ingredient comes from, from the tomatoes to the garlic, and give detailed information to the customers who are interested to know. Coluccio criticizes "those from Kentucky" for "landing in our market with low-priced products with the sole objective of eliminating us" and along these lines of attack he has the support of other family-run pizzerias in Sunset Park. Just within three blocks there are four of them and they too feel threatened by the fast-food places run by Indian immigrants. Gino Campese, owner of Scotti's Pizza explains the dynamics of what goes on along this street: "if they need some tomato or mozzarella at Johnny's Pizza we help them and we give them what they need as we've always done and they do the same for us. We've always raised or lowered prices in tandem with them because there's space for everyone in Sunset Park." Except for Papa John's Pizza that veils the threat of large-scale retailers that could kill what's left of the New York restaurant business economy that was built from scratch by immigrants. Sand-eep Sing, an India of about twenty who gambled his savings on the Papa John's franchise, counters that he "doesn't see the problem" and least of all the "pizza war" because "my dishes are different and intended for a different customer from the traditional restau-rants." As if to say that there is no need to quarrel in Sunset Park. Chuck Schumer, democratic Senator of New York, sees it different-ly. He was worried enough about what is happening on 5th Avenue to take a pen to paper to pay tribute to "mom and Pop Miniaci" as he remembered "when I was little they called places like these in Brooklyn the *great joints*" to underline how they all used to love to meet up there. Schumer is an authoritative presence in Brooklyn, but the Miniacis and the Coluccios know well that if they want to succeed in the fight against the very competitive fast-food business, they must play their cards well. This is why they decided to plant a flag with the stars and stripes in front of Johnny's Pizza because it has a story of patriotism. The flag was hoisted at Point Scorpion in Iraq by US Army Sergeant Abel Torres on a particular day: the 11th of September 2007, six years after the attack on the Two Towers.

Toyland in Dyker Heights

A month before Christmas, Dyker Heights is transformed and becomes the city of toys. It's a web of streets between 84th and 86th Streets at the intersection with 11th and 12th Avenues that sets itself apart from the rest of the Bay Ridge area because of the very opulent homes there. The residents are all Italian Americans who arrived in the Fifties and chose to transform this corner of Brooklyn into their village, resisting the choice made by friends, relatives and business partners to move south to Staten Island or New Jersey in search of even more beautiful, wealthy and isolated areas. To show its ownership of the area, this community, that shares southern Italian roots and high income, each year takes advantage of the holidays to decorate their homes, gardens, patios and fountains with Christmas decorations rivaling any Hollywood set. You just have to pass by there to see. Each home has different decorations that are over the top and perpetually in competition with what's in the neighbors' yard. The Spata family, on 84th Street, for forty years has populated its garden with plastic soldiers, angels, giant snowmen, Santa Claus and a myriad of Disney characters. The Rizzutos, also on 84th Street, surpass them with giant animated puppets that play Dickens' A Christmas Carol in a castle-like mansion adorned with tricolor flags that have a picture of Santa Claus. The Lombrones, on 12th Avenue, shroud their home in multicolor lights and they're not too far from 1145 on 84th Street where Toyland stands, the colonial house where Alfred Polizzotto, one of the most respected Italian businessmen of Bay Ridge, lived and died. Since his death, his wife Florence has not only maintained the Toyland playground that has giant images of horses, soldiers, wizards, Santa Claus and spinning carousels on every balcony, but she has also added the voice of her husband as a soundtrack that asks those who pass by to stop, enjoy the Toyland show and then donate to those who are in need. "Many of the residents here" explains Tommy Hahan who works for a local company that sells Christmas trees, "spend exorbitant amounts but then they collect money for orphans, the poor and the needy." To understand the value of Toyland, all you need do is consider that the average cost of some of the giant toys is 25-40 thousand dollars. Nobody steals here though, crime is nonexistent, Italian pride floods out the windows, cars and stores and the only regret that the elderly customers of Caffè Italia on 18th Street (better known as Cristoforo Colombo Boulevard) divulge is that "the number of Chinese and Koreans is increasing," taking land, stores and schools from Italians. But for the school children who come here all the way from Manhattan, Connecticut or New Jersey at Christmas to gaze at the statues and fountains of Toyland, the wars between immigrants are a thing of the past. All that counts for them is that the giant toys stay in the same place as the year before.

Little Italy besieged by assimilation

Between Mulberry and Grand Streets there's the corner of Little Italy where until 1932 the Banca Stabile stood. It was built in 1882 to guarantee the masses of immigrants, who were arriving at that time, the fundamental bank services such as providing small loans, giving access to translations and insurance, buying tickets for Europe and, most importantly, transferring money to relatives in Italy or to those who had settled in other parts of the US. Thus the founder Francesco Stabile contributed to giving a sense of security to the residents of Little Italy, but he wasn't spared during the storm of the Great Depression and he was forced to merge with the Banca Commerciale Italiana Trust Company. In that same building there is still the original safe of the Banca Stabile that today is one of the preserved remnants in the Italian-American Museum that the scholar Joseph Scelsa created to safeguard the memory of a fading ethnic identity. "Italianness for immigrants is linked to the home, the preservation of language, family customs and to food that they are most attached to, starting with pasta, but nowadays in New York you can eat a good plate of pasta in a restaurant for just 10 dollars." In a way, the metropolis has become Italian to the point that it has made the ethnic and family connections that used to prevail within the four walls of the home, now secondary. But that is not all. "Assimilation is apparent also in the attitude towards holidays. Now many celebrate Saint Joseph's day and Father's day together, as happens for example in Howard Beach," in Queens. Faith, on the other hand, unifies people much less than before. For the first immigrants, being Catholic was an element that distinguished them from the Protestants, now the situation is very different because "although most of them are Catholics they are not practicing Catholics, more women than men go to church on Sunday and some make mixed marriages with people of other faiths and race, even if conversions are very rare." What has emerged is that they form groups and make connections at work and in professional and business settings, knowing that "to count we must be united" because "even if this is a nation of individualists, to be successful we must be part of a tribe." In the "first generations, divisions based on the region, province, or little town that the immigrants hailed from, prevailed. Today Italian-American immigrants tend to unite in order to establish themselves better from a professional point of view." In doing this they become representatives of the values that they hold most dear (such as the family and the community), even if the job search makes them move from city to city "just like all other Americans do."

Scelsa speaks from within a reality that proves that Italian Americans are fleeing their own roots. Little Italy until the end of World War II was teeming with thousands of Italian families strictly divided by streets that mirrored their regions in customs, aromas and dialects. The Sicilians were on Elizabeth Street, the Campanians on Mulberry Street and the Apulians and Calabrians on Mott Street. Now there are only Neapolitan restaurants on the last few blocks of Mulberry Street going towards Canal Street, whilst Mott and Elizabeth Streets house boutiques, specialty food stores, pub and art galleries that make Nolita (North of Little Italy) one of the trendiest neighborhoods around Soho. 247 Mulberry Street is a representation of the transformation that has occurred. The Ravenite Social Club was based here up until the Eighties, where John Gotti, Gambino mafia boss, had his headquarters. Now the redbrick building houses rental apartments for young managers who work in the financial district, whilst at street level of the ex-bastion of the godfather (the FBI wiretapped this building to incriminate him) there is a women's shoe store, stiletto heels, flashy colors and high prices. Among the few remaining inhabitants of the area who remember the old Little Italy is eighty-six year old Moe Albanese, the last butcher to have worked on Elizabeth Street. His father Vincenzo arrived from Polizzi Generosa in 1923, he married Mary and they opened one of the six butchers' on the street where the Sicilians lived that supplied meat to the whole neighborhood. Now there is only Albanese Meats & Poultry at 238, and Moe is proud to "still serve meat in the same way" which means "cutting it in front of his customers from the original piece, because otherwise they might think that they're just getting leftovers." After the transformation of Little Italy, the clients of the old times have all gone and Moe Albanese, sitting on a chair in front of the entrance to his store recounts, "Once, everyone here was Italian, this street was full of carts and the houses that were for rent cost 55 dollars a month, and then after World War II the situation improved little by little, people started to make money and they bought houses in Brooklyn on 18th Avenue, they moved in groups following the respective club of their town of origin, then they moved from Brooklyn to more beautiful houses on Staten island and then to New Jersey. As a result, Elizabeth Street, Mott Street and Mulberry Street were left empty, the old buildings were bought and renovated and now "they rent them to young managers who are willing to pay 2,500 dollars a month, to Chinese families with a lot of cash or to shoe and clothing boutiques" just like the one in Gotti's ex-headquarters. "As far as I'm concerned," Albanese, whose store is quite unadorned with just a few photos of saints, some meat slicers and family memories, comments, "this caused all the Italians who used to eat the meat I serve disappear and now I manage to survive thanks only to the high-end restaurants, they come in the morning, they ask for quality meat and then they serve it and make their customers pay triple for it." Business isn't bad, but Moe with his blue eyes and pale complexion is nostalgic, "For the years I grew up here with Charlie Scorsese, Martin's father who together with his father, mother, four brothers and two sisters lived here, right opposite." Charlie and Moe were friends and when Charlie had "problems" with Martin he ran to tell him about them. "Charlie worked in the textile district, he worked a steam press, and they didn't have much money," Albanese remembers, "so one day he came to me and complained about his son who was wasting time dreaming about being a director without ever thinking about work, but I told him to wait and to have faith in him..." The last butcher of Little Italy speaks about the past as if it were immanent and for Scelsa it embodies a "heritage that belongs to everyone," but the reality of the situation is very different. The new generations, with houses on Long Island and Staten Island are trying to live together and resist the prejudice that hinders the road to assimilation.

On the small screen, the HBO TV show, *The Sopranos*, spread the belief that every Italian American is a Mafioso or a mafia boss whilst the MTV reality TV show, *Jersey Shore*, opens up a new front, presenting dozens of tacky youths that are derogatorily called Guidos or Guidettes, a title that highlights the fact that they are rude and uneducated and live in questionable situations on the fringe of society. "Before all Italian Americans were considered members of the mafia, now all Italian American women are potty mouthed voluptuous bimbos and our young people have to deal with these prejudices both in school and at university." Scelsa knows what has to be done in the face of these kinds of occurrences, "We have to fight in federal court, the law is on our side but it has to be applied." He admits that "we would need something like Abraham Foxman's Anti-Defamation League" to explain in school and on TV "the problems from which these prejudices arise," like how "at the beginning of the twentieth century the mafia had complete control over the immigrant neighborhoods and crime raged with the misdeeds of the Black Hand, but the turning point came when under the guidance of Joe Petrosino the police began to enlist Italians, finding inside the organization itself the answer to Cosa Nostra."

If this is the basis of integration that is tinted with prejudice, will there ever be and Italian American President of the United States? The answer is, "Most definitely! It could be somebody like Andrew Cuomo because he married and divorced a Kennedy and especially because he is an Italian American who decided not to define himself solely based on his ethnicity, just like Barack Obama did" and was criticized by many African Americans for not being "black enough." The irony of fate however has made Cuomo a democrat whilst Scelsa maintains that "our meeting of interests with liberals is over" because "republicans share our values of family, nation and business" even if "very often Italian Americans keep this fact to themselves because only those who support the Democratic Party make headway in New York."

Discussing "assimilation into American society" also implies examining the question of food, and here Scelsa clearly states that "local Americans are one thing but Italians are something completely different." This is because of the simple fact that "Italian American food is a cultural tradition that was borne out of the impact of the place." For example, to "make pesto they didn't have basil and they used spinach" and they didn't have "pinenuts so they used walnuts instead" creating different dishes from their homeland. But these dishes continue to be very popular like Veal Parmesan and Spaghetti with Meatballs, dishes that sprang from the fact that they liked to taste the ingredients of "separate dishes" together, creating upheaval in the kitchen.

West Village, target-shooting Bin Laden

Pat and Steve are two bulky ex-security officers and they spend their days helping guests shoot 22 caliber rifles in the shooting range with three booths located in the basement of 77 MacDougal Street, between Bleecker Street and West Houston Street. These are rifles with five-shot clips and a sight capable of enabling any member of the club (between one course and the next at dinner) hit the mark if they want to have fun with the targets bearing a picture of Bin Laden and the words "Osama Been Leaded." We're in the target-shooting club of New York, better known as the Rifle Club, the fortress of gun owners that was founded on August fourteenth 1888 by a group of Italian-American immigrants, avid hunters to whom Garibaldi had written in his own hand clearly encouraging them and informing them that being capable of using firearms would always be a useful skill. The call was heeded and Garibaldi gave one of his small revolvers in the sign of friendship. That revolver today is on display on the third floor of the club, where there's the private room for members only, beneath the shrine that also contains photographs of the US Army helicopter Alpha team that in 2005 flew over the Sunni Triangle (an Islamic guerilla stronghold) bringing the American flag donated by the 330 members of the Rifle Club as a sign of solidarity with the troops engaged in combat against the enemies of the state.

Italian heritage and American patriotism merge in the room where the bust of Leonardo da Vinci, photographs of marines, rifles hung on the walls, masterpieces with depictions of the Old Country and shooting trophies welcome members and guests in the same place where the tenor Enrico Caruso sang, Mayor Fiorello LaGuardia and CEO Lee Iacocca ate, and VIPs often come, such as Anthony Fauci, the leading immunologist in the fight against AIDS who runs the national institute for the fight against allergies and infectious diseases.

The National Italian Rifle Club was first housed at 407 Canal Street in what the founders called Mazzini Hall, but the construction of the Holland Tunnel forced them to move and in 1919 they relocated to MacDougal Street. This is a place that is steeped in tradition. Every Friday evening, it is considered a "good interlude" during dinner to go down to the shooting range and shoot with Pat and Steve. At Thanksgiving, families bring their children to shoot at the shooting range and the one who hits the bull's-eye wins a frozen turkey. Guests who are not members are permitted, but not encouraged. The greatest nostalgia stems from the shooting lodge that they owned on Staten Island, the island that welcomed Garibaldi, with a bounty of pheasants that could be hunted without restriction. But those times are gone, the lodge was sold, the team of Fusiliers nowadays prefers to play golf rather than shoot. LaGuardia's writing desk is beneath a dust cover on the second floor and there's no trace now of Mussolini's portrait. It's difficult to tell on which wall it hung until fascist Italy joined the war against Franklin Delano Roosevelt's America. On the other hand, those were troubled times: Italians were suspected of conspiracy with the enemy, the Rifle Club removed the word "National" from its title and some of its members, like Alfred and Charles Rossotti, were forced to provided documents to prove their loyalty to the United States. Then during the war, many members wore the uniform, participating in the liberation of Italy, as in the case of the Major named Toscani, to whom the army entrusted the temporary government of the small Sicilian town of Licata. This town had an uncommon problem: the church didn't have a bell because it had been melted by the fascists for their war effort, and the citizens felt lost. Toscani had the idea of mounting a new bell taken from a unit of the US Navy in the bell tower. His plan was successful and is still remembered as symbolic of the contribution of what Italian heritage can make to America. Nowadays, instead, it's philanthropy that holds sway: members deposit large sums every year and this means that the club can donate about half a million dollars to works of charity. Angelo Bongiovanni, the general manager who feels more conformable speaking English says: "One year we gave the money to the Casa Italiana of New York University, but usually the money is destined to pay tuition fees for children who can't afford the cost of private Catholic schools and so it's invested in the education of the new generations." The main offices of the Rifle Club are located in what is the combination of three pre-war brick buildings. The Columbus Club is instead located on 69th Street which is a short distance from Central Park. During the summer and vacation time, members of both clubs collegially offer each other free access because there is the age-old custom of shared endeavors that focus attention on Italian heritage in New York. Giovanni Lanzarotti prepares food for everyone in the kitchen at MacDougal Street. He is a chef from Parma who has been working here for eighteen years. Every evening, after packing up whatever he selects, he goes up to the second floor to bring the dishes that turned out best to at least two police officers who, in their light blue uniforms and holstered guns, confess to believing that his dishes are "the best in the West Village."

John's, Lucky Luciano's East Village

Italian American cuisine is a cross between the original Italian dishes that the immigrants remembered and the impact that the new country had both on the ingredients themselves and on the way of eating. Roasted peppers with anchovies, pasta with meatballs and chicken Parmesan with spaghetti: for less than fifty dollars, beer included, you can immerse yourself in Italian American cuisine at John's. At 302 East 12th Street in the East Village, John's has been welcoming customers with the same dishes for over 100 years. It opened its doors in 1908 and it has stayed as it was back then: wooden tables, coat hooks on the walls and a circular bar. The one new addition is a flashy neon sign and around it the Lower East Side has completely changed with the arrival en masse of Asians who replaced Italians and Jews. The decor on the inside faithfully exemplifies that of the restaurants that in the early 1900s were frequented by figures like Joe Masseria and Lucky Luciano who made history in the New York mafia. On the 11th of August 1922, Masseria, known as "Joe the Boss" of the Genovese clan, chose the tables at John's as the place of retaliation against the gangster Umberto Valenti who only 72 hours before had tried to assassinate him to insure himself control of Little Italy. Masseria knew that Valenti loved the meatballs at John's and he conveniently showed up to meet him. There was a very quick handshake between the two that Masseria used as a signal to the dozen killers he had lying in wait. As Masseria stepped aside, they riddled Valenti with bullets. The shower of bullets hit customers and passersby resulting in many injuries. In the general confusion it was Lucky Luciano who approached to fire the death blow and thus provide Masseria the revenge that he sought. This episode at John's that connects two of the most ruthless and powerful mafia bosses, was a defining moment because it marked the moment when Lucky Luciano chose to side with Masseria in the underground war pitting him against his rival Salvatore Maranzano, another equally ruthless mafia boss. In 1931, Maranzano was killed in his office on Park Avenue and many attributed his murder to Luciano who from that point on began the "Americanization of the mafia", or in other words, the elimination of old bosses who had immigrated from Sicily and their replacement with new recruits who were brought up or had even been born in America. This is the framework that explains why the producers of the popular TV series *The Sopranos* chose to set some scenes from the alternate life of the Gandolfini family at John's. On the other hand, this is the area of Manhattan where almost every corner reminds us of Cosa Nostra. At 11 on East 11th Street, a mutilated and tortured corpse was found in a garbage can on April 13th 1903. It was the body of Benedetto Madonia who at the time was involved in the trafficking of illegal goods with his bosses Giuseppe Morello and Ignazio Lupo. At 332 East, at the beginning of January 1908, the hatchet men of the Black Hand demolished the first two floors of a building to terrorize the residents of the homes to be able to blackmail them in the years to come. On the corner of 11th Street and Second Avenue on the 31 of September 1922, the alcohol trafficker Ignazio La Barbera was gunned down. On top of his lifeless body, the assassins left the keys to a nearby warehouse where the police found 39 barrels, each containing 20 liters of alcohol. They also found tools and materials necessary to run a fully functioning large still. Moving one more street south you get to 10th East where at 265 stands the building where the young Charles "Lucky" Luciano lived with his parents and family from 1906, when they arrived from Sicily, until 1926. It's a rundown apartment building and the few renovations done haven't made the inner staircases less fetid. This is where the boy who would become the most influential American gangster had his first introduction to crime. Back then they still used the name given to him when he was born in Lercara Friddi in 1897, Salvatore Lucania. As a child "Lucky" was an aggressive pickpocket but he soon progressed to the next level when he went to the nearby public school and began threatening his classmates to extort money from then in exchange for "protection." Meyer Lansky, a Jewish classmate from Columbia Street who was the same age as "Lucky," was one of the few to dismiss these threats and blackmail. On the streets of Little Italy and Chinatown they created, it is said, a legendary criminal duo chancing upon rivalries and business deals with other boys they became friends with, like Louis Lepke, Bugsy Seigel and George Uffner .

To try to get a feel for this world back then, besides the flavors and tables at John's, at the East Village Visitors Center, there are the *Gangsters and Murderers of the Lower East Side* tours. The tours are guided by Eric Ferrara who is a professor at Brooklyn College and the founder of the Museum of the American Gangster at 80 St Mark's Place in Noho. Or you could try Alberto Bonanno's stainless steel barber shop chairs at 2012 East 16th Street, on the corner with Third Avenue. Bonanno came from Cosenza in 1963 when he was eighteen years of age and he has never stopped cutting hair on his twelve-hour workdays since then. He recalls: "one time a mafia thug sent by John Gotti came in and offered me 5,000 stolen dollars in exchange for $2,500. I kicked him out and never saw him again." The old-style salon that he owns is a rarity in Manhattan nowadays, and one of the first people to discover it was David Letterman who found the place by accident towards the end of the Nineties. Letterman decided to set one of his shows there later on. Alberto Bonanno proudly states that he has "nothing to do with the mafiosi who share his name" and that he knows Americans "better than anybody else" for the simple reason that for forty years he has been "listening to them and talking to them" while cutting their hair. This is how he depicts them: "they talk about sports, politics and women. The sport is usually baseball, it's best to be careful about politics because they take themselves too seriously and if they're contradicted they're apt to get very angry. As for sex, women pull the strings because they like to have fun and men give in and get taken for heaps of money." Among his clients there are also some police officers and a while back one of them complained that the price he paid was unfair "compared to what was printed on the pricelist." When the plain clothed officer met Bonanno on the metro, he attacked him. The Calabrese barber with a slender body and grey hair is a black belt in Karate and the officer came out on the losing end. He later went on to sue the barber for the injuries he had sustained. Bonanno admits with a bitter smile: "A KO never cost me so much, I had to pay him 5,000 dollars."

43rd Street, the American Italians of the Calandra Institute

The bronze bust of John Calandra, a table covered with the latest editions of the local newspapers in Italian, a shelf with books about the New Orleans lynching and the heroism of Joe Petrosino, a gallery of posters on the immigration saga, yellowed passports with the crest of Victor Emanuel II, and photos of Madonna: We are at the Calandra Institute on the seventeenth floor of building 24 on West 43rd Street in Midtown. It is a research institute of The City University of New York, a laboratory of the Italian-American identity that is forever evolving. Heading the institute is Anthony Julian Tamburri, who has origins both in Settefrati (Ciociaria) and Faeto (Apulia) and who speaks with a Tuscan accent. He explains to students, researchers and anyone else who's interested, how prejudice, both positive and negative, doesn't stand up to the test of reality. "Only 65% of the Americans of Italian descent who study in New York schools identify themselves as 'Italian' while the remaining 33% define themselves simply as 'caucasian'" or in other words, as white, to distinguish themselves from African Americans or Hispanics. Not considering the Italian language that "the younger generations don't know" and the family traditions "that many forget." But this doesn't belie the fact that when the Calandra Institute mentors are sent out to the city schools, they are besieged by hundreds of school children wanting to relate to their "Italian cultural advisers." "It's not a contradiction," Tamburri explains, "but it confirms that a new type of identity that we can define as American-Italian, is asserting itself." American customs prevail although there is the need to "speak and have contact" with those of "Italian heritage," because this implies a "shared understanding" based on "knowing what it's like to live in an Italian family." The binomial "American-Italian" that Tamburri has in mind describes those who have Italian heritage–their family comes from Italy–or they were born in Italy, or grew up and graduated from university there, but have been living in the US for quite a number of years. For "quite a number" of years he implies at least 10, if these people carry out both their professional and personal activities for the most part in the United States, though they might take many trips home to Italy each year. Tamburri adds that "they are people who have put down roots in America yet still remain attached to Italy." This transformation fascinates the people working at the Calandra Institute because it lays out the challenge that this new phase of integration in America poses. Tamburri laments the fact that "in Italy, those who realize what's going on over here are few and far between." It's a "cultural amnesia" highlighted by the fact that "Italian-American writers are rarely published in Italy," as shown by the very few translations of Don DeLillo or by the fact that the novelist David Baldacci opted for the American name David B. Ford to get his first books published. Instead the subjects of a negatively biased literature seem to persist such as the writings of Giuseppe Prezzolini that describe the Italian emigrant as "mentally disturbed" in *The Transplanted* from 1963, or Emilio Cecchi who focused on *America Amara* (Bitter America) in 1939. Tamburri stresses the fact that "in Italy there is a dearth of research on Italian Americans and we see the consequences in the fact that a negative image of the emigrant to America is now ingrained and it dates back to the first half of the twentieth century whilst little attention has been given to transformations experienced by immigrants up to the American Italian phenomenon." He has written essays about Madonna, and he chose to go against the current in his approach to the controversy over *Jersey Shore*, the reality TV show on MTV that presents the lives of young Italians highlighting their many excesses. For many Italian-American associations, from the NIAF to Sons of Italy, *Jersey Shore* broadcasts the prejudice against *"thuggish Italians,"* or in other terms, "Guidos" and "Guidettes," the body-building guys with gold chains and the vulgar girls with breast implants. Tamburri maintains, instead, that a more appropriate interpretation of the Guido phenomenon is given by the CUNY sociologist, Donald Tricarico.

The theory that Tricarico presents to his audience at the Calandra Institute is that the cultural model of the Guido derives from the convergence of the Italian-American working class and pop culture that was brought to the screen by Hollywood in the film *Saturday Night Fever* in 1977. The protagonist of the film Tony Manero (played by John Travolta) always dressed in white, dances non-stop in the clubs of New York with Bensonhurst in the background, the neighborhood of Brooklyn where up until 1980 about 100 thousand Italians lived. "The consumption of the products of pop culture, for the working class, means becoming part of a higher class," Tricarico observes. He believes that it all stems from the Italian American's desire "to become somebody." Tricarico maintains that the term Guido can be traced back to "cugino" (cousin) that was very popular in working-class Brooklyn in the Eighties and was used as a distinction from the term Brother used by African Americans to show association with a group of friends. The popularity of Studio 54 at the end of the last century, TV series such as *Growing up Gotti, Mambo Italiano* broadcast on radio stations like Brooklyn's WKTU and social networks like Night Social Life, contributed to the transformation of Guidos into a mass phenomenon that spread all over New York following Italian Americans wherever they went. It started in Bensonhurst and South Brooklyn, it moved towards New Jersey when, between 1980 and 2000, thousands of families with higher incomes who were fleeing neighborhoods with African Americans and Hispanics chose to cross the Verrazano or to settle on Staten Island which immediately became known as "Staten Italy." Speaking of the *nouveau riche* with such a strong group identity that it rivals even that of mafia clans, Tricarico adds that "Guidos became a way for a particular ethic group of whites to have their version of hip hop culture." To support the idea of this tribal matrix, just as in the case of African-American hip hop followers, Guidos and Guidettes have exterior characteristics. "They are always dressed as if they are going to a night club or to the gym," they listen continuously to "freestyle and club music" and they pay particular attention to their hairdos: the men wear their hair short and fiercely jelled back whilst the women wear their hair "long and always straightened" with an array of different products that they carry with them at all times, requiring the use of giant handbags. Tamburri sees in Tricarico's description, one of the many examples of the convergence of *italianness* and American pop culture: Guidos and Guidettes carry the symbols of the Italian-American working class with them–the Italian flag, tattoos with Latin phrases and large gold crosses around their necks–and combine them with the music and consumerism that define the tribes of young New Yorkers. This means that it is necessary to "really understand what's happening among Italians in America without allowing others, even popular TV channels, to define ourselves."

Francesca, the life of undocumented immigrants

They say they are just "off the boat." They are undocumented Italian immigrants. In New York, there are hundreds if not thousands of them. They land at JFK and Newark International airports with the same determination to stay here as the immigrants who crossed the Atlantic on steamships and disembarked at Ellis Island at the beginning of the twentieth century. The only difference lies in the fact that in post-9/11 America, the anti-illegal immigrant laws are the harshest that have ever been enacted. There are some who have lived without papers from three, five or even up to fifteen years. They cannot return home, they have to live protected by lies, they fear the glance of a police officer and are persistently trying to find a way to solve unexpected problems like a sudden illness or the need to drive a car. Francesca is one of them. She was born in Latina in 1977. She got her sarcasm from her Tuscan mother and her light-colored eyes from her Sicilian father but she has a roman accent. I meet her in a pizzeria on the Upper East Side, the neighborhood that gathers the highest percentage of millionaires on the planet, where she has worked since arriving in February of 2001. "We had a pizzeria in Latina but business wasn't good, my brother had already made up his mind to come to New York and I decided to follow him." In the beginning it was "perfection": that's what the bus-girl says (the girl who shows customers to their tables before the waiter comes, or the coat-check girl.) Every evening I earned 110 dollars, we still had the lira back then…. That was almost 200 thousand lira a night… I felt rich, when I used to say that to other people my age, they didn't believe me." She was so happy that she didn't think about her papers. The three allotted months passed and she didn't even realize that she was now illegal. Summer arrived and brought additional work, then September 11. "That morning lots of people came up from Downtown on foot, they sat at the restaurant, they ate to relax and distract themselves, credit cards and computers weren't working, they were all crying, they thought that at least 20 thousand people were dead." The shock was so great that she decided to return to Italy. She removed the expired green stub from her passport, she went to Kennedy Airport "with her heart in her mouth" and when they asked her for the stub at the check-in desk, she replied vaguely: "I must have lost it... I don't know." It worked and she got though security, she returned to Latina, got a new passport and came back to New York with brand new documents. Now the choice to stay illegally was conscious. When the three months were up she knew what that meant: "no driver's license, no medical insurance and the risk of getting deported within a matter of days if the police find you without papers." But life soon proved to be less difficult than she had anticipated. "I went to the IRS and they gave me a tax number that allowed me to get a bank account and a credit card." She worked as a wine consultant going from store to store offering and tasting different products. She was paid well but had the constant problem of having her checks made out to a third party. She found an apartment for rent thanks to a relative who acted as a guarantor with the owner and she had enough money to work in Manhattan and even to go to the beach in Miami a few times. It's a precarious life, but "it works." She decided to go back to the restaurant where "being paid under the table is easier because there are no wages and money comes entirely from tips." She became a waitress and that meant earning more because each customer leaves at least 15 percent of the bill, and she could pocket 800-1000 dollars per week. Then in the most banal way, the unforeseen occurred: she hit her toe off the door and fractured it. She had to go to the hospital but couldn't give her real name, she lied and made up her personal details, "they have to treat you in the Emergency Room." Months passed and she had to go back to hospital a few times, for different reasons: she always gave a different name and changed Emergency Room to avoid detection. She did this too when she gave birth to her daughter with the young Egyptian Copt that she had just married. He is a perfume store designer with his papers in order. "The wedding at City Hall was fun, they only asked me my name and if I was already married and nothing else." She confidently states that "there are many like me," even though "most undocumented immigrants have been here for at least ten years because after 9/11 immigration checks have become much more rigid and fewer people are willing to take the risk." Among "the many Italians in my situation" there is a young Sardinian who "has been living here for twelve years, he doesn't have his papers yet and has his parents come visit him often but he really struggles with the fact that he cannot go back to Italy." And what's the worst thing for Francesca about being here illegally? "Not being able to go to the beach in Sabaudia, to Torre Paola during the summer…. To see the sea… here they don't have the sea, they have the ocean but it's really cold in August." Not being able to go to the sea "makes me cry like a baby every summer weekend." The light at the end of the tunnel is that her marriage to a legal immigrant opens the way for her to "sooner or later" get her papers in order. "I got married for love but many do it to become legal quickly," she states. This is why a clandestine market is now flourishing: "Most often Hispanics, both men and women, offer to marry illegal immigrants, the price varies from 7 thousand to 10 thousand dollars, half due at the wedding and the other half when the documents arrive which can be as many as three years later." The police at this point know how it all works and "when they get married they must show photographs of trips taken together, otherwise they don't believe you." The way illegal immigrants are pursued is suffocating. "If they catch you, they put you in a cell until they take you before a judge, then they find the first flight and they deport you. There are no exceptions, they are very strict." There are many Italians who like Francesca fear "being caught" and live in the constant fear of "making a fatal error" but they are reassured by the fact that "in this city nobody judges you or asks you, what counts… is that you work" and that "makes everything easier." The nightmare is the Arizona model, the state that passed laws that allow the police to stop anyone to check that their residency permits are on order: "It is shameful, this nation was built by immigrants and undoubtedly not all of them were legal from their first day of residence." The other thing that she can't stand is anti-Italian prejudice. "Here when they call you 'Guido' it is a very harsh insult." Then she adds: "Italian Americans are not like us. I lived in Queens for a while on a street that was full of them, they go around in sweats, they are vulgar, they say 'lobadroom' instead of 'bathroom'… in Italy we would say they are 'crude'," besides the fact that they "eat food that is all their own and has little to do with our cuisine."

Verdi Square, Upper West Side

Cesare Casella is one of the most esteemed chefs in Manhattan and Santino Battiata is the ex-mailman who sells pizza by the slice. They couldn't be more different. Casella is fifty years old, he comes from Lucca where he owned the restaurant Il Vipore that Henry Kissinger and Tom Cruise used to frequent. He came to Manhattan in the Nineties; he gave cooking lessons at the cooking school at Macy's (the largest store on the planet). He worked for the best restaurants in the city before he opened La Salumeria Rosi in 2009, designed by Dante Ferretti, where he sells Parma Prosciutto, mortadella, pork roast, pork loin and speck ham all strictly Made In Italy. Battiata, instead, comes from Castellammare del Golfo in Sicily. He came to New York in 1965 when he was fourteen. After a short stretch in the public schools in Brooklyn, he worked in a coat factory, he worked for the United States Postal Service, and opened a candy store before staking his bets on the pizzeria. New Pizza Town opened in 1985, there's nothing fancy in the décor and it's situated on the corner of Broadway and 78th Street. Since its opening he has had to contend every day with the homeless people that hang out on the sidewalk in front of the entrance. What the paths of the Tuscan chef and the Sicilian pizza maker have in common is their point of arrival. Twenty-four years apart they both landed near Verdi Square that encloses a small triangular park between 72nd and 73rd Streets and the intersection of Amsterdam and Broadway. The name is linked to Giuseppe Verdi, symbol of the Risorgimento, to whom a marble statue that was completed in 1906 by the sculptor Pasquale Civiletti is dedicated. He chose to add depictions of four of Verdi's most popular characters to the base of the statue: Falstaff, Aida, Othello and Leonora from the Force of Destiny. Dante Park is nearby, right in front of the New York City Opera at the Lincoln Center. Both for Casella and Battiata, opening their businesses near Verdi Square was just by chance, but their presence contributes to giving an Italian aura to this corner of the Upper West Side where there are also other points of reference: the Turinese ice-cream shop Grom, at the corner between Broadway and 76th Street, the Beacon Theatre, two blocks south, where well-known musicians from Renzo Arbore to Paolo Conte come to play, the Citarella grocery store and the Fairway supermarket that offer an updated selection of Italian products. Verdi Square, though, isn't another Little Italy because the Italians who frequent it belong to the new generation that is much different from the first generation of immigrants that arrived. They are mostly professionals who arrived from 1980 on and they go back and forth to Italy but aim to integrate into the fabric of life in New York. They don't express their identity with tricolor flags in their windows and they don't speak in dialect but they often gladly seek out tastes and smells of home if prepared properly. Cesare Casella who used the name Nabucco for the company with which he opened his deli says: "I like Verdi Square because it is like a little town right in the middle of the most cosmopolitan city in the world." Precisely because it feels like it's in the "town square" the tables of Salumeria Rosi, at 283 Amsterdam Avenue, offer products that you could find in the most traditional Italian deli. Casella reiterates that "Italian cuisine must be pure and that is why it is loved, it stands apart from Italian-American cuisine which is a different experience." The irony of fate has it that in New York today "the best Italian chefs are not Italian" he adds with a dash of self-criticism naming the Americans that he considers "absolute stars": Mark Ladner at Del Posto, Michael White at Marea, Scott Conant at Scarpetta and Paul Bartolotta who moved his Bartolotta's to Las Vegas. To understand Casella's approach to New York you have to go listen to him at his crowded classes at the De Gustibus School which is run by Salvatore Rizzo on the eighth floor of Macy's. Here he describes his adolescence "spent among pig farmers" from whom he learned that "the recipe for a good ham was and always will be one: salt, air and happy pigs."

Santino Battiata, instead, makes Margherita and Neapolitan pizzas with Italian products that he prepares himself. Over the years he has learned to choose "the right pizza sauce "either making it himself or buying the ones that "are closest in taste to the products back in Sicily" which are sometimes "Italian but can also be Spanish or Israeli sauces." The result is that Hollywood stars like Alec Baldwin and Whoopi Goldberg are regular customers as are officers from the Police Department. If you stop by New Pizza Town at any time of the day of night you'll see a police cruiser parked at the front or on the side with officers inside eating a variety of foods. "Yes, it's true" Battiata says gesturing with his hands, "police officers come here to eat between shifts, but they do it just like many other Americans who eat pizza for lunch because it's light and they can have it for dinner too." For Santino Battiata satisfaction comes from seeing the police officers crowd around his counter to buy calzones and pizzas with the strangest toppings because "when I opened there was a lot of crime here, drugs, no security, I needed a bouncer to be able to work and very few police officers passed by, and none of them came in. The change "came when our Rudy Giuliani became mayor," who with zero tolerance for crime rid the city of violent offenders and allowed Santino Battiata to increase his earnings, profits and investments. He states with obvious pride, "Today I have 6 or 7 houses and a villa in Pompano Beach in Florida." The difference between Casella and Battiata is in their relationship to New York: the chef is completely projected towards the future, to transforming Salumeria Rosi into a jumping off point towards an even more promising market, whilst the pizza maker looks back, he doesn't think so much about food anymore and he reveals a profound fear. "In twenty years there won't be any more Italian Americans here because emigration is over. Before, 40 thousand Italians arrived per year, most of them from Sicily and Campania, but now the standard of living has improved in Italy and they stay there whilst over here the young people assimilate, they are American in every way, they don't speak our language and they don't support our events like the Saint Joseph Day celebration on Long Island. Italians are growing old as the young people disperse, our identity is based on our language but our children don't care about it at all."

East Harlem, in Rao's world

At the intersection of 116th Street and Lexington Avenue there's The Lucky Corner, the corner of East Harlem where in the Twenties the young Republican Representative Fiorello LaGuardia chose to have his rallies and where later, when he became Mayor in 1934, he left it to his successor Vito Marcantonio who gathered Italians and Puerto Ricans there in one place and transformed it into the launching pad to get to Washington where he became one of the Representatives of the American Labor Party, the most leftwing party in the entire Congress. Also Edward Corsi, a contemporary of Marcantonio but a Republican, owed his fortunes to the Lucky Corner. If the intersection brings luck to Italian politicians, it's because it's situated in the heart of the most populous Little Italy in New York. In the Thirties, in the area bordered by 96th Street to the south, 125th Street to the north, Lexington Avenue to the west and the East River to the east, there were 89 thousand Italian immigrants. That was about 81 percent of the residents of the area, (in Little Italy on the Lower East Side it was 88% but the actual number of residents was smaller) and on some blocks the Italian presence was staggering: 672 Italians out of a population of 682, 703 out of 720 and 914 out of 932. This massive settlement, as documented by the research of historian Gerald Meyer from New York University, sprang from the arrival of the first immigrants from Polla, in the province of Salerno, in 1878. These immigrants settled on 115th Street triggering the replication of the topographical subdivisions of home that from the beginning of the twentieth century would begin in the other Little Italy. Those from Bari settled on 112th Street, those from Sarno in Campania on 107th Street, the Calabrians on 109th Street and 100th Street was divided between Sicilians on the first and second blocks and groups from northern Italy on the other blocks. They were a mass of farmers who couldn't find work in industry and thus created a local economy based on stores, bakeries, pastry shops, fruit shops, pizza parlors and small restaurants. Working in one of the many delis was Pasquale "Patsy's" Lancieri who on August 19, 1933, opened the "restaurant-pizzeria" that is still on First Avenue on the corner with 118th Street and boasts the "lightest" pizza "of New York" thanks to a wood burning oven that is still in the position where the founder wanted it to be. In 1933 a whole oven-made pizza sold for 60 cents. In the dining room of the restaurant an imposing portrait of Frank Sinatra hangs on one wall that is also covered with photographs telling the history of East Harlem starting with the Lucky Corner of LaGuardia and Marcantonio because it marked the debut of Italian Americans in the political life of the city. There are also numerous photos of Tony Bennett on the restaurant walls, a star whose importance rivals that of Sinatra. Two streets north, 116th

Street was the commercial drag of Uptown Little Italy where everything was sold and where the families of professionals who had established themselves more quickly, lived: doctors, lawyers, and teachers. The traces that remain are the biscotti of the Morrone Bakery at 324 East, and at 227 East the headquarters of the association named after the two political leaders LaGuardia and Marcantonio. In front of Patsy's Pizzeria there's Rex's, that sells lemon ice, and a block further south, at 2268 First Avenue, there's Ascione Pharmacy that welcomes its customers with the same sign "Purity and Accuracy" that it has used since it first opened. Then, on 115th Street, between Pleasant and First Avenues, Our Lady of Mount Carmel has stood since 1884. Italians built this church because they were not welcome to attend the Catholic churches run by the Irish. The rivalry was such that the Italian immigrants mobilized their community to build the church by themselves. The carters brought the material that had been bought with voluntary contributions and the builders built it with the help of artisans who worked with wood, iron and marble. Despite this, when work was completed on the church, Italians still continued to pray in the basement until 1919 when the first Italian priest, Gaspare Dalia, became Parish Priest. The statue of Our Lady of Carmel wasn't brought inside the upper Church until 1923 and the hard-fought battle explains why Pope Leo XIII decided to pronounce it a Basilica in 1903, and why the celebration of Our Lady Of Mount Carmel, which takes place every year in June, continues to attract thousands of believers from every corner of the United States. But an exodus of Italians from East Harlem which began in 1950 following a wave of petty crime brought by Hispanic gangs involved in drug trafficking, transformed the white marble Basilica into a cathedral in the desert of "Barrio" ruled by Porto Ricans. It is, however, still caringly adorned with tricolor banners by the students of the nearby school of the same name. The other educational institution in the area until 1982 was the high school named after Benjamin Franklin (today the Manhattan Center for Science and Mathematics is located on its grounds). The educator Leonard Covello headed the school from 1936 until 1956 and he made it a training ground for the children of Italian immigrants and then used this experience to the advantage of the new generations of Hispanics.

At the intersection between 114th Street and Pleasant Avenue, right opposite Jefferson Park, there's Rao's which is a much more lively, vibrant and popular spot. The restaurant which was opened by Charles Rao in 1896 is run by Ron Straci and Frank Pellegrino, better known as "Frankie No" because of his refusal to take reservations because his eleven tables are "always assigned" to individual customers who go there every evening, by themselves or with guests. Rao's offers the most traditional of Italian-American cuisine, from meatballs to Steak Pizzaiola with a spicy tomato sauce, just like the ones prepared by "Uncle Vinnie" Rao who, with a cowboy hat on his head, ran the kitchen until he passed away in 1999. The fact that it is a restaurant with "assigned tables,"–even stars like Madonna have been on the receiving end of Frank Pellegrino's "no", whilst Bill Clinton and Bill Gates were able to eat there only because they had been invited by others–turns it into a microcosm of characters who are frozen in time and who seem have just stepped out of a Hollywood film. This is true in the case of Louis Barone, better known as Louie Lump Lump. He has been a customer for more than forty years. He's 66 years of age and comes from a family suspected of having ties to the Genevose clan. Three nights before Christmas in 2004, he was sitting at the bar, he placed his order and then shot thirty-seven year old Al Circelli with a 38 caliber revolver because of some "unflattering comments" he made about a singer at the restaurant that Barone liked. A commotion followed, a pool of blood collected on the floor, and two plain-clothed police officers identified themselves and ran to apprehend the shooter. The incident, however, didn't have much of an effect on Rao's. Seven days later it was just as full as usual with the singer on duty belting out 'O sole mio' and Frankie on the phone repeating his usual line: "I'm sorry, all our tables are full." Five years later, Rao's was making headlines in the tabloids again. This time it was because of seventy-five year old Anthony Rabito, better known as "Fat Tony" because his weight is steadily over 100kgs. At the end of August 2009, he got out of Loretto prison in Pennsylvania after doing two years for extortion, racketeering and gambling and received what for him was the worst punishment. The Manhattan district judge in charge of his file, in an effort to keep him far from the Bonanno mafia clan, decided to "distance him from the world of crime" by forcing him to abandon the "traditional" gangster "meeting" places: restaurants. So he couldn't "patronize anymore" the four New York restaurants considered likely meeting points for suspected mobsters. The first on the list, it goes without saying, was Rao's where Fat Tony's favorite dish was lemon chicken that cost twenty-four dollars, prepared according to Uncle Vinnie's recipe with a special sauce made with lemon juice, red wine, olive oil and spices. "I've eaten at those tables all my life, what will I do?", the dejected gangster asked himself, forced to abandon the places that over time he had selected as natural alternatives to "Uncle Vinnie's." These places were Bamonte's in Williamsburg, at 32 Withers Street, for "a big plate of clams," Don Peppe , at 135 Lefferts Boulevard in Ozone Park Queens for linguine with lobster sauce, and Parkside on Corona Avenue in Spaghetti Park where they serve *chicken scarpariello* seasoned with rosemary, garlic, oil, wine and chicken broth. "Rao's is one of a kind" according to Fat Tony whose world speech is peppered with Americanized Italian words, for example, he says "checca" for cake, "bega" for bag, "storu" for store and "carru" for car.

Staten Island, from Jesus to Mazzini

Staten Island is better known by New Yorkers as "Staten Italy" because of the sheer volume of Italian Americans that live there. They are 34.8 percent of the almost 450 thousand residents, the county with the highest population density in the United States. Giuseppe Garibaldi arrived there after the fall of the Roman Republic inspired by Giuseppe Mazzini, and worked in the candle factory of the Florentine inventor Antonio Meucci who had fled from Italy after being arrested for expressing Risorgimento ideals. In his house on Staten Island, 420 Tompkins Avenue, Meucci successfully tested a rudimentary prototype for the telephone. At the end of the 1800s, thousands of immigrants came to the North Shore for the low housing costs, for the view of the Hudson Bay that brings to mind the bays of the Mediterranean, and for the possibility of living all together a little bit isolated from the big city just like in the towns back home. They came to live on the streets of Rosebank that since 1937 has had the shrine of Our Lady of Mount Carmel, at 36 Amity Street, the sacred place of New York that most resembles the grottos that Catholic pilgrims flock to in Europe. The Grotto stands a short distance from the ex-Meucci factory which has now been converted into a museum dedicated to Garibaldi. It incorporates the two original identities of the first immigrants who arrived at this outpost which was settled by the Dutch in XVII century: faith in Jesus Christ and trust in Giuseppe Mazzini. The Grotto was built by volunteers, both lay and religious people of the Our Lady of Mount Carmel Society, as a shared sanctuary, a place to go pray and meditate, just like at the nearby churches and little altars built at home. It contains a crucifix, a kneeler, a fountain, a monument and an altar to Saint Anthony of Padua. Work on the construction of the grotto continues to this day and the faithful decorate it with shells and bicycle reflectors, adding to the frugal look that makes it blend with the nearby meeting hall, built in 1914 by a few immigrants, used as a work hall during the construction and later transformed into another space for religious celebrations. Faith and History aside, life in Rosebank, the main Italian-American center on the island, is lived through activities linked to the catholic churches of St. Mary and St. Joseph and two annual events: the Rose Fair that takes place in October in combination with Columbus Day that celebrates Italian-American heritage, and the Feast of Our Lady of Mount Carmel that takes place in July with an impressive procession through the city streets that ends at the Grotto. It's an environment in which Catholicism and ethnic identity overlap and this explains why local residents, like those of nearby Snug Harbor, at the beginning of January, encourage schools and community centers to find a way to host performances and shows that focus on the figure of Befana. But all of this doesn't suffice to explain the high number of Italian Americans amassed on the island. As far back as the end of XIX century there was a significant Italian presence but what made the number take off altogether was the construction of the Verrazano Bridge in 1964. The bridge connected Staten Island to Brooklyn and to the rest of New York for the first time, where before only been ferries had been used. The bridge had a strong impact on the Italian-American population that, after leaving the Lower East Side for Brooklyn in the Forties, in the Fifties underwent the phenomenon of the *White Flight* with the relocation of little groups to more elegant and open suburbs on Staten Island and in nearby New Jersey. The bridge accelerated this phenomenon, adding to the Italian-American population from earlier migrations—new families or families that arrived between the end of the Forties and the beginning of the Sixties. From that moment onwards the Italian stronghold of New York didn't only grow in number but also in income, with the consequent political shift towards the Republican Party which was more focused on the economic interests of business owners and stockholders and was also defender of traditional family values that many Italian Americans consider their own. All of this bore political fruit in the most recent round of elections. In the presidential elections of 2008, Staten Island was the only New York district to favor the Republican John McCain and in November of 2009 the votes from Staten Island allowed the outgoing mayor Michael Bloomberg to be re-elected for the second time despite the surprising success of his democratic challenger William Thompson. Bloomberg won by just 50 thousand votes and it was the advantage that he gained on Staten Island, 31,125 votes, that proved to be critical.

The construction of the bridge that connects Staten Island to Bay Ridge, Brooklyn, was essential to the growth of the Italian-American community and the naming of the bridge was the result of a hard-fought battle. It was the unwavering John LaCorte, president of the Italian Historical Society of America who in 1951 proposed naming it after the Florentine navigator Giovanni da Verrazano. He had also been a key player in establishing the Columbus Day celebration and parade along Fifth Avenue. LaCorte's theory was that da Varrazano deserved the recognition because in 1594 he was the first to actually sail into the port of New York, well before 1606, when Henry Hudson repeated the route using the Florentine's navigational maps. Robert Moses, however, who was in charge of the building of the bridge as Chairman of the Triborough Bridge and the Tunnel Authority, opposed the name because it wasn't "well-known" and besides it was not very easy to pronounce for New Yorkers. But these were objections that didn't discourage LaCorte whose response was to launch a lobbying offensive that managed to first recruit the governor of the state, Averell Harriman, and then a series of towns along the coast and finally the whole parliament of Albany that approved a law in favor of the Verrazzano Bridge then enacted by the new governor Nelson Rockefeller in 1960. But the story doesn't end here. The assassination of John F. Kennedy in Dallas in 1963 caused the governor and Albany to consider changing the name in honor of the president. LaCorte went in person to plead with the only person who could help him: the minister for Justice Robert Kennedy. He convinced him. The brother of the assassinated president declared that he was in favor of the Verrazzano Bridge and he ended the controversy (instead the city airport up until then named Idlewild was given the president's name), allowing the inauguration of the bridge at 11:00 on the morning of November 21, 1964. Gay Talese, writer of New Journalism was one of the people present at the inauguration and he covered it for the *New York Times*. He wrote in his notebook: "the first toll of 50 cents was paid by twenty-two year old George Scarpelli, a council worker, driving a Cadillac with six passengers from Staten Island; the change was given to the collector Larry Chrusano who put it in his pocket and replaced it with his own." An all-Italian debut.

Faith

The Vatican flag on St. Patrick's

The white and yellow flag with the papal emblem waves at the main entrance to St. Patrick's Cathedral on Fifth Avenue and it can be found inside every Catholic Church in America. "Stand before any altar, from the heart of Manhattan to the smallest church in Wyoming, and you'll see the American flag in one corner and the Vatican flag in the opposite corner," says Archbishop Celestino Migliore. In 2012 he completed seven years in New York gaining experience as Permanent Observer of the Holy See to the United Nations and he's the person with whom the Catholic Church in American prefers to collaborate. He explains, "What distinguishes American Catholicism is that it's composed of believers who openly declare their faith to society around them," listing many examples. The papal flag in all churches is just one example, but there are others from "the Catholics who go around with a very noticeable cross on their foreheads on Ash Wednesday, to "the toast to the Pope on gala evenings," to "public prayers for soldiers in Iraq or Afghanistan that would be unthinkable in any European nation." American Catholics are "believers who don't hide their faith," they believe and "practice prayer" as "an externalization of their faith" and "they donate generously based on the *give back* principle that is firmly ingrained." What it means is this: those who are successful feel the need to make donations as a way of giving what they received back to God, and therefore they do works of charity." For Migliore it is "a practice that coincides with the original Christian sentiment that wasn't about sacrifice but instead about sharing with those who are in need, and so helping the poor." This *giving back* is possible thanks to the particular tax system that is in place in the US that incentivizes and facilitates donations to charity organizations, and it thus promotes the tendency to be "Active Christians" and "embody a profound sense of dependence on God." For Migliore, who was at Benedict XVI's side during his visit to New York in April of 2008, these are the characteristics that form the basis "of the solidity of Catholic Faith in America" and its importance to the Church is so great that there is the possibility of a future American pope. "After 475 years of Italian popes there was a Polish one and now a German, the preliminary question of geography has been overcome and it is now legitimate to ask "why not an American Pope? The salvation of the catholic faith could come from a religious country like this before coming from other places in the Third World, Asia, Africa or Latin America." When he speaks of a possible "American Pope" Monsignor Migliore, born in Cuneo and Titular Archbishop of Canosa in Apulia, emphasizes how "this nation is much less secular than Europe" and the fact that "the objections about the disproportionate concentration of power in the US don't make much sense because the Catholic Church can't be likened to the Security Council of the United Nations." On board the plane crossing the Atlantic for the United States, Ratzinger himself spoke about the deep religiosity that permeates American society and Migliore pauses to cite various examples that recall the war in Iraq. "It was 2003, I had just arrived, and I remember that in Ohio there was a public catholic mass for a soldier who had survived, in Italy there were people who ironized the event and made incorrect comparisons with the Nazi 'Gott mit uns' during World War II because they don't understand that in this county there is a strong sense of the presence of God in life." As a consequence, many Catholics in New York, Italian Americans first among them, often find themselves living a cultural discrepancy between Roman Law–which is the basis of Canon Law–and Common Law which is the architrave of Anglo-Saxon law. Or, for example, they find themselves having to confront a conflict of conscience in the case of nuns who after spending decades building important catholic schools and clinics in North America are now obliged to close some of them, to the detriment of the poor, because it is impossible for them to reconcile the principles of their beliefs with the civil laws that provide for the installation of condom machines in schools for example, or women's right to abortion.

Migliore's other role was that of "Observer" of the Holy See at the Uited Nations. "The term 'pontif' means builder of bridges and at the UN this is precisely the role played by the Holy See because it has an informal function and doesn't vote in the General Assembly." The fact that it's "informal" allowed Migliore to be protagonist in negotiations on various fronts: rights of the handicapped, the protection of women and against the new slavery of human trafficking and the arms trade. At times on topics such as the opposition to abortion and Gay rights, Migliore, who is now Apostolic Nuncio to Poland, found himself in the difficult position of having Muslim countries where the rights of Catholics are not respected at his side as allies "and I always chose to avoid decisions that could entail forsaking the defense of those who are persecuted or discriminated against." Migliore states that he lived "the most beautiful moment in my seven and a half years in New York," right in the hall of the General Assembly when Benedict XVI at the end of his speech received an extended a standing ovation by all of the ambassadors present. "There were people who cynically said that those same ambassadors the next day would start quarrelling again right away, but for me it was the exact opposite, the Pope's words embodied the ideals of the UN shared by all, and managed for once to identify a common ground."

Brooklyn, the faithful and the anticlerical

Nicholas DiMarzio, Bishop of Brooklyn and Queens, spends 16 hours a day at the main office of the diocese on the corner of Prospect and 19th Street. It is a red brick building that also includes one of the 200 catholic parishes that depend on him. From the windows, the highway that crosses through Brooklyn is visible. In the conference room there are crucifixes, icons, religious books, photographs

of Karol Wojtyla and Joseph Ratzinger, a *Zedakà* box (a Jewish dona-
tion box) and an Islamic picture showing the 99 attributes of Allah.
DiMarzio wears a cassock and speaks in Italian with a strong southern accent of Campobasso, Avellino and Salerno, his grandparents'
places of origin. Every morning he wakes up at 4:30. He goes to the
barber at 6:00, at 7:00 he celebrates mass and then he gets to work:
meeting with his congregants, visiting the parishes, making trips to
see mayor Michael Bloomberg in Manhattan to negotiate more aid
for schools that house 50 thousand pupils, 35 thousand in the elementary schools and 15 thousand in the middle and high schools
and their 3 thousand teachers. He heads one of largest dioceses in
America: 4.8 million Catholics that speak 29 different languages. As
he says himself, "It's a small country." How many of them are Italian? "About 400,000 because most of the Catholics, there, are Hispanic immigrants." And what kind of relationship do Italians have
to the faith? DiMarzio adjusts his glasses and opens his arms: "here
like in Italy, family is the most important thing for Italians, everything else comes after it, even their faith." On the other hand, when
the first Italian immigrants came at the end of the nineteenth century, "they were too hungry and too poor to think about their faith."
It was integration that led them to return to the Church. "This was
already the case with the second generation, with the third generation we started to get some vocations and that still continues to this
day." For Italian Americans the road to Catholicism was hindered
by the Irish. "When Italians came they encountered the Irish who
had arrived before them: they spoke the language, were more inte-
grated and had more money." So the churches split into two: in the
main church the Irish prayed in English, in the basement Italians
prayed in Dante's idiom or even in dialect. The difference in income
and culture evolved into a detonator for social tension. "There was a
lot of competition between us and them" the bishop admits. "Imagine that the first Italian-American prelate in the United States was
designated only after World War II," with the nomination of Bishop
Joseph Maria Pernicone. Nowadays, much of the tension is gone: of
the more than 200 parishes in the diocese of Brooklyn and Queens,
almost 40 have bilingual masses, the immigrants of the Sixties and
Seventies listen to the very popular radio programs of Radio Maria
(broadcast in New York by the Scalabrinian missionary priests and

directed by Walter Tonellotto) and the Italian language is the back-bone to the Italian identity of most of the Italians in New York "who suffered much more to preserve their language than the Hispanics do today who they can count on public aid and various forms of assistance." Bishop Nicholas DiMarzio often goes back to the topic of the suffering endured by immigrants: they were first discrimi-nated against by the Irish, then forced to survive with no help from Italy to preserve their language and identity, in short, they were left to themselves for many decades. It was a hard road but today "the faith is strong" in those who reside in the dioceses, "they care about the sacraments, they go to mass on Sunday and send their children to Catholic schools," and their identity "is founded first and foremost on the family, then on the Church and lastly on their nation, whether it is America or Italy." "Irish and Polish Catholics" are more nationalistic, whilst for Italians faith is manifested in the "value of the family" that causes them to be fierce opponents of abortion and gay marriage, generally. "For many the Church is the faith that forms the basis of family stability." This approach also ex-plains another difference with the Irish, because "Italians don't see political power in the Church whilst the Irish do." The "anticlerical culture is very widespread among immigrant believers and the de-scendants of immigrants, but that doesn't mean that the faith isn't strong." The co-existence of both identities which are seemingly opposed was evident in the warm welcome that Ratzinger received during his visit to New York in 2008. The visit culminated in a mass at Giants' Stadium: people flocked there and participated en masse, and they didn't see the Pope as the head of a State but instead as the embodiment of their faith.

The Bishop of Brooklyn and Queens, who has been head of the diocese since 2003 and who has years of experience in Newark and Camden behind him, has often happened to encounter the presence of "organized crime" or the mafia in some families. "It's always just one person, just as it is in the case of Italian police officers," he says, admitting that he has confronted, on occasion, the "Godfather pride," felt by some young Italians captivated by the dimension of power presented on the big screen by Francis Ford Coppola. "The Church did a lot to combat the mafia by speaking with people, es-pecially young people," even if in the American collective imagination Italians are still all mafiosi "as I realized myself on a trip to Australia when I was told that I had an accent like the *Sopranos*." After speaking for of two hours, the bishop apologizes and takes his leave because dozens, at time hundreds, of letters and emails from the church goers, who write to ask advice and very often to complain, await him. "They write without showing any respect, at times they ask me to get rid of this or that priest for trivial matters." DiMarzio answers all of them but often he just sends the most impolite letters back to the senders. The handling of matters relating to sexual abuse is completely different. In the diocese there have been 40 cases, all occurred before the Nineties except for one more recent case that led the bishop to remove the suspected teacher immediately. He says, "I met and continue to meet the victims and their families, I must listen to them, feel their suffering and express that the Church harbors them no ill-will. The Church must support these people who have suffered so much because of individual priests who took advantage of them when they were children." DiMarzio was born in America and he acts like an American: he shows neither reticence nor ambiguity in the face of the scandal but only boundless compassion, in an effort to rebuild the relationship between the Church and its followers.

Bensonhurst, the frontier priest

At 1230 on 65th Street in Brooklyn, in the heart of the neighborhood of Bensonhurst that once spoke Italian but that is now teeming with Chinese people, the church of Saint Rosalia-Regina Pacis stands, led by a frontier priest working with both illegal immigrants and the mafia. Reverend Ronald Marino has the collar of his cassock open, a smiling face and an office cluttered with objects that are there to encourage the faithful to join together in the sacrament of marriage. Listening to him means entering into the deepest recesses of New York City. Born in Brooklyn in 1946, father from Corleone and mother from Enna, he was the young priest who every Sunday in 1972 had contact with Carlo Gambino, the "Boss of Bosses" who supposedly died of a heart attack four years later. "He always came to the Church where I sometimes officiated when the pastor wasn't there, and at the end of mass he would stand at my side so that when the churchgoers came to shake my hand, they would shake his too." The mafia boss that Marino knew "always sent his men to the front and they always took up the first two rows "in the Church of Madonna della Grazia. "He was an old sick man, but he was highly respected and he made sure he was in Church every Sunday, to show that there too he was the most important." Between the little more than twenty year-old Marino and the "Boss of Bosses" born in Caccamo, there was more than just a little tension, "but he tried to ingratiate himself to me." This happened "one time when gas was scarce in the city and everybody was on line at the pump he told me to leave and he brought me to another gas station that seemed to be closed. I approached and a man came out and filled my tank and left." He was the boss's own private gas station attendant. When he was struck down by a heart attack in his house in Massapequa on October 15 1976, the priest "went to his wife and children begging them to make sure that the funeral didn't evolve into a garish Hollywood show." The deliberations were about the number and type of luxury car that would accompany the procession with the casket of the boss from Castellammare del Golfo. "The priest told them that they couldn't come to Church with more than twenty black limousines and ten loads of flowers, they agreed and on the day of the funeral that was the number of cars parked in front of the church," Marino recalls. "But at the end of the funeral ceremony, when the pastor went to thank them, they smiled at him, saying that they had left just as many a few meters away from the church, out of respect for his wishes." On the other hand, the Gambino clan was a force estimated by the police to be over one thousand "soldiers" strong and to keep them all in check was not an easy task. To discover who the most important members were at a particular time, FBI agents came to church every Sunday, before the Boss of Bosses arrived, and put video cameras everywhere. But Gambino's men knew where the cameras had been positioned and so they sat where they could pray without being seen.

Though he knows the mafia, Reverend Marino doesn't want to give it that name. He prefers the term "organized crime" because "the old mafia doesn't exist anymore, the new mafia is Russian, Chinese, Mexican and Jewish and most of the crimes committed are of a new generation, they deal with finance." He says "certain private companies make profits illegally, evading taxes and the law. They are financial crimes committed by people in suits; we don't see the old street assassins anymore."

The other front on which Marino works is the one that derives from his post as "vicar of migrants." There are prayers in Italian alternated with texts in Chinese at the entrance to his study because his principal daily duty has to do with immigrants: most of whom are illegal. "Among them there are many Italians." "It is good that in Italy they learn that many Italians are illegal immigrants," he says gesturing as he sits in front of a large religious painting, "because when you Italians pronounce these words you refer to Moroccans, Albanians, Senegalese and Romanians." Who are these illegal Italian immigrants? This is what he replies: "they are waiters, pizza makers, builders, factory workers, simple people that speak in dialect and have been here for five or ten years and became illegal when they arrived with a three-month visa and after it expired did nothing about it." It's a life that is made of hard work and sacrifices "because they cannot go back to Italy" and "they are disconnected from close family celebrations and funerals, and they suffer for it." There are those who "when faced with a traumatic event, like the loss of a parent, choose to return but then after the funeral, the American police prevents them for landing in New York and they remain separated from their wives and children here who very often are American citizens." But how many of them are there? "There are hundreds and hundreds, nobody knows the exact number but I believe it goes beyond 2,000 in all of New York. It is interesting to note that in 1994 the local police did an investigation that showed that Italians made up the highest number of illegal immigrants." Marino knows many of these immigrants "because they come to me, ask for help and ask for 'advice' on how to become legal but I explain to them that it doesn't work like that here and I tell them that the only way of changing their status is by participating in a government lottery that gives out Green cards every year." However, most of them don't follow my advice "because they are wary of giving their personal details to the government lottery, they're afraid that they'll end up in handcuffs, but they are wrong about this too because this is a country of laws and the lottery can't give the details of those who participate but only of those who win."

What worries the pastor of Bensonhurst is how "many of these illegal immigrants have been here already for more than ten years, they are not that young anymore" and they have formed "a community of middle-aged people living without papers." Many of them "are devout but not religious," or in other words, "they are followers of Padre Pio but then they stay at home to sleep on Sunday morning." When they set foot in the church and go to confession "they speak to me in heavy dialect but they want me to answer them in Italian." Father Marino stayed in Florence for a long time to study the language of Dante but when he came back to Brooklyn he discovered that of the 4,000 families in his parish most actually spoke Chinese. Italian immigrants in New York are the ones with the highest average age, but 56 percent of new immigrants are Chinese and very young. This explains why in an area where there are 28 parishes that provide mass in Italian, the young priests find themselves in reality dealing with Chinese congregants. Problems abound. Marino explains: "They are dysfunctional Catholics, because they come from a country where the official Church is allied with an oppressive regime and they don't practice their faith." To solve the problem, the decision was to "confront their culture" and so Saint Rosalia offered them what they needed most: an afterschool program where they could leave their children, as Chinese people work so much, almost 24 hours a day. This is why Saint Rosalia has become an Italian church that assists the Chinese, offering English courses, free rice for their children three times a day and recreational activities. "With the Chinese, our initiatives are preevangelical, we offer them services to connect them to the Church counting on the fact that the new generation will read the Gospel, we give services to the parents so the children of tomorrow will be the ones to pray on Sunday." It is this desire to "understand cultures to bring faith" that guides the credo and the works of Reverend Marino, who spends entire days immersing himself in the culture of the streets that are adjacent to Columbus Avenue where only Mandarin Chinese is spoken. Among the things that he has learned is the fact that "inside the home they use neon lights to save money and outside the windows they install heavy grates to protect the cash that they keep under their beds because they don't trust banks."

In the basement of Bleecker Street

At the intersection of Bleecker Street and 60th Place, in Queens, stands the church Our Lady of the Miraculous Medal, one of the parishes in New York where mass is celebrated in Italian. As it happens in lots of places, the religious congregation has two masses on Sunday, in the main church they pray in English and in the basement in Italian. It's a separation of languages and space that dates back to the time when Italians arrived en masse, between the end of the nineteenth and twentieth centuries. They weren't the first Catholics to arrive in America because the Irish were there before them and there were many clashes between them. Those tensions live on in many ways still to this day. Officiating in the basement of Our Lady of the Miraculous Medal is Fabio Flaim, an eighty-year old deacon from Tregiovo in the Non Valley of Trento. He immigrated in 1949 to Argentina, he spent time in Uruguay and in 1962 he arrived in America, where he got married and had five children. His followers are all Sicilian and they are all elderly. At the end of the religious service as he takes off his long white robe and speaks to the church regulars who treat him like an old friend he says: "Every Sunday about one hundred people come to hear mass in Italian, we started the practice after Vatican Council II, but now only the old people come, the younger generations go to hear mass in English upstairs." The deacon explains, in a feeble voice that lingers on the description of "the values of those who believe" like "faith in eternal life, in heaven and in the meaning of death, that here the faith is strong in those who come to church every Sunday but unfortunately most only come at Christmas and on the feast of Saint Joseph, it doesn't mean that they're not all Catholics, as is true of the mafiosi too." Among the topics that he most frequently discusses after mass with those who come to say hello is the persistence of anti-Italian prejudice in America. "It's true that it exists because initially people complained that Italians didn't work whilst now they complain because they've been successful, they are all just envious." But according to him, these diatribes don't count for much, "the truth is that Italian Catholics go to church and they are the ones who light the candles, donate flowers and they are the most consistent in making small offerings too." Members of the mafia "often come to church too, they have faith just like everyone else, but they make more substantial donations and organize big cel-ebrations." Standing nearby there's Battista Caruso from Torretta who's seventy years old with an impressive moustache and terse words who corrects the deacon: "there is no mafia here." But few people take notice of Torretta's objection because the topic that's of most interest to them is a different one. Antonio Barbetta, a seven-ty-eight year old barber, can't stifle his anger against "those who have it in for us": "We Italians make sacrifices, we save and don't squander money like Americans who spend everything on dinner or on having a good time and then they can't buy a house." The fact that they've been successful thanks to "hard work" is a source of pride that many share. Seventy-eight year old Vito Spampinato, from Regalbuto, started out as a shepherd when he was a boy in Sicily, once he came to New York he worked at dozens of jobs, from school janitor to chocolate factory employee, and now that he is retired he expresses his remaining energy by reciting poetry from memory in public, whenever he has the opportunity, in the café or in the church basement. One of the poems ends with the line: "This is America, one has to work, there is no other way."

Padre Pio Way, Williamsburg

Felice Manna goes by the name "Philip," he wears a black hoody when we meet on the steps of Our Lady of Mount Carmel, at the intersection of N 8th Street and Havemeyer Street in Williamsburg, Brooklyn. Mass is being said in Italian by a woman with only a few congregants in the main church. In the basement dozens of boys work every Saturday of the year preparing the frame to wrap the twelve sections of the five story-high tower (weighing 5 tons) that is carried on the shoulders of 320 men every summer in the Dance of the Giglio Feast. This celebration re-enacts a three century old tradi-tion from the city of Nola in Campania that is used to pay homage to the heroic deeds of San Paolino against the Visigoths in the Fifth century. The young boys, all of whom are fifteen or sixteen years of age, design the wooden structure of the tower piece by piece with a passion that leads many of them to participate also as "carriers," 50 in front and at the back and the rest at the sides. The *"capi paranza"* who in Williamsburg are called "lieutenants" lead the "carriers", and Manna has served as the First Lieutenant, or in other words, the "head" of the entire Dance of the Giglio. The fifty-three year old proudly recounts the tradition of his father and grandfather who arrived from Nola in the province of Naples, in 1910. Within the structure that holds up the tower there is a boat that recalls the voyages of San Paolino to North Africa. All year round the boat is housed in a neighbor's yard a hundred meters from Our Lady of Mount Carmel. Out front there's Padre Pio Way, the street that's named after the shrine erected for the most popular saint among Italian Americans in this area and this is where the Giglio Feast takes place, highlighting the establishment of the religious customs of the last immigrants to come here. Manna explains: "The new Italians came here in the last twenty years and they pray to Padre Pio whilst earlier immigrants when they came at the beginning of the twentieth century weren't familiar with him, they had the Madonna of Mount Carmel and the Giglio Feast" and therefore "they're the Italians from Italy who have brought us Padre Pio." In contrast to such enthusiasm and voluntary work from those who prepare the Giglio Feast or do upkeep on the Padre Pio altar, the priests are in short supply. There's just one priest who takes care of all of the Catholic churches in Greenpoint in Williamsburg and because there are so many of them one was given to the Lutherans and another to the Armenians. Manna emphasizes the fact that "there are more churches than priests and the Catholic Church has a low number of congregants because Americans only go to priests who are charismatic." One time the churches were surrounded by houses where Italians lived, small wooden houses, but as each owner died the big construction companies came in offering staggering sums to buy the properties, tear them down and build elegant condominium buildings, with more apartments, making millions of dollars. Young people come to settle in Williamsburg, the "hipsters," because it's one of the trendiest neighborhoods of today. From Driggs Street to

Bedford Avenue, the old Italian-Americans feel besieged by a reality that they don't recognize anymore because hipsters are artists, they get drunk at night, they dye their hair and they couldn't be further from the values of Padre Pio and from the traditions of the Dance of the Giglio. Without considering the tensions between the "new" and "old" Italians that Manna experienced firsthand when during a Columbus Day parade a young Italian who had been here only a few years approached him and said "you are not Italian." But the tensions dissipate when Manna goes into the studio apartment, a short distance from the road in front of the church where the annual festival takes place that houses Giglio Club. Inside there are photographs of Italian-American soldiers wearing the uniform of the Marines, autographed posters of Frank Sinatra and relics of baseball heroes and the music he listen to is the music "of Nola, which is really Neapolitan music" starting with 'O Saracino.

The dollars of San Gennaro

The ten rows of dollar bills descend the golden statue of San Gennaro that holds two ampullas of liquid blood in the left hand and makes the sign of the cross with the right. The rows of dollars are irregular, they overlap one another and little pins placed by the caretaker of the church of the Most Precious Blood on Mulberry Street (a few meters from the intersection with the Canal) hold them in place on a strip of red fabric. In the garden of the little church, a little bazaar dedicated to the Roman Catholic faith symbolizes this last street of Little Italy's link to Naples where the immigrants from Campania settled at the end of the eighteen hundreds. There are stalls with San Gennaro t-shirts, holy pictures of Padre Pio, religious books that recount the miracles and deeds of the most popular saints in two languages, numerous holy statues and a myriad of votive candles in all colors, sizes and price. The faithful pay for their purchases and then bring them through a little hallway into the church that is festooned with tricolor and American flags in honor of the Feast of San Gennaro that restores what remains of Little Italy to the splendor of the past. A human river of New Yorkers drifts along Mulberry Street during the eleven days of the Feast that begins with a little procession of the statue of the Neapolitan saint through Little Italy. Then the festival proper begins. Street vendor offer sausages, *zeppole, torrone,* and fried artichokes to eat on the street. Children can go to the circuses of *"Donna Serpente"* and *"Tartarughe a due teste."* There's a shooting gallery where goldfish are the prize. You can taste "Scarface's cigars" together with piña coladas. All while listening to Frank Sinatra's *New York, New York* over the loudspeakers or the timeless classics of Domenico Modugno and Umberto Tozzi from the stalls. New Yorkers, whether Italian-American or not, pour onto Mulberry Street from Prince Street, Grand Street, Elizabeth Street and Canal Street, they crowd through the little strip left between the stalls along the sidewalks. One way or another, they all aim at getting to the statue of San Gennaro at the entrance to the church on the Mulberry street side. It's the same statue used in the procession and on its left its caretaker sits wearing a brooch of the saint on his lapel and handing a holy picture to those who approach to add a dollar to the considerable cascade of cash. Standing there for just for a few minutes you see a parade of different New York Italian characters. A mother arrives with two small children in tow, designer bags and flip-flops, she attaches three dollar bills that she first has her children touch. Then it's the young thug's turn, he must weigh about one hundred kilos, his head is shaved, he has a thick neck and he's wearing a black t-shirt with "Italia" printed on it. He takes a dollar out of his wallet and while he pins it he looks at San Gennaro, showing sincere emotion that disappears the moment he turns and quickly leaves. Behind him there's an old man who speaks only in dialect, but he knows the process by heart: he looks at the saint as he would an old friend, he has brought many one-dollar bills to pin to the statue and then he leaves and does the same with the nearby statue of Padre Pio which is also equipped with red fabric "dollar-strips," but is much less adorned. The church of the Most Precious Blood has two entrances, and the one opposite Mulberry Street on Baxter Street is protected by security guards and a finely-dressed contingent of the Police Department made up of officers of Irish, Asian or African American heritage. In 2007, Mayor Bloomberg opposed a neighborhood committee that wanted to put an end to the tradition of the Feast of San Gennaro, accusing it of being too disruptive and controlled by the mafia. The mayor saved the Little Italy tradition but soon thereafter decided to increase the number of officers deployed at the Festival suggesting that not all of the objections raised by the committee were completely unfounded.

In 1996, 19 members of the Genovese clan ended up in hand-cuffs for a series of crimes that ranged from homicide to the undue removal of the dollar bills pinned to the statue of San Gennaro. In-vestigators showed that the Genovese clan ran illicit activities dur-ing the Festival, collecting payments from restaurants and street vendors creating a system of rent collection that brought in about one million dollars a year. As far as the San Gennaro dollar bills are concerned, at the end of the Festival they were taken and put in a bag by a cohort of Vincent Gigante, the boss who was known for strolling around Greenwich Village wearing slippers and a bath-robe and who died in 2005. In the films *The Godfather II* and *The Godfather III*, the San Gennaro Festival is the backdrop to two kill-ings that spark panic in the crowd: the young Vito Corleone's as-sassination of the local mafia boss Don Fatucci, and his nephew Vincent Mancini-Corleone's murder of rival Joey Zasa. And it's not just fiction. In more recent times, in 2004, Perry Criscitelli, presi-dent of the association The Sons of San Gennaro, was accused by the FBI of being a "soldier" for the Bonanno family. The Bonanno family had replaced the Genovese clan in the collection of "rents" that at Christmastime forced some restaurants pay sums of up to 15 thousand dollars. It's not surprising that there are some New Yorkers who anticipate the Feast so they can devote themselves to the tradition known as "Spot the Mobster" where they sift through the crowd looking for mobsters so they can photograph them and ask for an autograph.

The missionary of Flushing

Every Thursday from the microphones of Radio Maria, Al Baro-zzi speaks of the faith with New York churchgoers. The program lasts more than an hour. At the start the reverend from Trento con-fronts a difficult topic that can be anything from abortion to pe-dophilia, after which a question and answer segment follows with some listeners reciting prayers and expressing all sorts of passionate opinions. The faithful confess over the airwaves with father Barozzi, whose given name is Italo, because he is a priest of the people, he is always out meeting his parishioners, speaking about weddings and funerals, giving sermons at processions, dining in their homes and speaking about saints, schools, baptisms and also telling jokes that he has collected in one of his books. His style is what he learned from the Consolata missionaries in Turin. After he was ordained in Rome in 1965, he traveled the world with the missionaries, from the Amazon jungles in Venezuela to the Moroccan deserts of Marrakech. He came to New York in 1967 and here he studied journalism at Columbia University. He worked for Italian American newspapers and collaborated with RAI in Trento, coupling his faith with the knowledge of the importance of communicating with every single Catholic. His resulting conviction is that "when I find myself having to choose between rules and people, I always opt for the people." So if they force him to celebrate baptisms only until 2:00PM, he celebrates them until 4:30PM "because the baptized child is more important than the written rule." It is this approach that gives him access to the deep recesses of the Italian American community concentrated in Brooklyn and Queens on three geographical islands where the faithful seek out churches and priests who set themselves apart because they speak Italian: in Bensonhurst at the churches of San Domenico, Sant'Attanasio and Santa Maria and in Ozone Park where Saint Lucia and Saint Mel are located. At Saint Mel, the church that bears the Irish name of the nephew of Saint Patrick, Al Barozzi has his base that he leaves every morning with a different mission. This is how he describes his congregation: "They abide by traditions more than Italians do in Italy; they live gathered around social clubs that represent the towns from which they originate, they honor the saints and they struggle with the language question which is the problem at the base of the relationship between the young people and the older generations." The problem arises from the fact that "the elderly always spoke dialect thinking that it was Italian, so the young people never learned Italian and now that the older generation is disappearing they have no connection to Italy, they don't know how to read or write the language and they don't care about Raphael and

Leonardo da Vinci. Of course they know who Pavarotti is, but that's not enough." What is more, there are also the dynamics that "drive children to push their parents away because they feel more American than them and consider them relics of an old world." For fifteen years the diocese of Brooklyn and Queens has entrusted the task of taking care of its Italian congregants to him and Al Barozzi does this by immersing himself in their world every day of the year, without fail. He explains: "there is a lot of work to do because there are fewer and fewer Italian priests. At one time the vocations were in Italy but now they're in the Third World and so priests are African or Hispanic and Italians have been left without priests who are able to speak their language. In Brooklyn and Queens there are "many Italian churches without priests" that are given to Parish Priests who speak other languages "especially Spanish" and the result is that "the congregation doesn't know who to interact with." Barozzi is one of the few who goes from street to street, house to house, and what he sees is "a little world where immigrants from the North accomplished, in one generation, what it took people from the South to do in three." The result is that those who came from Piedmont or from Triveneto "soon became doctors or lawyers" whilst the immigrants from Campania, Sicily, Apulia or Calabria "have houses, pizzerias and restaurants." The latter "still live in a universe where the mafia is deep-rooted." Father Barozzi saw this firsthand when he went to preach in the club for immigrants from Corleone: "There are many reasons why people identify with the mafia. Some identify with it because of a sense of pride associated with their place of origin, some feel nostalgia for times past and others are attracted by the fantasy of being powerful, respected and even admired, not just like the bosses of the old days but like the representations of Hollywood such as Sylvester Stallone." Al Barozzi speaks of the mafia as an immanent reality, of bosses "who built churches with materials brought from Italy," of "extravagant annual dinners where everyone comes dressed in black," and of "streets scattered with stalls whose owners have to pay street rental to only one person." But despite all of this "family is what counts most of all" for Italian Americans, "even more than the Church" because "the parents' blessing is worth more than that of the priests." And now the seventy-two year old missionary priest, who goes everywhere on foot and jogs for at least an hour every day, speaks candidly about the priests who are "too vague," incapable of establishing relationships with the faithful because they are interpreters of an "inflexible credo" that "sometimes verges on the mystical." "In the past being a priest meant wearing the robes and repeating the rituals, today instead it's necessary to go out and meet the people, listen to them no matter what topics they talk about." Politics included. "In the clubs when they all watch Italian news programs together that discuss the quarrels between Di Pietro and Bossi, Berlusconi and Napolitano, people are upset, embittered, they would like to see an Italy that is integral, united and stable." As far as American politics is concerned, "for the most part Italians have conservative values even if they sometimes vote for the democrats, as he did himself in the presidential election when he voted for Obama. Last November, however, in the elections for Congress he switched party and chose the Republicans "because this President has just proven to be all talk, he didn't close Guantánamo, he carries on two wars, the economy is a disaster and he allowed himself to be too easily swayed by Nancy Pelosi" a staunch supporter of abortion. Al Barozzi knows a thing or two about the relationships between Italians and other minorities. Every year he celebrates between 30 and 40 mixed marriages with Jews "from New Jersey to Connecticut." All follow more or less the same ceremonial: he and the rabbi stand side by side underneath the canopy, with prayers from both faiths, readings from the Old and New Testament and lastly "the Lighting of the Unity Candles." This rite has the two celebrants give the mothers of the bride and groom their respective candles, they in turn give the candles to the bride and groom who light a third candle symbolizing the creation of the new family." The relationship with African Americans, instead, "is not very good and there is a lot of racism" due to the fact that "Italians made many enormous sacrifices to establish themselves in America, with the hard work of generations, and they have no time for families that for decades depend on the State for support, putting strain on the finances of everybody."

In the crosstalk with the faithful in church and also on Radio Maria, Al Barozzi often finds himself discussing the pedophile scandal and he expresses his theory candidly: "The difference is between priests who come from the university and those instead who go through the seminary because the former have contact with the female sex whilst the latter don't." When he studied journalism at Columbia University, Barozzi was courted and he also received an offer of marriage, but he chose celibacy. It was a moment that left its mark on him: "Celibacy should be a choice and not an obligation for priests. It's not written anywhere that priests shouldn't get married, it is something that has nothing to do with theology, the apostles were married, why can't we be married?" On one occasion Barozzi was in a church in New York where he had to deal with a priest who had committed abuse. "They told me that the system was what counted, I disagreed, the people count more than anything else." He goes further: "I'm in favor of women priests, we know that Mary Magdalene was the closest person to Jesus because she was the first to know about the resurrection" but "women themselves don't want women priests, they don't want the responsibility of it."

Yeshiva University

There is a member of the Italian Jewish community that has been studying at Yeshiva University for the past four years. His name is Umberto Piperno, the ex-chief rabbi of Trieste, who decided in 2006 to cross the Atlantic with his wife and three children following in the footsteps of another Italian rabbi, Alberto Somek, who up until the middle of 2010 was leader of the Jewish community in Turin. For Piperno, who was born in Rome in 1961 where his parents had a store near the Trevi Fountain, his arrival in New York wasn't completely trouble free. Although he had the title of Italian Rabbi he had to virtually restart his studies from scratch to obtain the Smichà (Jewish degree) to allow him to practice in America. That meant four years of study "learning new ways to expand on religious topics and acquiring a greater specialization in the rabbinate" because, just to give a few examples, "in America one of the priorities of the rabbi is the construction of a Eruv (an enclosure around an inhabited area that permits to transport goods during the Sabbath)" as well as the training of religious ministers "with specific expertise in the one task that they carry out, from hospital chaplain to religious officer in the Armed Forces or in the Fire Department." All of which occurs "within an environment where technology is the part of the daily routine because training is carried out by virtue of very advanced software." Umberto Piperno lives in Riverdale, in the residential area of the Bronx close to Manhattan where he leads a congregation of Sephardic Jews. He pursues a dream of "creating an Italian Temple" a "welcome, conference and scholarship" center for Italian Jews who live in the city "beginning with the many young university students who come to study here." It's a dream that he believes is "attainable here in New York." But why, in a city like New York that has the largest urban Jewish population would an Italian synagogue be a success? "Because Italian Judaism has characteristics that can be transformed into a bridge between different cultures" within the whole Jewish community which is "marked by sharp divisions between Orthodox, Conservative and Reform Jews." To explain what he has in mind, Umberto Piperno who was also a rabbi in Udine, evokes the example of the "Italian synagogues of the past that housed congregations with different observances" representing a model of co-existence that "can even today serve as a point of reference." It is also noteworthy that the magazine dedicated to Jewish thought directed by Donato Grosser, "Segulat Israel," is actually published in New York. It aims at reviving some of the most vibrant discussions that are occurring within American Jewish thought today and the fact that the magazine is in Italian expresses another example of this concept of the "cultural bridge." This is exactly the spirit in which, year after year, on Remembrance Day (the day that remembers the liberation of Jews from the extermination camp of Auschwitz on January 27th 1945) the Consul General of Italy in New York, Francesco Talò, stands beneath the Italian flag at the Park Avenue entrance and participates in the reading of the names of all of the Italian Jews who were deported by the Nazi-fascists. Arthur Schneier of Park East Synagogue which is twinned with the Synagogue in Rome observes: "It is a unique event in this city and it shows how beneficial the link between the Jews and Italy is to life in New York."

Italy

Italian flags on Fifth Avenue

The *Bersaglieri* in dress uniform carrying the Italian flag with the Mazzinian motto "God and Country" open the Columbus Day parade on Fifth Avenue. It's the time for Italians in New York to celebrate their heritage with pride and passion. Tens of thousands gather at the intersection between 47th Street and Fifth Avenue to march northwards all the way to 72nd Street, in an order that expresses their values, on the day when Americans pay homage to the Genovese navigator Christopher Columbus who discovered their country in 1492. Columbus Day falls on the second Monday of October, it is proclaimed by the President of the United States, it is considered a holiday all over the country and is celebrated by every city and urban area in a different way. In New York, the tradition of the parade dates back to 1866 and it has been repeated annually since 1929. It gives rise to a moment of ethnic Italian pride when those who originally came from the Old Country parade along the street past St. Patrick's Cathedral flanked by the crowd on both sides, surrounded by a multitude of tricolor flags and stars and stripes of every shape and form.

They say that every religious-ethnic group has its parade day in New York and among them Italians distinguish themselves in two ways: first because of the overwhelming presence of police divisions that symbolize the integration that they have achieved, and vintage cars, mostly Ferrari and Maserati, that are considered the stars of the Made In Italy brand.

Officers from the Police Department march in dress uniform on horseback, on motorcycles that bear the word "Sheriff," on foot with the band, or simply side by side: hundreds of them. Italian flags are everywhere, alongside the banners of selected units that fight organized crime in New Jersey, terrorism in Manhattan or financial crimes in Connecticut. They are veterans, officers, newly appointed agents and entire squads. In some cases they are inside the patrol cars that you see every day on the streets or squad cars from half a century ago, or even the black and white cars with iron grates that act as cells for the worst offenders who've just been arrested. The tribute that the crowd pays them shows the appreciation for the police corps that contributed to the social integration of the city and also worked to belie the image and prejudice of the Italian mafioso. Alternating between the blue uniforms are the black uniforms of the *Carabinieri*, followed by the Italian Police that highlights the solid alliance between two countries that guarantee the security of all. All of them are present in this colorful celebration that overlaps the Columbus Citizens floats with the ones that come from the Italian provinces, most especially from the South, that show the Venuses of the Gulf of Naples, the Bronzes of Riace, Sicilian carts and whatever else calls to mind the places that millions of Italians left to get to Ellis Island in the last 130 years. In the background the music that plays varies from *God bless America*, that for New Yorkers conjures the collective response to the terrorist attacks of 9/11, to *New York, New York* by Frank Sinatra to *Volare* by Domenico Modugno, but there are also Irish bagpipes, Hispanic tunes from the Brooklyn dance schools and even the *River Kwai March* played by the Tokyo police band (even though the song evokes a World War II movie in which Japan is described as the most ruthless of enemies.) This overlapping of colors and different identities is in the DNA of New York, it embodies the message that though this is a parade that celebrates Italian heritage it occurs within the frame of a metropolis that is proud to be multiethnic. In the middle of the procession the firefighters usually parade: the corps that was decimated by the attacks on the Two Towers suffering among the highest number of Italian casualties. When the red fire trucks pass with sirens flashing, the people on the sidewalks shout "God Bless America" and "Long Live Naples" almost as one voice. After them, it's the turn of the politicians and institutions, from both countries. Representing New York, the Mayor, the Governor, the elected officials of the State of Albany and the City Council march, followed by the Attorney General and a myriad of administrators. At the back of this group, if the parade occurs before an important election, there are also the candidates who are running for office in the major electoral races. There is no better time to campaign than at the Columbus Day Parade, when people from all New York neighborhoods gather along the parade route. The Italians are mixed in among them: sometimes there are ministers who have just arrived from Rome, mayors of important cities such as Rome or Milan, the Italian Ambassador in Washington or the Consul of New York. As they pass they are greeted with cheers and applause that public officials in Italian cities rarely witness. But the person who most encapsulates the identity of the parade is the Grand Marshall designated by the Columbus Citizens Foundation that, from its headquarters in an elegant neoclassical building on 8 East 69th Street, each year renews the tradition that was begun by Generoso Pope. He was the businessman who on October 12th 1929 led the first of these parades from East Harlem to Columbus Circle. The Grand Marshalls in the last ten years have differed a lot from one another such as Admiral Edmund Giambastiani, the queen of Italian cuisine Lidia Bastianich, the designer Roberto Cavalli and Maria Bartiromo, star of TV programs on the economy. What is most striking about the Columbus Day Parade is how it puts the spotlight on the unrelenting emotional divide between the Italians of America and those of the home country. Italian Americans become emotional when they see the Italian tricolor, they applaud with tears in their eyes, they look out for their children and relatives on the floats and in the symbols in *papier-mâché* they seek a reference to their own past. The Italians from Italy are for the most part tourists passing through the Big Apple, they've just come out of their hotels that morning to do some shopping on Fifth Avenue and they find themselves suddenly immersed in a celebration whose existence they ignore. They react to the parade with a mixture of surprise, sarcasm and cynicism. If you stand for a few minutes by the sellers of little Italian flags, you notice that most of the people who buy them aren't the Italian tourists who are passing through but they're the Italian immigrants who chose to stay.

In the trenches against prejudice

Vincenzo Milione is a researcher at the City University of New York and he has attached his name to the fight against anti-Italian prejudice launching the harshest of accusations at his own university: "You discriminate against us based on our heritage." To prove his assertion, Milione went to examine the university archives and he found that "in the last thirty years, the percentage of Italian Americans among the faculty and staff has remained stable at 5 and 6 percent whilst the number of African Americans, Hispanics and Asians has soared." The irony of fate has Milione pointing a finger at the Calandra Institute which was set up by CUNY to actually protect Italian heritage. The University denies any discrimination by citing other numbers, the number of white professors has declined by 20 percent since 1981 while the number of Italians has increased from 5.8 percent to 7 percent. Milione counters, however, that "the prejudice against Italian mafiosi which has been diffused by movies and TV has done damage also in the academic world" and he implies that he is willing to proceed bringing the fight into the legal arena where he believes Affirmative Action (the laws that protect the presence of African Americans in schools and public professions) will be necessary for Italian Americans too.

What is striking about the battle undertaken by Milione, a burly fifty-year old professor, is its convergence with the public relations battles carried out by the NIAF (the National Italian American Foundation which is the largest Italian-American organization) against movies, TV series and reality shows accused of presenting negative images of Italians. In fact, the theory of the NIAF is that it's the impact of TV and cinema that is at the root of this prejudice that is so entrenched in different generations of Americans. The most recent campaigns have been against *Jersey Shore*, the reality TV show broadcast by MTV, and *The Sopranos*, the TV series that was on the air for six seasons on HBO. The latter was hailed by both the public and the critics for its ability to tell the story, from within, of the family life of a mafioso in the wealthy suburbs of New Jersey, not far from Manhattan. Also in the sights of the NIAF are a few episodes of the ABC TV series *Desperate Housewives*, because one of the main characters is a bad-mannered woman, the ex-lover of a terrorist who is sexy in a vulgar way and speaks with a pronounced accent and cooks pasta with "the sauce learned from her grandparents" who is obviously of Italian heritage. The theory of Joseph Raso, president of the NIAF, is that "we are all under attack" by a "mass culture" that is the product of Hollywood oversimplifications that complicate the life of the young generations and also of professors like Milione by playing on images such as those of "Guidos." The Order Sons of Italy maintains the same argument singling out, as the biggest culprit, the "negative characterization of the Italians of America" in *The Godfather* trilogy by Francis Ford Coppola based on the novel by Mario Puzo. It was, in fact, precisely the success of *The Godfather* that generated a typology of film like *Analyze That*, *Good Fellas* and *Mickey Blue Eyes*, where the gangsters were exclusively of Italian origin, just as it was in the earliest films of this type that date back to the beginning of the nineteen hundreds, like *The Black Hand* (1906), *The Italian Blood* (1911) and *The Last of the Mafia* (1915).When asked what the accusations he advances are based on, Raso cites surveys done by Zogby International (one of the most respected opinion poll companies) that at the beginning of 2001 published a study on prejudice against ethnic groups that concluded that, for the majority of Americans, Italians are represented on screen by characters such as "mafia bosses, criminals, gang members and waiters." The Order Sons of Italy, moreover, identifies a further category in "the diffusion of prejudice" in the field of commercial advertising because, as a study from the summer of 2003 documents, "Italian men are presented as uncouth, dishonest and violent." As in the case of Godfather's Pizza whose slogan is the dialectal "Stay a home with da family" complete with a coupon titled the *Mob Pleaser*. Or the telephone company AT&T, that to advertise broadband, resorts to an ad in which two of the protagonists of *The Sopranos* threaten a teacher and force him to give good grades to a pupil.

What unites NIAF and The Sons of Italy is the memory of the offenses suffered because of prejudice of this sort. The first of these events occurred in New Orleans in 1891 when 11 Italians accused of plotting the assassination of members of the local police detail, were lynched by the crowd. Dramatic events such as this often return to the collective memory and are intermingled with everyday episodes that range from jokes about "Italian mafiosi" to the many depictions of Snooki (one of the protagonists of *Jersey Shore*) as an anti-star, expression of the middleclass on the outermost margins of popular culture.

Neglected for a century

The combination of two factors explains why a significant number of political leaders stop off in Manhattan to face animated Q & A sessions with the emigrants that are most interested in political affairs: the first is the increase in the number of Italians who have arrived in New York in recent years and the second is the electoral law that allows Italian residents abroad to vote for the Chamber of Deputies and the Senate. Romano Prodi stood before a crowd of more than 200 young people in a loft near Canal Street on the night before his decision to run in the 2006 elections. At different times during the last ten years, Francesco Rutelli, Gianfranco Fini, Roberto Maroni, Roberto Formigoni, and Massimo D'Alema have come to speak before an audience of New York University students in the auditorium of the Casa Italiana Zerilli-Marimò. There they've been often asked incisive questions also by other young Americans who are passionate about Italy. Marcello Pera, Giuliano Amato, Walter Veltroni, Carlo Azeglio Ciampi and Giorgio Napolitano have been ceremoniously welcomed in the setting of the Italian Academy of Columbia University. Marco Pannella and Nichi Vendola have chosen restaurants that are well-known by their compatriots where they were embraced by small crowds of supporters who identify with their respective political platforms. Not to mention the flock of political leaders, from Pierluigi Bersani to Ignazio La Russa and Mara Carfagna, who year after year stop off in New York for a few days making time for events with the emigrant community that share the same political ideology, place of origin or passion for soccer.

In general, events such as these are very well attended by the public. In the Winter of 2010, a crowd came to listen to Fini discuss Italian identity in the reception rooms of the Hyatt Hotel: the crowd was too large even for the ballroom reserved for major events. When Vendola came to New York, the Matilda restaurant on 11ᵗʰ Street couldn't accommodate the large number of patrons in attendance, and in the case of D'Alema there was a full house at the Casa Italiana. Pierluigi Bersani stirred up a lot of interest in Brooklyn as did Clemente Mastella when he participated in the Columbus Day Parade. Not to mention the lecture hall packed with students, not all of whom were Italian, at New York University to hear the Head of State Giorgio Napolitano discuss the topic of the future of Europe. But despite the high attendance at events such as these, when it comes to voting, the percentage of those with the right to vote that actually fill out the correct ballots and mail them is just above 30 percent. In the 2006 elections, 17,242 voters out of the 54,596 constituents (31.58%) cast their ballots for the Chamber of Deputies and 16,645 out of 52, 139 for the Senate (31.81%) and two years later the numbers were almost exactly the same, 17,405 voters out of 52,765 constituents (32.99%) for the Chamber of Deputies and 16,673 voters out of 50,605 (32.95%) for the Senate.

To understand the cause of this apparent contradiction we need to leave the George Washington Bridge behind, cross the Hudson into New Jersey and drive for about an hour to get to 72 Franklin Turnpike in Waldwick where Antonio Ciappina lives in a low-set white house surrounded by a patchy garden. He's the veteran reporter for "America Oggi" the Italian-American community's most popular newspaper directed by Andrea Mantineo. Ciappina who was born in Messina in 1925 is an ex-interpreter for the Americans in Sicily during the war, an ex-importer of wood from Alabama to Genoa and ex-proofreader for "Progresso Italo-Americano" which preceded "America Oggi." He refuses to use digital cameras, recorders or computers and he always takes notes by hand. He has a passion for processions and county festivals at which priests and prelates are always at the fore. He travels around the world despite his age and ailments, and he has a Franciscan friend in the Andes whom he often visits because he promotes fundraisers for his humanitarian activities. He collects bread that he delivers to the needy, in the past he taught Italian and everyone, even the editorial staff, calls him "professor" as a sign of respect for his age, his works and his devotion to his community.

Entering his house is like taking the pulse of the world of emigration. In the basement of the house that he built himself brick by brick, there are walls covered with history books, flags, maps and a myriad of awards received from "societies" like the Mutual Aid Societies created by emigrants who wanted to congregate in groups according to their place of origin. Riccardo Chioni a writer for "*America Oggi*" confirms that "nobody knows the spirit and the history of the Italians of New York better than Antonio Ciappina." Ciappina explains the limited involvement of Italian Americans in Italian public life with "the existence of a very deep wound, buried within thousands of families."

He goes on to explain: "Emigrants began to arrive here in around 1870 and for more than a century Italy didn't bother with them except in case of working through, with great difficulty, paperwork related to passports and pensions." "It was a long and harrowing period in which thousands of families felt neglected, betrayed and ignored by their country of origin." The creation of "societies," clubs named after the cities of origin, "helped make up for the absence of Italy" that "was even worse when combined with the memory that most Southern Italians had (the vast majority of emigrants were from the south) of the human catastrophe that had followed Italian Unity when the Northern Italians came to the South, not to build factories, but to collect all sorts of taxes."

Though, in the century that followed the Breach of Porta Pia, Italy began a progressive–yet still incomplete–integration of the North and the South, the communities of emigrants "lived a different history, based on a different sense of neglect."

The turnabout "came in the eighties, firstly with the setting up of AIRE (the registry of Italian citizens residing abroad), and then with the election of COMITES (the Committee of Italians Abroad) who represent them," giving rise to a "new process, of greater identification between emigrants and the country of origin." But, Ciappina points out, "that didn't bring a strong interest in Italian politics because of two different problems." First of all: "The limited knowledge of Italian by second and third generation immigrants (the children and grandchildren brought up in families that favored integration into American society in response to Italy's neglect of them) and the effect, that we must come to terms with, is that the younger generations consider the language of Dante an obligation rather than a pleasure and therein lies the difficulty to follow what's happening in the Italian political sphere." Secondly: "In Rome political leaders change too often, we don't even have time to learn their names, people get confused and because of this they drift away." Besides, "we've seen all sorts of ludicrous things, from town-twinning attempts that went up in smoke because of the sloppiness of the Italian administrations or because of actual fraud as it happened in the case of an entrepreneur from New Jersey who went to Palermo to donate one thousand dollars to every virgin girl and they ended up extorting more than 100 thousand dollars from him." "It's sad but true, the bond to Italy is shared by a very small minority of emigrants and they're usually the ones who have arrived very recently, in the last twenty years. All of the others are skeptical and therefore they don't vote. When they say 'we' they refer to an Italy that is immersed in the memories of the past and certainly not the political life of today." This concludes Ciappina's account as he sips a glass of wine with ice that was poured for him by Cindy, "my fiancée of seventy-four years of age that our priest introduced to me when I went to her husband's funeral." That historic wound that the aging journalist talks about is hard to heal because a century of neglect has caused a cascade of consequences (starting with the new generation's limited knowledge of Italian that makes identification with the Old Country more difficult), even if attempts to earn trust and credibility in recent years have been made by the State, not only the setting up and support of COMITES but, also, through symbolic gestures like the decision of the Consul General of New York, Francesco Talò, to travel by boat to New York for his assignment in order to retrace moments and sensations that marked the arrival of millions of his fellow citizens that crossed the Atlantic.

Mulberry Street doesn't vote

"Here nobody votes." Ciro Silvestri, wearing a red Yankees baseball cap and holding a coffee cup in his hand, is the owner of Caffè Napoli on Mulberry Street that's at the center of a snow-covered Little Italy. Ciro says: "I'm thirty seven, I've been living in New York for sixteen years, I love Italy and especially Naples, my city, but don't ask us to go vote in the elections because it's clear to everyone that none of the parties care about us." In the area surrounding the Big Apple that includes New York, New Jersey and Connecticut there are just over 3 million Italian Americans and 75 thousand of them are eligible to vote. To explain the skepticism that surrounds the right to vote (ratified for the first time in the elections of 2006) Quintino Cianfaglione, president of COMITES in New York and Connecticut states: "The voting system is a complete joke and, besides, candidates for all parties are chosen from the top, based on decisions made in Rome, so is there any reason why people here should feel politically engaged?" Cianfaglione supports the center-right coalition and in 2006 he was a candidate on Tremaglia's ticket. His perplexities about the electoral system are the same as those expressed by Graziella Bivona who ran for the center-left coalition in 2008: "Ballots that are unnumbered and that anyone can copy and reprint are sent by mail, then they are filled out and sent back without being inspected and when they get to the Consulate—from where they are then forwarded to Rome—nobody can verify that the people who actually voted were the eligible voters who received the ballots." Cianfaglione adds: "Besides being susceptible to vote-rigging, sending ballots by mail is very expensive; each envelope ultimately costs 20-30 dollars. Opting for electronic polling stations would save a lot of resources, but it's as if the State just wants to throw money away." The other issue is candidate selection. "In the 2008 elections, the district of North America elected two candidates from Canada and one from Philadelphia though most of the people who are eligible to vote actually reside in the New York region: isn't that an obvious contradiction?" Stefano Vaccara, who followed the campaign for America Oggi, asks. Tony Di Piazza, Vice-President of COMITES adds: "The candidates, whether they're right-wing or left-wing, don't represent the electoral base, they are chosen by the parties in Rome that make the selection based on favoritism, choosing the people that they are close to. It would be very easy to have primaries but nobody wants them." In 2008, Gino Bucchino from Toronto (Democratic Party) and Amato Berardi from Philadelphia (The People of Freedom) were elected to the Chamber of Deputies, whilst Basilio Giordano from Montreal (The People of Freedom) won the Senate seat. Bivona, a popular host on the Italian-American radio network ICN in New Jersey adds: "The only thing that party secretaries in Rome care about is who has enough money to run, because in a constituency that stretches from Canada to Co-starica only candidates with extensive funds can afford to campaign, I only had 10 thousand campaign dollars and in just one trip to Toronto they were all gone." In Canada the perspective on the situation isn't any different. Angelo Persichilli, a reporter for the Corriere Canadese in Toronto says, "I followed the 2008 campaign from start to finish but there were next to no public events and following the election, political life went back to being practically non-existent: you couldn't really expect it to be otherwise considering that the voting system is a joke." At the counter of Caffé Napoli about a dozen regulars have gathered and Ciro speaks for all of them: "What the party secretaries should be worried about is the fact that the people not voting aren't the immigrants who arrived here half a century ago, the immigrants who have become American, but Italians like us, the most recent generation, who started to arrive in the Nineties, who go back and forth, who follow what's happening in Italy and often consider returning there for good." Surrounded by the general consent of everyone present, the Yankee fan with a Neapolitan accent concludes with a crescendo: "The parties don't care about us? And we feel the same about them." The conversation ends here because Ciro and the others must hurry to shovel the snow-covered sidewalks of Little Italy before the dinner-hour customers arrive.

Food is more important than language

Franco Zerlenga was born in Torre del Greco and came to New York in 1968. In 1977, when he was working at the Italian Cultural Institute on Park Avenue, he came upon a document from the Farnesina that made him wince. "It was a newsletter from the Ministry of Foreign Affairs that suggested the Director of the Institute not have any association with Italian Americans" he recalls, revealing intense emotion in his voice, a combination of anger and misbelief. "More than a century had passed since the arrival of the first Italian immigrants in America, but Italy didn't trust them because of the hostility that had surrounded their mass departure" he explains, tapping into the knowledge and research that have brought him to teach at NYU. Since then a lot has changed: Ambassadors, Consuls and Directors of the Cultural Institute now compete to strengthen and renew the bond with Italians abroad, but to understand that initial fracture it helps to understand the genesis of the "fragile Italian" immigrant "identity" that has been passed on to generations of descendants. "It all started with that initial fracture as hordes left the South because they didn't identify with the Unified State, Italy suffered the phenomenon of mass emigration as a betrayal, not only of the ideal of Unity but also of the very concrete interests of the land owners who watched their workforce flee across the Atlantic, the workforce that was considered invaluable to economic development." There is, therefore, an original hurt in the relationship between Italy and the Italians of New York to which Zerlenga adds another element: language. "When the immigrants arrived, tens or even hundreds of thousands spoke the dialects of their villages and not Italian, because they didn't know it, and as a result when first and second generation Italian Americans spoke of 'Italy' they were really referring to a very restricted geographical and linguistic matrix." This is the reason why third-generation Italian Americans know only a very small amount of the language of Dante "because they learned it in America as a foreign language." This rediscovery of Italian today distinguishes many educational institutions in New York and in the United States, "but it's happening very late" Zerlenga (born in 1942) states, and therefore "for millions of immigrants, food substituted language as a bond to their villages and families of the past." Regional dishes that were the expression of dialect cultures, and not the Italian language, informed the collective memory of an immigrant population originating from a fragmented territory. All of these elements accelerated integration that, according to the sixty-nine year old former professor, "explains why Italian Americans actually consider themselves American Italians. They have never lamented their lot even in the face of the prejudice that surrounds them, and with their hard work they have become successful protagonists in every sector of life in New York, from business to politics." Though they may "have a fragile Italian identity," their American identity "is very consistent" thanks in part to

the "patriotism" shown by many Italians who don the uniform of
every corps, from firefighters to police officers to the Armed Forces.
"World War II was a crucial moment. Many Italian American soldiers were sent by the army to fight in Italy because bombarding
their home country was proof of their loyalty to their new country,"
Zerlenga remarks as he speaks of a "painful yet common" phenomenon that "succeeded in forging the American identity of the new
generations," and contributed also to "abandoning things of the
past such as anti-Semitism and racism towards people of color that
the immigrants had brought with them across the ocean" as well
as terms such as "mulignane" (black eggplant) to identity African
Americans. Born in an Italy that was still at war, educated by the
Jesuits and a former student of theology, Zerlenga arrived in New
York in 1968 "in search of a truth that he had not found within the
Church" and, progressing from a understanding of Erich Fromm to
that of Allen Mandelbaum (the supreme American Dante expert),
he studied theater with Herbert Berghof and Uta Hagen. He received a teaching position at New York University after September 11, 2011 to teach the history of Islam at the urgent request of
a university that recognized in him the possibility of expanding
the awareness of new threats. It's his multifaceted experience that
distinguishes Zerlenga's New York identity. Whenever he can, he
takes refuge in the Neapolitan restaurant Kestè on Bleecker Street,
a name he explains "comes from the Neapolitan 'chist'è,' meaning
'that's it'."

The Baroness of NYU

You can see Central Park visibly extend all the way to Harlem from
the windows of the elegant apartment of Hampshire House where
Mariuccia Zerilli-Marimò has been living since 1987. Original art-
work, ceramic vases, art books, antique furniture, red wallpaper
and the inseparable Portuguese housemaid, all create an atmosphere that evokes the early twentieth century Lombard upper
middle class. These are the origins of the wife of the former CEO of
the pharmaceutical company Lepetit, Guido Zerilli-Marimò, who
died in 1981. The baroness, as everybody in New York calls her

with a mixture of affection and respect, arrived in Manhattan for the first time in October of 1950. She arrived on board one of the ocean liners that left Southampton, England headed for the Hudson Bay. Among the things she is proud of is the fact that "she has tried them all," from the *Andrea Doria* "on which we travelled through an epic storm that we suffered through because of the poor quality of the stabilizers" to the most recent *Queen Elizabeth II*, that she describes as "much more solid and welcoming" than its predecessors "although it does have one black mark against it – it was built in French and not Italian shipyards- a fact that I was sure to mention to the captain." "Arriving in New York from the Atlantic is a unique emotion and as soon as I can I will repeat it, even though now I prefer to travel by plane" she confirms, speaking about the "Ocean breeze" and the "thrill everyone feels when they glimpse the outline of the Statue of Liberty on the horizon." Born into the Milanese Soncini family, right after the war she met her future husband through their shared support of Giovanni Malagodi's Italian Liberal Party. She considers herself a representative of the legacy of a man who made his fortune in the pharmaceutical industry, bringing American products and scientific discoveries to Italy to help the national Reconstruction. Mariuccia Zerilli-Marimò confesses that she immediately felt at home in New York and because of this she moved there in 1987, buying the apartment with a view of Central Park thanks to the sale of the family home, an elegant residence designed by Gio Ponti set in the middle of a garden right in the center of Milan, just behind Manzoni Street.

She focused on New York University to find a way of honoring "the memory of my husband and my love for Italy," and she decided to create the Casa Italiana that would house the Department of Italian Studies just as had been done already for French, German and Jewish studies. The Provost, John Brademas, liked the idea, the university board took it on, and the baroness combed Manhattan until she found what she was looking for in Greenwich Village: a little area that in the past had been home to one of the first Little Italys. Three years later, in November 1990, she inaugurated the Casa Italiana in the little six-floor building at 24 West 12th Street, near Washington Square, that had originally been built in 1851 and had been property of the Mexican war hero General Winfield Scott. The Casa

Italiana of New York University is still today the most vibrant point of contact between the culture of the Peninsula and the students of the Big Apple. Every year it hosts between 90 and 100 events that offer the students of New York University the opportunity to immerse themselves in both Italian memories of the past and current affairs. The Italian Academy of Columbia University distinguishes itself by hosting Italian professors and researchers (according to an agreement between the university and the Italian government), the Italian Cultural Institute on Park Avenue promotes events that are selected and financed by Rome, the "Zerilli-Marimò," instead, is the result of entirely private donations guaranteed by the baroness and the fund she created has triggered a self-financing mechanism to which NYU contributes the upkeep costs. Many people of note have appeared on the stage of the Casa Italiana auditorium: Vittorio Gassman recited Dante's *Divine Comedy*, Giorgio Strehler discussed Pirandello, Giuseppe Tornatore talked about his works, Martin Scorsese described his approach to cinema, the musicologist Fred Protkin interviewed Opera greats, the banker Giovanni Bazoli spoke about faith, peace and war during the war in Iraq, and hordes of politicians (from Gianfranco Fini to Massimo D'Alema, along with Letizia Moratti, Francesco Rutelli and Achille Occhetto) have sat to answer the pointed questions of the young Americans and Italians of New York who share both curiosity and perplexity about Italian politics. It is precisely this interaction between American students and Italian people of note that makes the "Zerilli-Marimò" unique. The baroness remembers every single event over the more than twenty years of activity as if it were yesterday, but she reserves a special place for Gassman: "He was old, he spoke to the students like a father does his children and he knew how to transmit a great love of life to them." His recitation of Dante also struck her as "a way of bringing the students closer to the language of our country." Stefano Albertini, who has been the Director of the Casa Italiana since 1994, has had a pivotal role in the organization of the activities successively presented, but what stimulates him is the unremitting passion of the woman who describes herself as "proudly Italian." She goes on to explain: "Although today it's not fashionable to be proud of our country, I am, and very much so. I'm proud of what we did during the Reconstruction, at the end of the war the country was destroyed, there was nothing left, 62% of the city of Milan was reduced to rubble, we turned up our sleeves and Italy rose again, we did it, and it was never a forgone conclusion, it came about because of hard work and, for this reason, every time I see the tricolor or I hear the national anthem here in New York, in Buenos Aires, in São Paulo or in any other place, I am deeply moved." The Casa Italiana helps the Baroness "convey knowledge and pride of Italy, its culture, history, and art so as to share it with New York, where I feel just as at home as I do in Milan."

On the desks of Rutgers University

Frelinghuysen Hall, Classroom B1, 4:30 PM. The Italian Studies professor Vincenzo Pascale walks into the classroom of Rutgers University where 37 students between the ages of nineteen and twenty six come three times a week to learn more about the "history of Italian culture" by reading classics, analyzing historical events, watching movies and discussing current events. Most of the students are of Italian origin but from different generations—some have only grandparents or parents who immigrated—with Asians, Latin-Americans and Middle Eastern students mixed in. They all share an interest in Italy and they would like to know more about it though they are unfamiliar with its language. The topic of the lesson is Italy. Jessica Saliba takes the floor, she's from a Syrian-Lebanese Christian family: she has no Italian relatives but she is very lucid in stating that "from what I know and from the people I spend time with, Italian identity is based on three things, family, food and Catholicism." As she pronounces the last syllable Lauren Luthman who has an Italian mother and Swedish father, interjects: "it's all true, it reminds me of my maternal grandmother, she used to say that family was number one in everything, she wanted everybody to eat together and to go to church on Sunday, and I'm in this class because she gave me so much." Lauren goes to a catholic church every Sunday to "pray and to feel Italian." Gabriella La Spina also speaks of her grandmother "who passed away recently": "She was proud to be Sicilian, I remember that she used to make me drink coffee when I was only three years old, that taste has never left me" and so she grew up convinced that "Rome and New York were very similar." At the desk next to hers Stephanie Chen, an Asian student, speaks about Italy as a "combination of art and food." Elisabeth Rooney who comes from an Irish family with just one Italian aunt, has never been to Italy but she explains that she is "attracted by the way Italian do things, by the way they are, by how they are always welcoming and friendly." Charles Tremato, a muscular veteran of the US Army with an untrimmed beard, sits in the front row. He speaks about Sicily as the "land from where my grandfather came and that my father loved but where I have never been" and he explains that because of "this strong bond of history and identity" he has decided to dedicate his professional future to a degree in Italian studies." Tremato is sorry that nobody ever taught him Italian, as is Anna Chrysantopoulos who has a Greek father and Italian mother. She describes her family as "very united as far as the holidays celebrated by both cultures are concerned, but I've never understood why Greeks preserve their language so much better, showing they are more aware of their roots." The chronicles of New York recount many episodes of ethnic tensions between Greeks and Italians, just as between the Irish and Italians, but Anna and Elisabeth speak of them as events of the past that have been overcome by family integration, to the point that their decision to dedicate themselves to Italian Studies was strongly supported by both their parents.

The image that Italy projects on the students is shaped by their respective experiences. Sachelle Vasquez, a Hispanic of Cuban origin, sees it as a place "where the people are united, they stay together and a sense of community prevails" and that attracts her because "in the rest of the world there's just endless fighting." Ana Quitana, from Peru, considers it a "source of possible future earnings because it has a flourishing economy," Peter Plumeri maintains that "the knowledge of Italian will help me become a good doctor," and Lauren confirms that "for many people Italy is like the Venetian hotel in Las Vegas." But Gabriella Basile, daughter of Calabrian immigrants, who goes to Italy almost every summer, speaks much more concretely: "The differences between the North and the South are striking, when I go to visit my relatives in their village in the mountains of Calabria, far from everyone and everything, I ask myself how can they stay in places like that." "It's all true," adds

Satei DiLeonardo who has a Filipino mother and Italian father, "but it's also true that Italians live better than Americans, they are more relaxed, they enjoy what they have more, and above all else they are less stressed."

Whether they are first, second, or third generation Italian Americans, they are all a little upset by the "stereotypes that surround them" beginning with those that have been "disseminated by movies and TV shows about the mafia" says Anthony Comuniello, regretting the fact that "when I speak to my friends after an episode of *The Sopanos* or *Jersey Shore*, I realize that they know nothing about the mafia or the Black Hand, they ignore its origins and they only talk about crimes and violence." Alex Amoroso, a second generation Italian American interjects: "When I'm confronted with such prejudice I feel proud, and it's that same pride that brings me here to study in this classroom." Charles tells a personal anecdote to "explain the harm that falsehoods about Italians can do": "My grandfather never wanted to see *The Godfather*, he refused, he felt it was offensive, an evil capable of harming all of us because it spread a distorted image of Sicily that is not a land of criminals but is home to people who spend their whole lives working hard, just like the immigrants who came to America." Gabriella Basile has something to say about grandparents too because hers, Salvatore Basile and Augusta Colosimo, both from Cropani in the province of Catanzaro, couldn't be more different in their relationship to America. They emigrated from Cropani in the Sixties laying the foundation for the integration of their children and grandchildren. The student recounts: "Nonna Augusta remembers the voyage by ship as a nightmare, she does nothing but repeat over and over how she misses the warmth of her neighbors in Cropani and says that the only thing that keeps her here is the fact that her children and grandchildren are all in America, whilst Nonno Salvatore, instead, frequently states how grateful he is for everything that this country has given to him, and every time he goes on vacation to Cropani he can't wait to leave."

The UN Veteran

There is a tribe of 124 Italians within the ranks of the UN in New York and for all of them Giandomenico Picco, known as Gianni, is the example to follow. In the little town of Enemonzo where he grew up, Soviet tanks were about 40 minutes away by road and Yugoslavian tanks about 45. In Carnia, the area between Soviet-occupied Austria and Tito's Slovenia, Picco's childhood was influenced by the daily tensions of the Cold War that his parents experienced very differently. His mother would wake at night fearing the Soviets or Tito's army, convinced that the border was too close. For his father, instead, that cramped geographical space and such proximate dangers made him reflect on the fact that, when all is said and done, all men are the same. Picco discovered politics in 1956 when he was just eight years old and learned that the Soviets had invaded Budapest, the city where his maternal grandfather had gone to school as a boy. When he grew up he chose to study abroad, in Ireland, the UK, Czechoslovakia, California and then in Amsterdam, where he received an offer that marked a turning point in his life: to go work at the United Nations. The DNA make-up of Enemonzo could have borne either a nationalistic fervor or the impulse towards internationalism, and when he arrived in New York in 1972 it was the latter that asserted itself, though still during the tensions of the Cold War. He was the only westerner to become part of the department dealing with the Security Council that was dominated by Soviets in that very delicate balance that had even the UN building divided into sections between the USSR and the West. It was crazy there: his boss was a soviet diplomat who behaved like a bulldog, he was a double agent who had been there for sixteen years, and then one day he just vanished into thin air, he deserted and went over to the Americans with his stock of information, whilst his two subordinates were exposed as spies in the following months, one of them was captured by the Americans as he exchanged secret documents hidden in milk cartons in a supermarket in New Jersey and the other one was forced to flee. Working side by side for years with diplomats from the Kremlin helped him and the UN. When they sent official delegations to the funerals of Leonid Brezhnev, Konstantin Chernenko and Yuri Andropov, he was the one who went as the youngest functionary, forced to wait long hours for the funeral processions to pass in Red Square. And when the time came to try to find an exit strategy for the invasion of Afghanistan, it was Picco who, during a flight from Rome, wrote the four points that years later offered the diplomatic way out of a conflict that had already been lost in 1989 because of the effective resistance of the Mujaheddin.

Speaking with a glass of beer on the table in front of him in a little reception room on the first floor of the Century Club on 43rd Street—the club that has had nine ex-presidents and dozens of ex-ministers of the United States as members—Picco tells the story of his life in the service of the UN just like the veterans of military conflict do: many details, a lucid memory and little emotion. His emotions filter through when he talks about one of the success stories that had an effect on the Middle East: the last phase of negotiations that brought an end to the war between Saddam Hussein's Iraq and the Ayatollah Khomeini's Iran. It was 1988 and Picco was attending the talks on behalf of Pérez de Cuéllar—the Secretary General of the UN with whom he had connected many years earlier during a shared mission in Cyprus—when the American Secretary of State George Shultz threatened to "slice him like butter" if he didn't get out of the way and allow America's ally Saddam Hussein to launch a new offensive. Picco consulted with de Cuéllar, who at first left the decision about what to do up to him and then, seeing his readiness to challenge Schultz's reprimand, told him that he had to achieve peace within six days. The objective was achieved due to a lightning-fast (and action movie worthy) race to the finish, that had its turning point when Picco asked himself "how can you end a war when one of the sides abandons the negotiations?" He found the answer in the history of the Renaissance when the armies stopped fighting only when the nations and commanders exhausted the funds that had been guaranteed them by the banks. This time it was the Saudi King Fahd who paid Saddam, and de Cuéllar's envoy dealt directly with him, negotiating a compromise that was acceptable to the two belligerents. It was a call from King Fahd to the Secretary General that gave the green light for the end of the war, but de Cuéllar objected: "I need to hear it from Saddam Hussein." The Rais called from Bagdad just five minutes later: "I subscribe to everything that His Excellency has said to you." And so eight years of war ended, and the Iranians who were exhausted by the conflict and in need of peace owed a great deal to Picco. But when, a few years later, de Cuéllar's envoy was sent to negotiate with Iran to obtain the release of western hostages (held by Hezbollah) in Beirut, there was no acknowledgement of what had happened before in the response that came out of Teheran. Picco had to go back to square one. He was successful once again. The hostage operation in the Lebanon was the event that marked and changed his life because he went through so much there: he was taken in the middle of the night, blindfolded, and transported by car to unknown locations never knowing if he would get out alive. The rescue was a success, but Picco never went back to sitting behind a desk in the UN building. Life changed because of the death threats that he continually received, some airports in Europe became off limits during certain periods, and the experience he gained in those impossible mediations led him to help the UN free another fourteen people. These experiences, that remind him of his father's teaching that "we are all important and no one is indispensable," have made Picco a witness of the most critical international crises.

With more than three decades of conflict resolution and a myriad of assignments for the UN behind him, Picco now represents only himself and is still an indefatigable negotiator. He often leaves his office in Connecticut for quick trips to different continents, where the meeting agendas are always top secret. And when he stops to look beyond the horizon of the international balance that is starting to ferment, he sees two processes in action. The first one, in the short-term, is a "return to the past," or in other words, a world order that is product of the balance of many powers, as it has always been, except for the "lengthy exception of the Cold War." But looking further into the future he perceives the inclination to "move beyond the idea of the State that came out of the Treaty of Westphalia in 1648 that saw nations, founded on the compactness of identity, ethnicity, and religion, come into being." "The idea of the State has often changed throughout history, before Westphalia it was completely different, and then came the nation based on one distinctive identity and today it is changing again," he says indicating the revolutionary elements of communication, transportation and the discoveries of the age of globalization that "have brought people who are geographically very far apart closer to one another." What brings people together isn't the fact that they live in one territory but rather the activities that they engage in and the interests that they share. "Individuals have the upper hand as each one of them creates his/her own network of reference that often goes beyond the rigid national boundaries that once confined Enemonzo and that still influence the relationships between States." After thinking forward to what the rest of the XXI century will bring, Gianni Picco leaves the Century Club and heads towards Columbia University, where a Think Tank on the Middle East awaits him. But before he says goodbye he is careful to define himself as a "marginal Italian" because although his education in Italy allowed him to resolve the Iran-Iraq war by helping him take inspiration from the Renaissance —and this is only one of the many possible examples—his relationship to his home country has never been in the foreground. Whether marginal or not, Picco is still an example for Italians who choose a career at the UN because, as Furio de Tomassi, who is president of the Union of Italian functionaries in international organizations, explains, "he is the Italian who has reached the highest level of professionalism, competing in popularity with the Secretary General himself," embodying "the dedication to UN ideals that all the other Italians who work there share." Among them there's Staffan De Mistura former head of UN headquarters in Bagdad and today in Kabul (where he now represents Sweden, the country where he was born), Patrizio Civili who reached the level of assistant Secretary General, Laura Vaccari director of Political Affairs, Vincenzo Aquaro the director of Economic and Social Affairs who is also in charge of projects, plus a myriad of statisticians, economists, experts in human rights, international analysts, development aid workers, convinced that the United Nations can "guarantee transparency and stability in international relationships" as de Tomassi observes. De Tomassi himself was the protagonist of a legislative battle to obtain recognition for the official figure of "functionary of international organizations" from Parliament. At least three thousand Italian graduates apply for positions in one of the agencies linked to the United Nations through a program created with funds from the Development Cooperation, it offers only 20 positions. But those who do get in rarely leave because, despite the fact that the salaries are lower compared to other international organizations, they believe in the possibility of becoming the next Gianni Picco of the XXI century, of being able to reinterpret and renew the idea that in 1942 led Franklin Delano Roosevelt and Winston Churchill, who were capable of looking beyond the horizon of a conflict that was far from over, to imagine the United Nations.

At the gate with Benigni and Manfredi

For the thousands of Italian Americans who choose to return to Italy each year just as for the myriad of Italian tourists who arrive in New York, the trip begins in JFK or Newark airports, where Alitalia flights land and take off every day under the direction of the traffic control officer Gaetano Messina. In Messina's office decorated with famous autographs, awards and mementos of every kind, the photographs of Roberto Benigni, Pelé and Pope Ratzinger stand out.

Gaetano's New York story begins when he left Castellammare del Golfo in Trapani and arrived with his parents, Castrenze and Francesca in Brooklyn in July of 1972. He went to live in Bensonhurst in a small house at 1935 West 6th Street. At fourteen, Gaetano went to attend Lafayette high school where he describes the initial period as "really terrible." He recalls: "I spent the weekends locked up in my room listening to the Beatles and the Rolling Stones and I wanted to go back to Italy at all costs." The only time during the week that he tried to socialize came when he played soccer with kids his own age. Every day, as soon as school was over, Gaetano went to play soccer and that's how he made his first American friends who were actually from Greece, Poland, Yugoslavia and the Caribbean. At that time, racial tensions were very high. Many schools bused African Americas from black neighborhoods to schools in white neighborhoods trying to foster integration, but often this practice turned out to have a boomerang effect and instead generated fights, brawls, and verbal abuse between opposing groups. Messina witnessed, with disgust and anger, the beatings of African Americans by whites. "For me, skin color was never an issue, we were friends, we played soccer together, we tried to win the game and that was what counted, playing soccer was the most beautiful thing." The time spent in high school proved to be formative for him. "The good road ran parallel to the bad road; it was very easy to make the wrong choice, with all the drugs that surrounded us." Soccer saved him again though he continued to spend his weekends in total solitude, overcome by nostalgia for the land of Sicily that he had left. Thanks to soccer, he was chosen among the best soccer players in the school and in the city, the All City Team, and he met the coach for St. Francis College in Brooklyn Heights who offered him a scholarship to cover the entire cost of his academic studies. This was the moment that changed his life. University opened the doors to a world that he didn't know and led him to play on the fields of Princeton, Penn State, Albany and Hartwick. He traveled, discovered new worlds, and explored New York: Little Italy, Broadway, the Village, the East Side, the West Side, and Chinatown. The solitude he had felt at 1935 West 6th Street became an ever more distant memory. He went to Madison Square Garden and finally managed to hear the Rolling Stones, Eric Clapton, Stevie Wonder, PFM, and many others live. "College was the best period of my life." What he is most proud of is that he became an All American, one of the forty best soccer players among college students in the entire United States. It was the summer of 1978 and when the coach asked him if he wanted to be Pelé's assistant at Soccer Camp he didn't think twice. He certainly didn't believe that he would ever meet the Brazilian champion, but it was enough just to be on the same soccer field as him. On the first day he was assigned to the juniors, the youngest kids. He explained the rules of the little campus, leading them around to explore it and when they got to the cafeteria they came face to face with the living soccer legend, the three time champion of the world, Edson Arantes do Nascimento, also known as Pelé. "I told him that it was a pleasure to meet him and I was about to shake his hand when he put his arms around me, it was unforgettable." That night Pelé felt like singing, he picked up the guitar and began to play, bringing everyone along with him. When it was time for an Italian song he looked at Gaetano and asked him to strike up a tune. He decided to sing *Volare* because everybody knows it. "It was an unforgettable night; I went to bed thinking that I was the happiest person in the world." The camp lasted a month,

Pelé spent a lot of time with the young players who adored him. On the last day they bombarded him with so many requests for autographs (on soccer balls, t-shirts, pieces of paper and all kinds of objects) that he postponed his departure just to make everybody happy. "This is the reason why Pelé is the greatest, besides being a great soccer player, he is above all else a great person." When he finished university, Messina played for three years on the New York Eagles team, among the semiprofessionals of the American Soccer League, but in 1982 the league was almost bankrupt and he was forced to find a job "off the books." A friend of his father had a restaurant where the Queen of Holland and many Dutch VIPs, including the directors of KLM went to eat. He was the one who suggested he find a job with the Dutch company explaining that "they are very good business people." But the initial impact was harsh because at the interview the manager said to him: "This isn't the job for you because here we work all the time, Christmas, New Year's and Easter." Messina accepted the challenge, he began at the check-in desk where he asked passengers "smoking or nonsmoking?" and he took care of the people who needed wheelchairs. Because KLM checks in passengers for Korean Airlines, Olympic, Lan Chile and Viasa, he learned how to ask the same question in Korean, Greek, Spanish and Portuguese, exemplifying the "KLM style" that is very rigid in its respect for rules and passengers. KLM also has a soccer club and this was his opportunity to nurture his passion playing with champions like the Brazilian Carlos Alberto and the German Gerd Müller who both came to North America like Pelé to solidify the popularity of the sport in the United States where the World Cup was going to be held in 1994. In 1990 Messina became the KLM Duty Manager and he was so popular at that point that his name appeared on the in-flight menu with "Cannelloni Gaetano," but it all came to an end when KLM transferred management of the American market to Northwest Airlines: he changed company too and three years later, in 2000, he came to Alitalia. "My family was happy, but I came from a northern European mentality and it took me some time to adapt to a more flexible way of managing work, I wasn't used to being in front of passengers who said 'I got your name from…' or asked me 'what region are you from?'" On September 11, 2011, he was working on the afternoon shift and outside the shut-down Kennedy airport handling a handful of can-celled 747 flights within the space of a few hours: after three days of grounded flights there were thousands of passengers on the ground, he was afraid that the whole system would collapse, but when they re-opened, it just took three flights to get through most of the passengers because "the people that left were the ones who were returning home," all of the others had decided to stay. It was a watershed moment. "Before then it was possible to get on board a plane with a ticket bearing one's maiden name, now, instead, iden-tity is checked four times, security has redesigned our jobs and x-ray machines have brought about the restructuring of airports. It's not hard to imagine that the system will continue to improve in the future, when the whole process will be run electronically without the need for any personnel, from the moment of online check-in at home to boarding.

This greater focus on security has changed Gaetano Messina's life and work. He describes Alitalia as a "unique company" because "the Italians of America consider it a first step towards home, they ask to travel only with us and on board they feel like they're with family," and this creates a "unique and inimitable bond between the company and its customers." It's within this context that Mes-sina has met and accompanied the most diverse group of people to the gate: Mick Jagger, Eric Clapton, Bocelli, Domingo, Berlusconi, Prodi, Casini, Bill Clinton, Tony Renis, Bonolis, Pino Daniele, Prodi, D'Alema, Fini, Totti, Batistuta, Milito, Del Piero, Krasić, Collovati and "two very classy people," Paolo Maldini and Ciro Ferrara. But, out of all of them, the encounters that most left their mark were his meeting with Roberto Benigni, Nino Manfredi and Benedict XVI. Benigni arrived in Newark in 2004. They met when Benigni was getting off the plane and a few days later the popular actor him called him from Chicago looking for help to reschedule his trip. "I did what he asked me to do and a few minutes later he called me in person when I was in my car on the Goethals Bridge, he thanked me and asked me 'can I use the *tu* form with you?' and that left me speechless." Five years later they met again when Benigni came to Manhattan to perform *Tutto Dante*. Messina accompanied him to passport control and he noticed that something wasn't right. The customs official disclosed to him that "Mr. Benigni is traveling with a stolen passport." The actor didn't protest, he followed the procedures trying to figure out what could have happened and he went to the office of the head of customs that in the meantime had gotten in touch with Interpol. After a few minutes the suspense was lifted when they told him that "there has been an error, there's a difference of just one digit with the stolen passport number, you can go." Years earlier he met Nino Manfredi who at that point was almost completely confined to a wheelchair. Messina was the one who brought him in person to the plane and his care was such that to thank him Manfredi kissed his hand. In 2009, shortly before landing on a flight from Washington to New York, Benedict XVI asked to meet Messina to thank him for taking care of his air travel arrangements on his first papal mission to America. Among the many anecdotes of the air manager who guards the "doors to Italy," the one that he keeps closest to his heart and that he loves to recount to his children Isabella, Bianca and Marco, dates back to his arrival in New York: "It happened on board the ship, it was dawn when I saw the Statue of Liberty, I will never forget that emotion."

1. At the Feast of San Gennaro in Little Italy the faithful, as a sign of devotion, pin dollar bills to the base of the statue of the Saint.

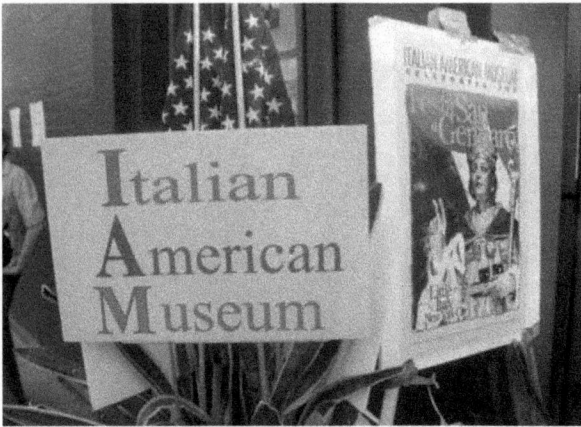

2. The Italian American Museum at the intersection of Mulberry and Grand Streets. It is located in the place that housed the Banca Stabile until 1932.

3. The Feast of San Gennaro on Mulberry Street.

4. Borgatti's Ravioli and Egg Noodles has been packaging handmade pasta for over seventy years. Old Glory flutters in the wind outside the storefront at 187th Street in the Bronx.

5. The pasta machines inside the store.

6. The deli counter of the Arthur Avenue Retail Market in the Bronx that was inaugurated by Mayor Fiorello LaGuardia.

7. The Made in Italy products on display at the entrance to Teitel Brothers on Arthur Avenue.

8. The Casa della Mozzarella on 187th Street in the Bronx. New Yorkers come here from distant neighborhoods to buy Italian food in Arthur Avenue's Little Italy.

9. The Carabinieri band at the Columbus Day parade on Fifth Avenue.

10. The bust of Christopher Columbus at the Columbus Day parade that celebrates Italian heritage each year in America.

11. When the end-of-year holidays arrive, the wealthiest Italian-American families of Dyker Heights decorate their homes with colorful lights and giant toys.

12. The Giglio Feast takes place on Padre Pio Way in Williamsburg in July.

13. The bas-relief and the plaque that at the Italian Consulate on Park Avenue commemorate the many victims of the September 11 attacks in 2001 that were of Italian origin. (Photo by Vito Catalano).

Politics

Passion and independence

The Italian presence in New York public life is considerable and it suggests that Governor Andrew Cuomo, who was the Attorney General from 2006 to 2009, isn't an exception. 22 of the 150 Representatives, 13 of the 62 State Senators, as well as 7 of the 51 town councilors of the Big Apple, 2 of the councilors of Staten Island, 2 of the 16 in Brooklyn, 2 of the 14 in Queens, 1 of the 8 in the Bronx, are all Italian. The only exception is that neither of the 2 councilors of Manhattan is Italian. To these numbers we have to add that the State of New York elected 3 Representatives of Italian descent to Congress, Mike Arcuri, Dan Maffei and Eric Massa, and also Eliot Engel who officially became Italian when he earned the title of Cavaliere of the Italian Republic for promoting laws on the recognition of the civil liberties of Italian Americans that were violated during World War II, and on the designation of October as Italian heritage month in America. Just like Andrew Cuomo who is champion of the safety of minors who use Facebook, the most influential Italian politicians of the metropolis set themselves apart for their shared passion for the defense of citizen rights. Thomas DiNapoli has been the State Comptroller since 2007 and is responsible for monitoring State accounts, an elected office that he attained because of the credibility he earned for combating overspending and redressing the budget of Nassau County on Long Island, whilst Bill de Blasio

has been the Public Advocate since January of 2010, the guarantor of the rights of residents when in conflict with city government
activities. On his curriculum he cites decisions such as the one giving every New Yorker access to public day care, and limiting the
number of children in elementary school classrooms to 20. There
are also some emerging figures and they are very determined to
prove themselves, such as Republican Enrico Anthony Lazio, called
"Rick," born in 1957, who in 2000 lost the Senate seat race against
Hillary Clinton, his fellow Republican Carl Paladino, the sixty-five
year old businessman supported by the Tea Party who survived
a duel "in the name of the Constitution" with Andrew Cuomo in
the race for Governor, and Democrat Regina Calcaterra, born in
1966, who ran as a candidate for State Senate on her success as a
court lawyer who defended the rights of the victims of financial
crimes committed by the managers of Wall Street giants such as
WorldCom and Merrill Lynch. Calcaterra who grew up with her
four brothers in an institute for abandoned children, is now a regular participant in charity work combatting the abandonment of minors, and she collects big private donations each year and earns the
growing praise of the city media.

Civic passion sets the Italian politicians of New York apart, and
the electorate that they have behind them is multiethnic. In fact Italians, for some time now, haven't been a compact electoral group in
so far as they vote primarily to promote their own interests just like
all other Americans do. And their interests are connected to the territory: on Long island and Staten Island, Italians live in elegant suburbs, they belong to the upper middle class, their incomes are above
average and they vote mostly for Republicans whose overriding
priorities are the lower taxes, opposition to abortion, the support
of private education and preserving the death penalty that was re-
introduced by former governor George Pataki whose Greek name
conceals an Italian heritage. In Queens, Brooklyn and in the Bronx,
Italian constituents live, instead, in urban areas where the middle
class prevails and they are more in tune with the Democratic base:
from public education to the protection of abortion rights to immigration reform. Manhattan is a separate case because now most of
the Italians that live there came in recent years and they don't have
American citizenship. John Calvelli who was the assistant to Repre-

sentative Engel until 2000 and the man behind the idea of October as Italian-American heritage month explains: "On the whole, the Italian vote in New York is equally divided between Republicans and Democrats, but in both camps the attention of voters focuses on the improvement of education in general and on the diffusion of the Italian language in particular which they consider as vital to the preservation of their identity." Frank Macchiarola, who was the New York City School Chancellor during Ed Koch's administration, explains how the differentiation of the Italian vote began, as follows: "Italians supported the Democratic Party up until it distinguished itself as the defender of worker and immigrant rights, but when the Democrats, in the Sixties, became the party of minorities, from African Americans to Hispanics, and began to choose very liberal positions on abortion and gay rights, it lost many of its supporters who shared a catholic identity that respected life and the family, issues that were certainly more in tune with Republican values." Victor Kovner, who has been a Midtown lawyer for fifty years and an informal advisor to most liberal city leaders, notes that what also damaged the relationship with the Democrats was the fact that "Italians weren't on the front lines of the battle against segregation or of the civil rights movement because of the rivalry that set them against African Americans, a rivalry based on the competition between the less well-off classes of the time in areas like Greenwich Village." For Maria Laurino, the author who was the speech writer for Mayor David Dinkins, "the choice of the Italian electorate to move from the Democrats to the Republicans originates from a type of distinction within American society: the more economic and professional success people have and the more they progress into the upper class, the more they identify with Republican values." They voted for the Democrats when the issues that needed defending belonged to the class of poor immigrant workers; now, instead, because Italians live mostly in the suburbs, in homes that they own and send their children to the best universities, their values converge with those of the Republicans. What illustrated this shift in votes from left to right, was when in 1981 Alfonse D'Amato became a Washington Senator after an electoral campaign that had its headquarters in Nassau County, Long Island, in the suburbs populated by Italian Americans. A few years later, it was D'Amato, a staunch supporter of Capital Punishment, who advised Reagan to place Rudolph Giuliani as third in command at the Department of Justice thus reinforcing even further the relationship with conservatives. Mario Cuomo, who in 1983 was the first Italian American to become State Governor and observed the political transformations that occurred, speaks of Italians as "voters belonging to the category of independents, who vote according to their interests at the time." And who often end up have the deciding vote.

The reformers of Tammany Hall

"We Italians arrived in New York between 1880 and 1925. Way back then everything began, and nobody talked of politics." John Lo-Cicero is eighty years old and for six decades he has been one of the leading spirits of the Democratic Party in Manhattan: he participated in election campaigns with Eleanor Roosevelt, for John Kennedy and Bill Clinton, and most importantly, he grew up on the Lower East Side "where everything began." "When the immigrants arrived, they didn't have a political conscience because they bore the legacy of an idea of the State as enemy that distanced them from public life" and besides that "the Irish dominated politics in New York as they did the city Church, and they certainly weren't ready to give way having suffered so much to gain a foothold in spite of the protestants." The Lower East Side in the Twenties was a web of streets where every region and city of origin was represented by a certain number of blocks, "so it was impossible to even consider talking about the Italian vote: there wasn't even the sense of being Italian, everyone spoke a different dialect and in my house it was Sicilian." So "when somebody needed something, he'd go ask the Representative named Foley, who was Irish." The first turning point was when Italians "left the cart behind and began to work as laborers" and they became Union members. "Many went to work in factories, there were many factories in East Harlem and so many people moved from the Lower East Side." The Great Depression transformed this new generation of workers into indigents, they needed everything and they realized that the State could help them. In the Thirties, Vito Marcantonio—the Republican

Representative who then became an important exponent of the Labor Party giving voice to labor radicalism—shaped the idea of an
Italian vote bound to the necessity of defending the interests of the
workers who were being thrashed by the economic crisis." "Besides
East Harlem, Italians in the Twenties and Thirties moved towards
Brooklyn, to Bensonhurst, that was in the middle of the countryside
back then" LoCicero adds explaining that "one of the advantages
of going down there was the absence of the Black Hand," precursor of the mafia. The Forties belonged to Mayor Fiorello LaGuardia
"who found space in the Republican Party because the Irish still
refused to let us into the Democratic Party," but when World War
II ended, the most visible political leader was Carmine Gerard De-
Sapio. "He came, like me, from the Lower East Side," in 1949 he
ably trounced the Irish and became the youngest leader of the Tammany Hall society—the democratic electoral machine—and in 1955
he appeared on the cover of Time in a celebration of his power. In
the Fifties he was the deciding figure in the nomination of mayors,
governors and local administrators, but he had made a fearsome
foe: Eleanor Roosevelt, widow of the President who had crushed
Hitler. She reproached DeSapio for having blocked her son Franklin D. Roosevelt Jr.'s run for governor in 1954. The clash between
the Roosevelts and the DeSapios led the new generation of Italian politicans, LoCicero among them, to side with the former First
Lady who wanted to launch a series of reforms within Tammany
Hall, to "renew an antiquated party and make it more liberal." The
battle was won in 1961 when DeSapio left Tammany Hall after his
defeat in the democratic presidential primaries in 1960 when he
supported Lyndon Johnson, whilst Roosevelt and the young leaders of the Reform Democrats movement rallied around John F. Kennedy. "It was almost like a quake in New York. We reformers united around Koch who was fighting for civil rights, abortion, divorce
and respect for gay people," LoCicero remarks as he speaks about a
"term marked by losses and defeats" until Koch was elected mayor
in 1978. "Ed was fighting on issues such as abortion, divorce, sod-
omy… so it's really not surprising that in the Sixties there was some
resistance against him." However, Koch had Mario Cuomo as his
democratic rival. The two clashed, they supported different candidates for city offices and they didn't like each other because they

couldn't have been more different. "Koch was a reformer, Cuomo instead didn't want to break with the old guard, so much so that to block Koch, he coined the phrase 'Better Cuomo than a Homo,' a slogan that better suited the Republicans" because it focused on the homosexuality of his rival. But for the Italians involved in politics on the democratic side, those were the years of triumph and redemption, "even the Mafiosi, I'm thinking of the Gambinos for example, realized that it was better to send their children to college to open up carriers for themselves as businessmen and lawyers." LoCicero, the Korean War Air Force veteran, has his own interpretation of the genesis of the Democratic Party transformation after the Second World War with the "collapse of the old barons and the rise of the liberals thanks to Eleanor": "A lot happened because of the GI Bill, the law passed by Congress to help the veterans of the war, it guaranteed the possibility to buy homes and to have a better education, there were hundreds of thousands of veterans of Italian heritage who took advantage of it and that changed the Italians of New York, they had gone to war often barely able to speak English, and they returned and became part of the middle class," bringing new energy even to the political arena.

From Koch to Bloomberg

Besides being the descendant of one of the best-known families of Little Italy in the Bronx, Peter Madonia Jr. is the brains and the brawn of the Rockefeller Foundation. He has an L-shaped office with a breathtaking view of the Midtown skyscrapers on the twentieth floor of 420 Fifth Avenue. He became Chief Operating Officer of one of the largest philanthropic institutions in America after holding the position of Chief of Staff to Michael Bloomberg and before that, at the time of Ed Koch, he was second in command of the Fire Department. He comes from the Bronx, where his father opened Madonia Brothers Bakery on Arthur Avenue in 1918. The bakery still operates to this day and Peter himself managed it for a time during a career break. He is tall, fair-skinned with light brown hair, he carries himself like an athlete and he sits at his round table as if he were a cowboy. His Italianness is in the values that he in-

herited from his father and they can be summarized by the term
loyalty, loyalty to the *unit* to which one belongs or, in other words,
to the family as a company. It's a principle of belonging whereby
"even if there are different opinions and at times there are argu-
ments, loyalty towards the others always prevails, in an effort to
build a future and confront difficulties." And this is the approach
that guided him through his political career in New York, from one
mayor to the next. He reiterates that "disagreement doesn't compromise loyalty" explaining that "discord is often healthy because
the best ideas emerge out of sincere differences, provided that everyone involved is always loyal." And he was loyal to the Democrat
Ed Koch from 1979 to 1988 just as he was with the Republican (then
Independent) Bloomberg from 2002 to 2004. "Being Mayor of New
York entails governing the melting pot, which means conciliating
ethic communities, being in the thick of things, in the laboratory of
humanity, and you notice this when you go abroad because when
you say you are American you get a cold reception but when you
explain that you are from New York the reaction is that people embrace you, which is what happened to me in Kampala in Uganda
where a bartender said to me 'I have a cousin in the Bronx too.'"
Both Ed Koch and Bloomberg embodied the role of "mayors as interpreters of a city of immigrants, worthy successors of Fiorello La-
Guardia," as they confronted the different reconstruction agendas
that they had to face. "Koch took over a city in which crime was
very high and the infrastructure was in ruins, metro, trains and garbage facilities had to be updated. He had to get the city on its feet
again. It was really tough. Everything was falling apart. The key
was to motivate the young people, transform them into the driving
force behind the regeneration of the city. I was just twenty-three
years old, I remember that feeling well." Bloomberg, instead, took
office after the attacks of September 11, 2001 and "had the problem
of the financial meltdown, the greatest strength of the City was now
its weakness and he worked as a businessman, getting economic
growth back on track with a host of projects, even if some worked
and others didn't: the new Waterfront and the rezoning of the city
but also the failure to construct the stadium on the West Side as
well as the unsuccessful Olympic bid." On the whole, however,
Madonia confirms that "Bloomberg managed to re-launch New

York just as Ed Koch had been able to revive it" and "the response to the 2004 black-out" proves it, "because everything was better organized compared to what had happened in 1977, it could have been the coup de grace, but it wasn't."

As for the role of Italian Americans, Madonia points out some differences between the two mayors. He recalls: "I was walking down Mott Street in Little Italy with Koch 10 years ago and he said to me, 'you know Peter, Italians have been the last of the immigrants to leave Manhattan for the suburbs, they've stayed, they are an important part of the fabric of New York.'" For Bloomberg, instead, Italians aren't immigrants anymore. "But it's because the last wave of Italian immigrants dates back to the Fifties and Sixties and so much time has passed, for him the Chinese, South Asians and Central Americans are the immigrants. He no longer distinguishes between Italians and Americans."

Since leaving City Hall, the new dimension of Madonia's public service lies within the Rockefeller Foundation for which he promotes programs for climate protection and the development of health reforms in Third World countries. It was this great charitable institution that successfully eradicated yellow fever. But what does leading a foundation mean? He answers, "Looking for models that have been successful and then trying to replicate them," and he makes reference to certain health programs in Rwanda and in some coastal communities in India and Vietnam where projects are in progress that aim at protecting the inhabitants from the risk of flooding if sea level rises significantly.

The jewel of the Foundation is the Bellagio Center, but he admits that "if I had to start all over again I wouldn't build it" because of all of the obstacles that go hand in hand with operating in Italy. "We have 32 employees with very high costs, we have to pay health and life insurance and 14 salaries every month, the labor laws are too onerous, and for this reason American entrepreneurs don't invest in Italy. The problem is that if you hire somebody for six months you have to keep that person on for life incurring very high costs." Italy today, from an economic point of view, doesn't convince him much, but as far as identity is concerned he has no doubts: "My father Peter came from Sicily, my mother Josephine from Senigallia, in the Marche region, and she grew up in Canarsie,

Brooklyn, where she suffered discrimination only because she was Italian, one of my aunts actually died because she went to live in a New York neighborhood where everybody spoke English. I feel Italian."

Cuomo and Giuliani

The Italians of New York have served as mayors, governors, Representatives, Senators, and in a myriad of local administrative positions, but the two leaders who best personify their political passion are those who came close to the dream of becoming the first Italian American to sit in the Oval Office. Besides their presidential bids, Democrat Mario Cuomo and Republican Rudolph Giuliani couldn't be more different, because they represent contrasting ideas of America, they are champions of opposing values and their lives show different bonds to their cultural heritage. Both their trajectories, however, help understand just how far-reaching the participation of Italian Americans in public life actually is.

Mario Cuomo was born in 1932 in a house in Queens, his father Andrea Cuomo came from Nocera Superiore and his mother Immacolata from Tramonti. The Cuomos had a big family that they supported with the earnings from a store in South Jamaica. They raised Mario speaking to him in dialect until they sent him to school at age eight without any knowledge of English. In an interview with American Heritage Magazine in December 1990, he reveals that the public schools taught him what America was, "seeing that my parents and the priests in my Church hadn't done so." Rudy Giuliani, instead, was born in Brooklyn in 1944, the son of Harold Angelo Giuliani and Helen D'Avanzo who were both born in America of parents who came at the end of the eighteen hundreds. The fact that they spoke English at home shows that this family was a little further ahead on the path to integration. This didn't help them much though from an economic point of view, they made ends meet moving from one job to the next. To make matters worse, Harold Giuliani was convicted of assault and robbery, he was put behind bars and when he came out of prison he became the bodyguard of his brother-in-law who was involved in gambling and loansharking.

For both Cuomo and Giuliani, their childhoods were marked by hardships and difficulties that led them to prove themselves by way of their studies (Cuomo at Public School 50, Giuliani at Bishop Loughin Memorial High School) opening the doors to careers as lawyers. Mario's career in law began with Judge Adrian Burke after he graduated from St. John's University, and Rudolph's began with Judge Lloyd MacMahon after he finished law school at New York University.

Though twelve years apart, both Cuomo and Giuliani began their public service activities in the courtroom. For Mario it was the natural progression of his studies whilst for Rudy it was a choice made following lengthy reflections about entering the priesthood, which he ultimately decided to renounce. Giuliani's relationship with the Catholic faith is very strong, and was reinforced by his studies at Bishop Loughin, whilst Cuomo lives his faith as a family tradition, distinguishing it from his education which he received mostly in public schools that instilled in him a belief in the separation of Church and State.

As a lawyer, at the end of the Sixties, Cuomo emerged on the city scene when he defended the Corona Fighting 69 which was a group of 69 property owners in the Corona neighborhood in Queens that had been threatened with eminent domain by the City plan to build a new high school. It was a legal battle that transformed him into a champion of the middle class that, after another two similar cases defending small property owners in Queens, brought Mayor John Lindsay to assign him the management of property disputes between residents and owners in Queens in 1972.

Giuliani's debut, instead, was marked by the fight against crime because MacMahon was the Judge for the Southern District of New York that includes Manhattan, and he assigned him some cases dealing with drug trafficking that brought him attention and led him to become Chief of the Narcotics Unit in 1973.

In the Seventies, Cuomo and Giuliani advanced on parallel paths: dedication to the rights of the less wealthy transformed Mario into a rising star of the New York Democratic Party (until he lost the race for mayor to Ed Koch in 1977), whilst Rudy staked everything on city security, he left the Democratic Party, he became an independent and entered the government for the first time during

Gerald Ford's administration as Chief of Staff for the Vice-Minister of Justice, Harold Tyler. What turned them into direct opponents was the Reagan administration: the President whom Cuomo, now Governor of New York since 1982, despised, attributing an ideology of disparity to him, whilst Giuliani (almost a Republican at this point) owed him the nomination as Associate Attorney General, the third highest position in the Department of Justice, in 1981. At the Democratic convention in San Francisco on July 16th, 1984, the candidate Walter Mondale assigned the keynote speech to Cuomo, which he shaped as an anti-Reagan manifesto in which he criticized the sitting President for "not seeing the desperation of those who are excluded from your shining city." "The Republicans believe that the wagon train will not make it to the frontier unless some of the old, some of the young, some of the weak, are left behind by the side of the trail so that the strong can prevail" he said from the stage in San Francisco, " but we Democrats believe in something else. We democrats believe that we can make it all the way with the America that includes blacks and Hispanics, people of every ethnic group, and Native Americans, and all those struggling to protect their families."

The content of his speech along with his eloquence, projected Cuomo into the leadership role of the Party after the clear defeat of the ticket with Mondale and the Italian American Geraldine Ferraro (another New Yorker from Queens). Four years later, when the Republicans chose George H.W. Bush as their candidate to succeed Reagan, many democrats backed Cuomo, convinced that he had the right profile to win the Oval Office, not only because of his liberal values but also because of the positive results of the employment recovery that the State he governed was experiencing. But Cuomo resisted all adulation, he was hesitant to talk about putting himself forward as a candidate and he left the field open for Michael Dukakis, who was later defeated. His lack of decisiveness left New York democrats perplexed and earned him the title of "Hamlet on the Hudson," which was even more justifiable when, in the middle of the Nineties, President Bill Clinton thought of nominating him as Supreme Court Judge and once again he retreated. "To avoid saying no to Clinton, Cuomo didn't take his call" says a veteran of the New York City Democratic Party who confesses that he "still doesn't know what the reason behind such incomprehensible be-havior was." In 1988, Cuomo's excessive caution made the hope of having an Italian American President vanish into thin air, whilst twenty years later, the prospect of Giuliani vanished for the op-posite reason: too much self-confidence. In the electoral campaign after Bush, Giuliani presented himself with the most solid creden-tials on security: as US Attorney for New York in the middle of the Eighties he had tackled organized crime within the context of the inquiry known as Pizza Connection, and as Mayor he had led the response to the terrorist attacks of September 11, 2001, after ridding the city of crime in the Nineties by applying the Zero Tolerance doctrine based on the idea that by arresting those who commit petty crimes, an increase in more serious crimes is prevented in the long term. In January 2008, when the primaries began, Giuliani thought he had the Republican nomination in the bag, and he raised mil-lions of dollars. Among the biggest donors were Italian American groups in New York, Pennsylvania and Florida that identified with him, though he had difficulties winning the ethnic vote as, unlike Cuomo, he doesn't speak Italian. But it was this overconfidence in his abilities that caused him to slip. He chose a suicidal electoral strategy by not participating in the primaries in Iowa, New Hamp-shire and South Carolina and instead focused everything on Flor-ida where he was later soundly beaten. He got to the Convention in Saint Paul, in Minnesota, with only one delegate, after spending 50 million dollars in campaign funds. The presidential nomination that just a year earlier he was sure he had within his grasp just faded away and all he could do was play the role of the anti-Obama attack dog in a speech that galvanized the audience of conserva-tive delegates. The stinging defeat of Giuliani who after September 11 had been defined "America's Mayor" and crowned "Man of the year" by Time Magazine, brought the other side of his life into the spotlight: from his father's involvement with the mafia to his three marriages (one to his third cousin which was annulled), from liv-ing with two gay friends in Manhattan to his political and personal connection to Bernard Kerik, the ex-New York Police Chief who was embroiled in a scandal about the renovation of his apartment paid for by a mafia boss.

In the space of two decades, first Mario Cuomo and then Rudy

Giuliani lost the possibility of running for the White House because of a combination of uncertainty and bad decision-making that resoundingly clash with the many clearly confirmed accomplishments of both men in their respective fields. But that doesn't mean that their candidacies, whether openly declared or held to be credible, have made the idea of a future Italian American candidate for the Presidency of the United States taboo. The challenge has been placed in the hands of the next generation of leaders.

Referendum on identity

For the Italians of New York, Election Day 2010 proved to be a referendum on their own identity. For the first time, the candidates for new State Governor, Democratic Andrew Cuomo and Republican Carl Paladino, set a clear choice before them between two opposing ways of embodying the values and the ideals of Italian Americans. It was an unforeseen situation that came about by surprise when Paladino, the businessman from Buffalo, backed by the Tea Party, won the Republican primaries instead of the favorite Rick Lazio, also Italian but minus the ethnic slant. Paladino presented himself as the synthesis of all of the most common stereotypes of Italian immigrants: his election meetings took place in Buffalo, in Upstate New York, in a restaurant named Sinatra's whose regular customers wear gold chains around their necks, have tattoos and whose mannerisms evoke the style of the Sopranos, and the social club that he frequented is called Big Tymers where the customers are mostly factory workers of southern Italian descent who "are all really loud, they all speak at the same time and nobody listens," as Guy Molinari, former Borough President of Staten Island, wrote in the New York Times (11 October 2010). Paladino comes from a family of immigrants from Molise that arrived at Ellis Island in 1926. Every year he returns at least once to Santa Croce di Magliano, he speaks dialect with ease and he is a proud consumer of the local cuisine that he loves to describe when he talks about himself. It's a way of being Italian that he flaunted during the Columbus Day parade on Fifth Avenue, when his younger supporters marched wearing *Jersey Shore* t-shirts. To all of this we can add that Paladino, who was born in 1946, is married to a woman who is well aware of all of his infidelities (even the secret child he has fathered with one of his mistresses) and so it isn't hard to understand why the Republican businessman embodies a way of life that many Italian Americans consider excessive, vulgar and essentially harmful to integration in America.

Andrew Cuomo, born in 1958, is the polar opposite of all of this. Though he is the son of ex-Governor Mario (the protagonist of many battles against anti-Italian racism) and of Matilda (the sponsor of countless associations and events of Italian interest), Andrew leaves those origins in the background. His first wife was Kerry Kennedy (daughter of Robert and Ethel Skakel) and his current partner is Sandra Lee the White Anglo-Saxon Protestant with blond hair and light-colored eyes who is the host of cooking programs on the Food Network. As New York Attorney General, he avoided behaving in a way that could be construed as too ethnic. He commissioned a survey in 2002 that revealed how stereotypes about Italians as Mafiosi and thugs were still so ingrained that they could damage his political career. When the race for Governor, in the fall of 2010, turned into an all-Italian challenge (with other races for administrative offices that were also dominated by Italian names), he didn't hesitate to confess to his closest collaborators that he feared a negative boomerang effect on his popularity. To explore the Italian American identity of Andrew you must meet his mother Matilda, an elegant New York lady who juxtaposes her pride in her Italian roots (her mother was born in Merì, in the province of Messina) with frequent references to the example of Eleanor Roosevelt, not just as First Lady, but in her dedication to others. During a breakfast gathering at the Regency Hotel on Park Avenue, Matilda explains that "the new generations are what count most for the future of New York, because when my husband was governor, the biggest social problem was homelessness, today, instead, it's abandoned children who find themselves in this situation because their parents turned their backs on them after they were born." There are "thousands of cases" that Matilda says can be helped by creating a "support network" founded on "families, schools and the community," by rejecting now in the context of the XXI century, the "example of my grandparents and parents." She goes on to explain: "My parents came from a nation where it was necessary to do everything alone, and after arriving in America they continued to do everything by themselves, working hard to bring up their children, but nowadays it must be the State that bears this legacy of dedication and determination to help children without parents to whom we must give a future." These are words that describe the transmission of Italian values into the heart of the American system. If for Carl Paladino being Italian means extolling one's own ethnic characteristics, for Andrea Cuomo integration prevails, the convergence of values. This led Paladino to mock Cuomo's heritage when he sarcastically stated that "perhaps Andrew was adopted," and was Italian only in name. But when the polling stations opened and New York chose its next Governor, it was Andrew who prevailed. The reasons for Paladino's crushing defeat (34% to 61%) shouldn't be individuated in the duel of identity for the very reason that Cuomo became popular as Attorney General because of his investigation of Wall Street criminals and because of his defense of the rights of consumers who had been devastated by the economic crisis. But if Italian Americans clearly prefer him because he exemplifies successful integration, it's because he's capable of allowing his ethnic origins to coexist with the American lifestyle. It's no coincidence that Victor Kovner, a veteran of the New York City Democratic Party, speaks of Andrew as the "first Italian who could really become President of the United States" because "he is like Barack Obama in that his ethnic identity is important, but it doesn't define him, the most important factor is being American." Those who voted for Paladino did so as an anti-establishment protest, in response to the pleas of the Tea party on a national scale, but also to restate their pride in their ethnic origins in opposition to the diktats of American society. It's a difference that is reflected in the socio-geographical distance between the two candidates, because the Italian Americans of Manhattan to whom Cuomo belongs are considered outsiders by the members of the Buffalo clubs which are for the most part made up of middle-class families who have unskilled jobs and live far from the lights and affluence of the Big Apple.

Business

Maria "Money Honey"

Italian is spoken on Wall Street because of the achievements and success stories, over the last thirty years of CEOs like Gil Amelio at Apple, Lee Iacocca at Chrysler, Carly Fiorina at Hewlett-Packard, Bob Nardelli at The Home Depot and Leonard Riggio at Barnes&Noble, and because of the image of the New York Stock Exchange itself which, for most people, corresponds to the face of "Money Honey." This is the nickname of the indisputable star of financial TV news programs who is the sexiest economist on Wall Street. Maria Bartiromo was born in Bay Ridge Brooklyn in 1967 into a middle-class Italian family that supported itself on the income earned from Rex Manor, a restaurant bearing the name of the ocean liner that set sail from the Bay of Naples in 1919, bringing her grandfather Carmine to America. Bartiromo grew up in a house in multiethnic Bay Ridge where Italians were 16.6 percent of the 70 thousand residents, the largest ethnic group, followed by the Irish, Arabs, Chinese, Greeks and Hispanics. When describing her family, with her father Vincent from Naples and her mother Josephine from Agrigento, she speaks mostly of the abundance of food and the scarcity of financial resources. When she was little, she went to an all-girl Catholic school, her first job was as the coat check girl at the family restaurant. During her tough adolescent years the only moments of relief were the Saturday evenings that she spent at the disco with her sister Theresa, where she danced so much that she earned the nickname "Disco Queen" from her friends. She never thought that at forty years of age she would be the best-known financial journalist in the United States. Fame, success, and wealth have grown out of her ability to "work hard like the immigrants did at the beginning of the XX century," an ability that she learned from her parents and that led her to graduate from New York University with a degree in Journalism and Economics. She explains it as follows: "my strength comes from my upbringing, no matter how much success I have, I feel very connected to my origins, I come from a very close family, my mother is my best friend and my sister closely follows, I still see my father work at Rex Manor wearing a white bandana, sweating, never taking a break from the long hours. These humble beginnings are what make me appreciate life's little pleasures." This is how she laid the foundations for her career. She started as an intern at CNN in 1987 and then she worked alongside Lou Dobbs as a producer for *Money Line*. The turning point in her career was when she became the first reporter to broadcast live from the New York Stock Exchange floor. That day she tackled the topic that was headlining all newscasts, the nomination of Jack Welch as CEO of General Electric. The stockbrokers were the first to be skeptical about a woman discussing financial matters and they crowded around her position shouting uncivilly at her "this is no place for you, go away." But she stayed; she ended the live TV report for *SquawkBox* on CNBC and came back the next day and then the next. She created a new kind of financial journalism that after fifteen years is now virtually unrivaled: the financial news programs, with live comments on trends in stocks and transactions with real stock quotes displayed on the screen. Richard Grasso has fully supported her since she got the go-ahead for her first show. He was born into a family of Italian and Maltese immigrants in Queens, and was President of the New York Stock Exchange from 1995 until 2003. At the end of the Nineties, reporting on the economic boom of the Clinton era on live TV, Bartiromo earned the nickname "Money Honey," but it didn't bother her too much because she wants to "turn business into something sexy." It is true that nowadays many tall, blond, athletic women have become popular faces on the big network TV programs that discuss sports and politics, and Maria Bartiromo doesn't see anything wrong with somebody like her (5′ 4″, green eyes, a shapely figure, and Mediterranean coloring) becoming the Sophia Loren of Wall Street. The number of viewers that her morning show, *The Wall Street Journal Report*, and her afternoon show, *Closing Bell* (that she anchors on CNBC) attract, shows that her popularity is still rising, backed by praise from the critics, journalism awards, books on the secrets of finance and a host of city offices, from member of the Board of Directors at the New York City Ballet to Grand Marshall at the 2010 Columbus Day Parade when she wore the tricolor sash. For "Vanity Fair," her beauty makes her the "Sophia Loren of journalism" and her financial prowess "the economic version of Barbara Walters." The two tragedies of the beginning of the century had her witness news-stories firsthand: the terrorist attack of September 11 (her birthday falls on the same day) happened when she was inside the Stock Exchange and she watched the plane crash into the second Tower, and the Wall Street crisis that followed the collapse of Lehman Brothers on September 15, 2008. Bartiromo's New York is all on the Upper East Side where she lives in a building worth 6.5 million dollars with her husband Jonathan Steinberg (son of financier, Saul), she uses the breakfast hall of the Regency Hotel for her work meetings and plans her workdays during which (and her colleagues at CNBC attest to this) "she is capable of working faster than anybody else." Her work ethic and accolades though didn't spare her a difficult period in 2007 when the top manager of Citigroup, Todd Thomson, was accused of flying from Beijing to New York on a private jet after leaving all of his colleagues on the ground just so he could travel alone with Maria, with whom it is said he had a relationship. The suspicion of complicity with a Wall Street VIP had her fear the worst for a few weeks. But her decision to never comment on the story, and the unwavering support that her TV employers publically expressed, paid off. And she was able to get back to gathering breaking news stories and interviews (from Alan Greenspan to Condoleeza Rice with all of the major Wall Street CEOs along the way), dedicating her free time to go visit her oldest relative to whom she is very close. It's her "Uncle Charles" who is 103 years old and he often describes what New York was like when Rex Manor first opened. In the *American dream* that is Maria Bartitomo's story there is, however, a looming threat embodied by

the only financial TV reporter capable of stealing some of her viewers and attention: Charles Gasparino. He was born in 1963 in the
Bronx and when he worked at CNBC he praised "Money Honey"
as a "good journalist," but when he went over to Fox he started to
challenge her so vehemently that he earned the nickname "Rocky
Balboa," evoking the boxer brought to life on screen by Sylvester
Stallone.

The "Street-fighter" generation

The Italian Americans who've made headway in the Wall Street
business community, weren't born, as they say in English, with a
silver spoon in their mouths, but they're people who came from
poor families and they proved themselves with hard work, they
made tough sacrifices and escaped a background of poverty and
of immigrant families who as soon as they arrived became factory
workers and builders. Charles Gasparino is one of the people who
recounts both the suffering and success of this generation of *streetfighters*, because he has direct experience with it. His grandparents
arrived penniless from Naples but he is now the face of Fox Business Network TV. "Today in New York, the anti-Italian racism of
times past doesn't exist anymore, and the mafia stereotype rarely
surfaces, as it did for example on the New York Times when Dick
Grasso was described as a "world boss," a term used to indicate a
Cosa Nostra gangster, Gasparino explains. "But when this generation of businessmen first came to Wall Street, they had to confront
prejudice because they weren't American and they weren't Protestants. Nobody trusted them." They were successful despite the
fact that everything was against them and they are Richard Grasso,
who was President of the New York Stock Exchange, the investment banker Kenneth Langone, one of the founders of the home
improvement giant The Home Depot, Leonard Riggio, owner of
Barnes&Noble bookstores, Samuel Palmisano, CEO of IBM, Lawrence Auriana, manager of the Kaufmann Fund and leader of the
Columbus Citizens Foundation raised in East Harlem, and many
many more. "They made it because they are all *streetfighters*, honest
but tough. Nothing was ever handed to them, they had to earn ev-

erything, starting with little or nothing." For the most part they are businessmen with parents, grandparents and great grandparents who came from Southern Italian regions, they grew up very poor, with the ambition of doing better than their parents had done, by the only means given to them: hard work and doing the right thing. "These are people of a harsh and concrete cast, and it's because of these characteristics that they've been successful," Gasparino confirms.

But there have been some black sheep too. Angelo Mozilo, CEO of the mortgage giant Countrywide, is the face of one of the speculators who destroyed the stability and wellbeing of millions of American families, just as Raffaello Follieri is serving a sentence of four and a half years for a multi-million dollar real-estate scam that he had managed to put in place, at age thirty, deceiving numerous American bishops and the Clinton Foundation. "These are people who've been imprisoned in a different way by the housing bubble, everyone knows what they are guilty of but nobody accuses them because they are Italian American, and this confirms the fact that prejudice is on the wane," the financial anchorman states, pausing to note that "what strikes Americans much more is the fact that the billion-dollar fashion industry speaks Italian, you just have to walk around New York to notice it." Italian banks are few and far between on Wall Street, and Made in Italy high finance doesn't have a strong presence, but "this shouldn't be such a surprise because, when all is said and done, this sector of the economy is in decline, consumers continue, instead, to spend on fashion and that's where Italy is very strong." Along with Gucci, Fendi, Loro Piana, Armani, Max Mara, Dolce e Gabbana and Bottega Veneta holding court on Madison Avenue and Fifth Avenue (despite the crisis that hit other luxury brands), the other new element of the New York Made in Italian business is the real-estate sector. Daniele Bodini and his Continental Properties is now a well-established presence and in recent years the Sorgente group has taken over Flatiron (one of Manhattan's iconic buildings) and Bizzi & Partners has inaugurated a skyscraper at 400 Fifth Avenue and many other Italian companies have amassed acquisitions, businesses and investments. Gasparino states that "it's a sign of the times, real-estate in Manhattan costs less now that it has in the past and Italian entrepreneurs are right to take advantage of this precious opportunity." Gasparino's grand-parents came to New York from Naples. His maternal grandpar-ents went to live in Lower Manhattan, in the Sullivan Street area, whilst his paternal grandparents went to the West Village, to Little Italy, and they later moved to East Harlem and to the Bronx where he was born. His father who worked the most menial jobs to sup-port his family was the one who instilled in him the importance of the business world, and along with his passion for journalism, Gasparino's studies at university did the rest. His debut during the financial scandals of the Eighties and Nineties served as a jumping off point for his TV career. The fact that he has successfully estab-lished himself in financial TV journalism is for Gasparino a suc-cess that parallels the achievements of the Wall Street *Streetfighters:* he explains, determined to free himself from the "the poor-person mentality that he came from." He speaks of it firmly but without bitterness: "I come for a family that recommended we work for the Department of Sanitation in order to have the security of a full-time job, and they thought that because they were poor, factory workers, they believed that a city job was the highest aspiration they could have, but my brother (who became a doctor) and I and many more of us chose a different path, we wanted to test ourselves and try to build a better future. And we did it." The true words of a *street-fighter.*

Italy vanished from Wall Street

The headquarters of Lincoln International, on the top two floor of 400 Madison Avenue, is furnished like an apartment, with warm paintings, colored desks and a perfectly functioning kitchen. Look-ing out from the terrace you see the headquarters of Lazard, JPM-organ and Deutsche Bank. Despite the fact that this is a hub of fi-nancial gurus, the atmosphere is relaxed, almost family-like. The managing director, Federico Mennella, is from Milan where he studied at "Leo XIII" Jesuit high school, and he came to America after what happened on August 13th 1975 when his maternal uncle Gianfranco Lovati Cottini was kidnapped by the *"banda dei giost-rai,"* the first major kidnapping of a businessman in the Veneto region. Lovati Cottini recognized his kidnappers and he was found dead on August 18th. For Federico, who was seventeen at the time, it was a shock and his father, owner of a plastic toy and educational toy company, reacted by sending him to America. He arrived in New York on August 25th having studied English for only two years in high school. Guido Calabrese, a Yale law professor who had fled Italy thirty six years earlier (because of racial laws), saw his own situation mirrored in Federico's odyssey and he was the one who helped him. Calabresi's advice and encouragement accompanied Federico on his studies and he achieved a degree in Economics and Political Science at Yale where Calabrese, in the meantime, had become Dean of the Law School. He began to work at Oppenheimer on Wall Street, he went to the Harvard Business School and, after a short period at McKinsey in Milan, he went back to Wall Street. He consulted with the banker David Rockefeller who advised him to go work at Lazard Frères, but the desire to go back to Italy was still very strong. In the Eighties, he did an interview with Mediobanca in Milan but they had a host of objections to his appointment: they doubted the true value of degrees from Yale and Harvard (that at the time weren't recognized in Italy) and they asked him if he could be considered Doctor (the title given to all university graduates in Italy at the time), they wanted certificates that attested to his "knowledge of languages" and they were dubious of the earnings that he had reported on Wall Street. Thus he decided to stay at Lazard (in New York, Frankfurt and then back in New York again) for nine years and then he moved to Deutsche Bank and JPMorgan where he dealt with mergers and acquisitions until 2005 when he set up the New York office of Lincoln International.

Putting down roots in New York, though, did mean following in his family's footsteps because his grandfather (whose name he shares), arrived at Ellis Island in 1913 to open the American branch of the family company producing Neapolitan foods. The bond between the managing director and Italy is strong, almost visceral, so when it comes to explaining the lack of business investments in America he speaks with restrained but noticeable bitterness: "The problem is that many Italian businessmen, when they decide to make investments in America, don't use American advisors, they want to have people they trust at their side, they give more importance to knowledge of the language than competence, and they often prefer to pay less for a less qualified person. Sometimes, they even suggest doing transactions in an 'Italian way' presuming that here in America there are also some underhand accounting schemes which surprises their American associates and often scares them away."

Mennella describes how the "disappearance of Italians from Wall Street" came about in the following way: "Fifteen or twenty years ago, Italian, French and German industries and banks in New York shared the same level of industrial importance and financial clout. In recent decades, the importance of our companies has significantly diminished. Back then we had big industrial groups like Olivetti, FIAT, Ferruzzi, Finmeccanica, Pirelli, Telecom, whilst today only a few of our great mainstays remain, like Valentino, Armani, Prada and Ferragamo, individual businessmen or families such as Del Vecchio who own Luxottica and Brooks Brothers, Colaninno, the president of Piaggio, and Benetton that controls the clothing chain of the same name and the Autogrill/Host Marriott group, as well as smaller companies such as Citterio and Binda. I have noticed now too that Italian private equity fund firms, like Investindustrial among others, are starting to open offices in the United States. What's missing is an organized presence of the big industrial or state groups," if you exclude FIAT that has just recently undergone a merger with Chrysler bringing it back to North America. Behind this scant Italian presence, there's "a managerial and/or strategic failure, due to the fact that there hasn't been the drive to invest in the USA through acquisitions like foreign groups such as Saint Gobain, Schneider, Siemens, Deutsche Bank that bought Bankers Trust, Credit Suisse that merged with First Boston, and UBS that merged with Paine Webber and SBC. Many Italian banks, instead, like Monte dei Paschi and Intesa Sanpaolo, have reduced their presence and their importance in the American market." His conclusion is merciless: "We were tactical and not strategic, we carried out single transactions that were of small import and not far-reaching. For example, many years ago both Comit and Deutsche Bank had the same stock market value and the same share in Lehman Brothers. Deutsche stayed and got to know the American market and built its position of importance, whilst Comit sold its part and got out." Another emblematic case is that of the Jolly Hotel that "bought a hotel on Madison Avenue but never built a chain of hotels." Yet another example, "Olivetti was among the first personal computer companies but it wasn't able to take advantage of the situation." Mennella believes that behind the reduction in Italian investments on Wall Street there's "a fundamental problem: Italian companies weren't able to attract top Italian or foreign managers with a truly global vision, where time spent in the United States was seen as an essential part of one's career. In general, the logic of Italian businessmen prefers build over buy, the idea that it's better to build a little company of your own rather than to buy companies or banks, there hasn't been the will to enter into American business in a strategic way. The choices that were made in the Eighties and the Nineties created the current situation," as is illustrated by the fact that "De Benedetti made many acquisitions in Europe, not in America." What weakens management is also the fact that "in Italy many private companies choose children and grandchildren, they don't look for quality external managers" and the result of this process, that has lasted over twenty years, is that "here only a few industrial companies remain like Eni, Enel, Finmeccanica, and Chrysler thanks to the exemplary business dealings of Sergio Marchionne for FIAT." But "these are really the only few exceptions." As a result, many top Italian managers chose to build their careers in foreign companies, from Lamberto Andreotti at Brystol-Myers Squibb to Francesco Granata at Biogen Idec, and Vodafone's Vittorio Colao.

Completing the picture is the "Milan Stock Exchange that when it comes to do its *roadshow* in New York only invites Italians, like when Gianfranco Fini and Letizia Moratti came to promote investments there were almost no American stockbrokers in the audience to listen to them." "There aren't many Italian companies listed on the American Stock Exchange" and that shows that American investors aren't interested in our country. Mennella concludes: "How can this surprise us when we have so much bureaucracy in Italy, labor costs are extremely high, there's too much politics, the banking system is muddled and scandals such as those of Cirio and Parmalat have left a lot of nervousness hanging in the air?" Harsh words and biting criticisms but the top manager confesses that "despite everything, I'd be ready to go back to Italy" if "it were possible to trade on the market like it is here."

The mistakes of Made in Italy

There are many young and successful people in New York. New York teems with managers between the ages of thirty and forty-five years who after graduating in Italy (many of them from Bocconi) or after their first job experiences in Milan, Triveneto or in Sicily, came Stateside and established themselves in the business community. Their stories of sacrifice, hard work, and ingenuity allow us to explore two phenomena: the difficulties that Italian companies encounter in America and the reluctance of American businessmen to invest in our country. When I went into their offices, and listened to what they discussed and explained, these were the two topics that most often recurred.

Let's start with the difficulties of the Made in Italy brand. Nicola Gallotti, general manager of the Geneva Watch Group, the American division of Binda (a watch company based in Milan), gives examples that explain how important it is to understand cultural differences even before having a good strategy, or else you can't even "begin to play the game." Example 1: American pragmatism means that "if you want to sell me something, I must be able to see it." The principle of accessibility may seem banal, but our business culture doesn't always completely embrace it. "Very often, going into a jewelry store in Italy is like going through customs at the airport! You have to, at least, ring the bell; in some cases you even have to leave your fingerprints. Here everything is open and stores invite customers to enter: if the doors were locked here everyone would automatically think that the store is closed. It's simple and practical," Gallotti says. What should we learn from this? "Brand name and quality aren't enough to sell a product, you have to seek out your customer, apply some fundamental rules to find him/her." We have companies armed with sophisticated strategy plans that fail because they make the most common mistake of doing what they do in Italy. "And yet, the use of a little spirit of observation and some common sense would be enough." Example 2: what Gallotti calls the "Little Italy context," or in other words, that deep-seated tradition that Italian companies have of packing their American branches with dozens of Italian managers ready to repeat what they've learned and tested back home. Gallotti, whose office is on the fourth floor at 1407 Broadway just two blocks from Times Square, is the General Manager of a company where he is the only Italian among more than two hundred employees in America. He explains: "cultural isolation allowed me to listen and to learn the basics quickly, it helped me avoid committing costly blunders; everyone knows that to learn English it is essential to be surrounded by native speakers and to avoid your compatriots: why should it work differently where business is concerned?"

You can get from Times Square to Rockefeller Center in just 10 minutes and there, in the building standing at 1, in Suite 2404, there's the Chiomenti law and financial firm where Salvo Arena works. He's from Catania, he has a Master's from Harvard Law School and he specializes in the mergers and acquisitions sector where you really see how Italian companies can do business in America. "The truth of the matter is that here in new York only 10-15 big companies like Eni, Enel and FIAT remain, and three big banks, Monte dei Paschi, Intesa-Sanpaolo and Unicredit, and the rest is a desert, or almost so," he explains, indicating Luxottica that's "the only company that made significant acquisitions with Ray-Ban and Brooks Brothers." It's a situation that "springs from the fact that Italian firms don't do business because they don't expand, they just limit themselves by maintaining what they inherited from family enterprises." American businessmen are always looking for opportunities "to grow, innovate and change," Italian businessmen "are capable but they hold themselves back too much." The approach of many businessmen is too timid, it's enough for them to get a shoe in the door in the New York business community, open a store, create a company or send an agent from time to time, but then "they don't build" and they don't establish themselves, unlike the Germans and Asians do." He adds that "recently, there has been a light shift in the current, with a discreet wave of small and medium sized enterprises especially in the distribution sector, and with an interesting project that has just been finalized in the real-estate sector by the Bizzi group." Diego Piacentini, vice-president of the internet giant Amazon, goes even further, stating that "one of the major weak points of Italian companies in America is customer relations" because "this is a market where nothing is more important than the consumer, and to put the consumer at ease investments are made in personnel and advertising, whilst many Italian companies be-lieve that this way of doing things will only lose them money." It's a difference that "springs from a different idea of profit," because "Americans think of long term profit whilst for most Italians the profitability of the individual sales quota prevails."

As for the absence of American investments in Italy, there is an even greater convergence of opinions among the managers. For Piacentini (who Jeff Bezos called to his side in Seattle and put in charge of international activities that make up 50% of Amazon), "the reality is that there are no incentives to invest in Italy" because "even if we are the eighth economic power in the world and we have high revenue and significant potential, the tax burden, over-regulation and lack of work flexibility" cause American entrepre-neurs to keep their distance. Not to mention, Piacentini adds, "the lack of local incentives that encourage investors to go to Ireland, Canada and Australia instead." Amazon has opened distribution centers in Europe, in Wales and in Leipzig, and in the former East-Germany, whilst investors have only started to come to Italy re-cently because, for example, "even setting up a call center is com-plicated," and "though the Italian postal system is improving, there are still serious logistical problems," meaning that it is still difficult to commit to delivering items within a certain number of days or to track packages online.

Global managers

He doesn't like to speak from the podium, he defines himself as a "global manager" and he runs a pharmaceutical giant with a mar-ket capitalization of over 43 billion dollars. Lamberto Andreotti, born in 1951, is, together with Alberto Cribiore who is the vice-president of Citigroup, the Italian who has most successfully es-tablished himself in the world of Corporate America. His arrival in the pharmaceutical sector was rather by chance: he had stud-ied Engineering at MIT but things got off to a slow start before he took a leadership role at Montedison which immediately went through bankruptcy. This forced him to move to the Spanish com-pany Farmacia that he left almost thirty years ago after accepting a lower level position at Squibb. He climbed the corporate ladder at Squibb becoming its CEO in 2010. "The decision to leave Farmacia for Squibb was not an easy one, but life teaches us that sometimes humility pays, and that's what happened in my case," he says as he meets a group of ex-Bocconi students at the mezzanine of Le Cirque, the flagship restaurant of Sirio Maccioni. For an evening under the roof of Le Cirque, Maccioni sits wearing a very glamorous white jacket, Cribiore wears the blue suit of a Wall Street *streetfighter*, and Lamberto Andreotti refuses to take the podium "because it doesn't make me feel at ease" and he instead moves about the tables of the thirty or so invitees with the microphone in his hand. He has learned to live with the fact that any Italian he meets immediately thinks of his father Giulio Andreotti. But freedom from his father's shadow came with his integration into the very restricted community of Corporate America VIPs. "Above all else, I consider myself a global manager, I live in New York just as I could work in any other part of the world. My last name? Of course, I know in Italy it is very well-known, but here in America they often mistake me for a relative of the racing driver Mario Andretti." Just like Madonna, Sarah Jessica Parker and Woody Allen, for Lamberto Andreotti living in New York is easier than anywhere else, because it's a metropolis where there are so many stars and VIPs that they almost become anonymous, and can lead an almost normal life. In the question and answer session with the ex-Bocconi students, themselves emerging managers in the Manhattan business community, Andreotti pauses to describe the values that he believes in. There are three of them. The first is team work, because it's the best recipe for confronting global competition. "I often say to my close collaborators that they can be the best, I spur them on and believe in them because nowadays it's impossible to establish oneself alone, it's team work that makes a company strong." Then there's "integrity," that is "a number that isn't often factored in to graphs and statistics but that is very important in the success of an individual just as in the success of a big company." For Lamberto Andreotti, having "integrity" means "dedication to work" and "personal honesty." But all of this isn't enough without "the third value" in which he believes the most, "being passionate about the work you do." He built an "identity" on these three pillars "in which being a manager counts more than being Italian although I am very well aware that having an Italian passport is a rarity in the world in which I live that is populated by White Anglosaxon Protestants." What thrills him most about his work is the fact that he contributes to create "products that have a concrete effect on people's lives." When he was studying at MIT he never thought that he would have launched himself into the pharmaceutical industry but his Bristol-Myers Squibb today has the numbers of a giant in this industrial sector: 28 thousand employees, sales of 20 billion dollars a year and a well-established presence not only in North America but in Western Europe, Japan and Australia and also in the largest emerging economies like China, India and Russia. On the desk in his office at 345 Park Avenue, data and studies come together to give a picture of the health, wellbeing and difficulties of billions of people and that allows him to check the pulse of the planet on a daily basis. To his mind: "Despite all of its difficulties, America is still a nation that combines the most ability and innovation, but if I were twenty years old I would go live in China, in Shanghai, because the future will come from there." A reflection about the country he was born in is inevitable: "There are many Italian managers of quality, in my company alone there are at least twenty of them, our weakness, however, lies in the fact that we don't have many Italian multinational companies and that brings a scarcity of local opportunities to accumulate global experience." Hence the result that "although Italy has excellent researchers and a good number of excellent minds" Italy lags behind in the global business community "for its absence of entrepreneurs who want to be entrepreneurs without help from the state." The evening comes to an end with Cribiore posing a question to his manager friend on the most difficult issue: "How do you manage the research and development sector?", or in other words, how does a top manager lead a team of scientists intent on projects and inventions that could prove fundamental for the health of human beings. "It's true, it is the most difficult thing to manage" is his answer, "and the only way to confront it is to speak candidly with those who work there and to diversify your investments as much as possible," investments that in the case of Bristol-Myers Squibb amount to 700 million dollars a year.

High finance and old books

Pino Torinese as the launch pad towards the World Financial Center in Manhattan. The American adventure of Alberto Cribiore, vice-president of Citigroup who also served as interim president of Merrill Lynch, began in the small Piedmontese town of Pino Torinese because that's where he decided to live when in 1971, at the age of twenty five, Gianluigi Gabetti hired him to work at IFI, three years later he sent him to America to work at the newly created IFI International. Cribiore accepted the challenge and moved to the United States with his wife Raffaella and his children Federico and Martina who were then still very young. They arrived in New York with Italian passports but they decided not to live in Manhattan but in the verdant Westchester, because they wanted to experience real American life, the one that pulses far from the skyscrapers of Midtown Manhattan. Integration into the fabric of American life was rapid and intense. A while back, Cribiore compared the impact of the reality of New York to smoking: "At the beginning you cough, but then you smoke two or three cigarettes and you can't quit anymore." In those years, between 1974 and 1976, New York was very different from how it presents itself today: it was a less international city, very American and yet very open and welcoming towards immigrants because America likes having new people because they guarantee it a constant input of new ideas, nourishment, vitality. From the outset, the challenge of the Midwest proved to be all-consuming because those who worked in finance in New York had the habit of sitting in their offices and waiting for investment opportunities to come them, but Cribiore went back to basics and went straight to the source to seek out those opportunities. In the Seventies, the Midwest was the most productive and creative part of the United States, that's where value was generated, and Cribiore delved into that reality and discovered it to be a fount of significant innovation and economic opportunity, and also delightful and creative in the character of the people who populated it. Numerous episodes describe the welcome that he received in the Midwest. Like when Cribiore and Gabetti arrived at their hotel in Lafayette, Indiana, and were asked the obvious question, "are you Italian?" and they replied with an amused "No, we're Irish" that allowed them to break the ice immediately. When they came to America the Cribiore family planned on staying three to five years, but they discovered that they felt really at home overseas and they decided to stay, to put down roots. But to be successful they had to integrate and the top manager took the next step of going to work in an American company: it was Warner Brothers headed by Steve Ross. He had met Ross at a number of earlier meetings about a specific investment. He stayed with Ross for four years and from there he moved to the investment sector of Clayton and Dubilier: he was one of the three original partners and together they managed a fund that grew to 45 million dollars, the second or third largest in the United States at the time. There weren't many others like him on Wall Street, and his success there paved the way for the founding of the firm Brera followed by his move to Merrill Lynch as interim president where his office was located at 250 Vesey Street, in the World Financial Center building 4, not far from Ground Zero. Then, in September of 2008, he moved to the headquarters of Citigroup, at 399 Park Avenue, where he was assigned the task of managing institutional relations. Not only Alberto's but also Raffaella Cribiore's experiences have been essential to the integration of the family. She is a scholar of ancient books and she has held prestigious positions at different universities, from Princeton to Columbia, and she currently teaches at New York University. In recent years she has authored three books that have impacted Classical studies in America: *Writings. Teachers and Students in Graeco-Roman Egypt, Gymnastics of the Mind: Greek Education in Hellenistic and Roman Egypt,* dealing with Hellenistic and Roman education in Egypt, she co-authored *Women's Letters in Ancient Egypt: 300 BC-AD 800* with Roger S. Bagnall and her latest volume, *The School of Libianius in Late Antique Antioch,* has been published by Princeton University Press. Milanese by birth but a New Yorker by adoption, Alberto Cribiore has been connected both professionally and personally to Gianluigi Gabetti for more than forty years, and he often thinks back to the years he spent in Pino Torinese after finishing his studies at Bocconi University – a school he still considers to be excellent. The also lived is Rome: he went there at the age of eight when his father got the position of head of the local Banca Popolare di Milano. Ten years later he returned to the city of his birth to study at

Bocconi and that academic experience is, still to this day, the foundation of the professionalism that is part of his DNA. He recommends Bocconi to young Italian managers as exemplary in learning how to confront the global economy.

Columbia Business School

Italians are consistently among the top performers at the Columbia University Business School, which is one of the four highest rated business schools in the United States along with rivals Harvard, Wharton and Stanford. In the rankings of students who take Master's level courses, Italians make up a staggering 60 percent of the 10 percent of students who achieve the best grades. If you try to identify them you find some well-known last names–Draghi, Scaroni, Stanca, Scognamiglio–but others too that are less familiar. Silvio Palumbo is part of the latter group. Born in 1977, he graduated from RomaTre with a business degree and then he left his own business in Rome to study at Columbia. Having earned his Master's, he now travels all over the United States as a financial consultant. "Everybody knows that Italians are among the best at the Business School," he explains as he drinks an espresso at Lalo–the café on the Upper West Side where the movie *You've got mail* was filmed–"and the reason is that in our schools and universities students who take subjects like Business and Engineering receive a really solid education" and when we're compared to Americans "we easily emerge, as happens with others too, like Brazilians and the French, for example." But why leave Italy for New York? "The reason is because our higher education provides an exclusively theoretical training, there's no practical preparation, and this really complicates entry into the work place, whilst in America learning is based on the analysis of specific cases and that's how you prepare for what you'll have to do when you start to work." But that's not all, because the other element that encourages these students to leave Italy is the financial compensation. For example, the consulting firm McKinsey offers a Columbia graduate the following options: 125 thousand dollars annually to work in America and 68 thousand euros (plus a car) if they opt for the Italian branch, and at the Boston Consulting Group the difference is pretty much the same, 125 thousand dollars in America and 70 thousand euros in Italy, excluding the end of year bonuses. Palumbo confirms that "on the balance, if a Columbia graduate stays here, his salary is more than double what he would get if he went back to Italy" and he believes that "the financial crisis that everyone talks about was felt here, but not too greatly" and that even if "there are fewer jobs available now," the compensation "remains high, especially in the banks." It's a system that allows students who have to take out loans to pay for their degree at Columbia–two years of Business School can cost up to 150 thousand dollars–to pay it all back within about 24 months because "there is always work." About five months after starting their first year, students have their first interviews with financial firms that offer jobs, then they do a summer internship that makes for their first solid networking experience, and then the second year of the Master's becomes, in many cases, a path towards an objective that is already secure. Among the Italians who follow this route there are those who take out loans from Banca Sella or from other banks, but in the end almost all of them decide to stay in America "and especially in New York, where there's a cultural atmosphere that allows everyone to find their habitat." The one piece of advice that Palumbo feels he can give to young people interested in taking a gamble just like him is "to study English well in school, from high school, spending time abroad to study because one of the weaknesses of Italians compared to other foreigners is that they learn English (not only spoken but also written) much later. Admission is contingent upon the following criteria dictated by the top schools: any degree with an excellent grade, if possible from a prestigious school, a high score on the GMAT test (the 92nd percentile an above), qualifying professional experience and time spent outside of one's own country for work or study. Essentially this means that the combination of a degree from Bocconi, Luiss or Politecnico, an Erasmus experience, and a job linked to projects abroad, improve the chances of getting into the Master's program at Columbia, a program that each year admits about 900 students out of 17,000 applicants. The path that they have to follow helps explain why many of the Italians at the Business School are ex consultants (at McKinsey, BCG, Bain, Booz&Co, Roland Berger etc.), because very often these firms select job candidates, following similar parameters (the school attended, grades, capacity for logic, knowledge of languages), by skimming through the candidates for university admission. Firms such as these fund the Master's degree for their own employees (McKinsey permits career advancement only with a Master's from a Business School), so the Italians at Columbia are often company sponsored or financed by their families and therefore very few of them actually get into debt. Regardless of where they come from, however, once they arrive on campus in the north of Manhattan, there's the Italian Academy founded in 1991 that hosts conferences, presentations, public events and also private events like wedding receptions, for example. Among the students there are also those who choose to get married in the Columbia Chapel with a reception that follows at the Italian Academy that offers a very popular catering service.

The entrepreneur who fled Italy

We meet at Sant Ambroeus at 1000 Madison Avenue in the center of the Golden Block that records the highest percentage of wealthy people on the planet. Gherardo Guarducci is sitting at one of the tables at his Bar-restaurant, one of the highest rated in Manhattan, drinking a mineral water. He's still upset after just returning from his father-in-law's funeral, he was very close to *Cavaliere* Gaetano Caltagirone. Guarducci is one of the most successful entrepreneurs in the restaurant business but he is still a "fugitive." He was born in 1966 into a family of textile manufacturers in Prato, his life changed in 1975 when he was little more than eight years old: a gang of Sardinian kidnappers abducted his neighbor's son (the Baldassini family), a few days later they found his mutilated body dumped in a manhole. Investigations showed that the kidnappers were working for the Red Brigades, in search of funds to finance their terrorist activities. The tragedy of the massacred young boy devastated the Guarduccis. The head of the family, Felice, made a few quick phone calls and decided to go abroad, as soon as possible, as he feared that his wife or children might suffer the same fate. He gathered the family together at breakfast and simply said "tomorrow we're leaving." There wasn't time to talk or to think. The break from Prato was clean. They headed for the first available destination which was Edmonton, in Canada, but for the young Gherardo it was just *America* that he only knew as the place of "battles between cowboys and Indians," nothing else. The move to Edmonton was difficult.

Gherardo remembers it like a "type of Siberia" light years away from the mild Tuscan climate. But it wasn't just the bad weather that complicated their relocation to North America, his father's business didn't go well either: his investments in oil and real-estate plunged. From that moment on Gherardo began a series of relocations: he left Canada at fifteen years of age to go to school in Switzerland, he left Switzerland in 1984 to complete his studies in Massachusetts. He then gave into nostalgia in 1988 and tried to go back to the family business–The Azienda Tessile Pratese–but realized within a short few months that "working in Italy is impossible because of the reach of politics and because of social envy and the short-sightedness of labor unions." In 1990 he returned to New York and put everything he had into the food business, and today he owns the Sant Ambroeus restaurants–upscale Milanese style restaurants–and Casa Lever, a top rated restaurant in Midtown on Park Avenue that is decorated with Andy Warhol paintings that are on loan from the most important art collections in the world holding an estimated value of over 35 million dollars. He also owns establishments in other parts of the States. Success, marriage and children make him a well-established American manager, but deep down there's still the adolescent boy from Prato scarred by the unexpected necessity to flee Italy and abandon the world of his childhood. "Having to run away weighed on my life, I left my country because the streets weren't safe, because of the Italian political system and the spectre of Communism, and after many years, every time I go back I realize that we lack a national identity to free us from these bonds." I have four children but I haven't talked to them yet about the years of terrorism (in the Sixties and Seventies) because I want them to grow up "feeling free." In Manhattan he's not the only "fugitive." "There are many like me," he confirms. His wife Ginevra, daughter of Gaetano Caltagirone, "had to leave Italy when she was only eight year old because the communist magistrates were persecuting her father." His attempt to go back to Italy in 1988 wasn't successful because, the reach of politics aside, he encountered an economic reality that he didn't understand: "Globalization wiped out the advantage of Italian textiles–the production of quality materials at a lower price –because now there's competition from China and Turkey that exploit their workforce in a way that for us would be impossible." But the decision to leave still weighs heavily: "I remember the years of terrorism, for me it is a memory of fear, I lost so much, many bonds were broken, friends, the smells of the Mediterranean Spring, and there's been no closure." Returning to Italy isn't completely out of the question but for the moment the most important challenge is to get his business through the trying times of the worst recession since the collapse of 1929. It's a risk that he believes in. "I chose to put everything into the food business because my childhood memories are all linked to the dining table, with my father. I've been working in this sector since 1990 and I believe that the recovery is close at hand." The Sant Ambroeus restaurants, Casa Lever and the Felice Wine Bar on First Avenue, allow him to test the health of the market from different perspectives though it means he has to confront significant risks. But in his mind he has a "recipe for success": "To make it in New York you need to stay for at least five years, your stay here must be well-planned, when you decide that New York is your life you understand that the only thing that counts here is your work ethic, nothing else."

The lawyer who knew Sindona

George Pavia comes from a Genoese Jewish family with roots in Casale Monferrato and an ancestor, Mosè Pavia, who was adviser to the Pope. The description of his ancestry is his way of introducing himself as he sits at the table in his office on the twelfth floor of building 600 on Madison Avenue, between 57th and 58th Street, in the heart of Midtown. "In 1938, after the Munich Pact on the division of Czechoslovakia, my father Enrico decided to leave Italy and brought our family to London," he remembers, "and when Italy joined the war alongside Hitler in 1940 we were interned on the Isle of Man, because all Italians were considered enemies." Long weeks passed before the commander came to realize the obvious:

Enrico Pavia was not only an antifascist and a Jew, but he was also the ex-lawyer of the London government in Genoa and he posed no threat to public safety. To set the Pavia family free, however, the officer had to invent "a health condition" that allowed him to release them, and a few days later they were on board the *Western Prince* that crossed the Atlantic unescorted. The ship's return voyage to Great Britain was less fortunate; it was attacked by German submarines and sank. After they arrived in New York, the head of the family worked for the federal government whilst Giorgio–now called George–studied law at Columbia. He then enlisted to fight in Korea but he never actually got there because his commanding senior officer discovered his legal talents and set him on the path to the Pentagon, where he began his first assignment in the Department of International Affairs. His job was to make the Generals in Korea respect the Geneva Convention and that's why, he confirms, "I don't like Guantánamo, I didn't like Bush who created it, and Obama doesn't convince me either because he is in favor of military courts that are very questionable, insofar as the lawyers must always answer to their superiors." For George Pavia the Geneva Convention is the most important agreement ever created to protect rights in war zones, he speaks of it with such conviction that he becomes really animated: "It is a unique instrument because it makes the interest of the State prevail over military interests in war zones." After he left the military he tried to return to Italy, between 1954 and 1955, and he wanted to become a lawyer back in Genoa but American law prevents anyone from taking the bar in a second country. At that turning point he crossed back over the Atlantic to set up –with a few associates- the law firm in New York that still bears his name. As a lawyer he defended FIAT, between the Seventies and the Eighties, in almost 60 lawsuits by customers enraged by the deficiencies in service of the company that earned the derogatory acronym "Fix it again Tony." "After these tough battles, FIAT decided to leave and it was the right thing to do because the American judicial system rewarded the bad faith of debtors, and because the major problem was the structure of the car which was too small to handle American roads." But the court case that left the biggest mark was the case of Michael Sindona.

"I was Sindona's lawyer when the banker refused extradition

to Italy," he recounts as if it had just happened yesterday. "Sindona had facilitated a merger between two banks but the truth is that he was born a crook, I've met three or four people like him in my life, they're always helpful, easy to deal with, friendly, smart but crooked, with no ethics in their brain, just born that way." In the case against extradition, Sindona told Pavia that he wanted to defend himself but the ploy didn't work. The lawyer is convinced that the Sindona case still holds some hidden truths. For example, "I remember that the inspectors of the Banca d'Italia came before the case broke and strangely enough they found nothing" about the illegal activities committed "by a banker who was in business with organized crime and the mafia." But the excess power of Sindona was of little use to him in court: "He was losing, he would have been extradited and for this reason his friends killed him in prison," the lawyer maintains. Since then America has changed and the Italian presence in New York has transformed, grown weaker. "Italy today is represented over here by fashion, many banks have left, the Banco di Sicilia, the Banco di Napoli and BNL aren't here anymore. Industry is also in a tough spot because India, China and Germany have gained the upper hand in different sectors with lower prices and perhaps better products." Therefore, "only fashion remains and it's powered by good taste." The names of his clients reveal the Italian financial presence in New York: there's Unicredit among the banks, whilst in the Made in Italy sector there are many companies like Dolce & Gabbana, Keaton, Brioni, Ferragamo, and there was also Fendi at one time. "Designers and good taste are Italy's remaining strengths," he concludes with a bitter smile, because everything he says and does exudes love for the nation that he had to abandon when he was little - even his tie with its light blue background and tricolor band.

Where Anna Wintour reigns

Fashion shows, nightclubs, luxury products and the omnipotence of Anna Wintour. This is the New York of an Italian chief financial officer who requests anonymity when he describes his experience in one of the fields where competition is the fiercest. He arrived in Manhattan in 2006, he lives in an apartment near Times Square and he travels continually between the United States, Canada, Mexico, Brazil which are the main markets for luxury products in the Western Hemisphere. When we meet at the bar of the Tribeca Grand Hotel, near Canal Street, he has just returned from São Paulo. He's enthusiastic about it: "the Brazilian economy is growing steadily; only China's economy is stronger." As the waiter offers the trendiest drinks of the moment he responds with a courteous hand gesture: "Just a Coca Cola, please." Living in this exclusive world of luxury products "means keeping a low profile and staying backstage" he explains, emphasizing how "America is crucial for us insofar as we register 20-25% of our sales here," but to be able to navigate your way through the commercial network "it is necessary not to get distracted and to stay focused on the objective." What does this mean? "It's a matter of the difference between Madison Avenue and Fifth Avenue" he replies, describing what's happening in the two commercial zones of Manhattan: "Madison is a street where wealthy New Yorkers want to shop without having to deal with tourists but it was badly hit by the financial crisis that had an effect on the wealthiest bracket of residents," whilst "Fifth Avenue is a completely different story, it has held up better due, especially, to the low dollar exchange rate that encourages tourists to spend a lot." The balance between Madison Avenue and Fifth Avenue changes all the time and "to stay in step with consumer tendencies you must follow it carefully." These days that means "betting on the crocodile handbags on Fifth Avenue and surviving on clothing and a few accessories on Madison Avenue." The litmus test for market orientation is rental price: 2000 dollars a square foot on Fifth Avenue compared to 1000 on Madison Avenue, 600 at the Meatpacking District and 560 in Soho. The CFO speaks of trends, costs and consumer indexes "because in America the luxury sector is finance whilst in Italy it is creativity." It is, however, "a delicate balance, because Italy stands on shaky ground with the Chinese emerging, all they lack are big designers and when they get them it will be a significant challenge for us." In the Manhattan market what he sees is "a consumer who pays great attention to the quality of service, who wants to be treated well and who spends over time," requiring the seller to provide "a level of customer care that doesn't exist in Italy" because "in Italy it's a matter of the seller and the buyer cheating one another, whilst here it's a question of commanding respect." Making headway in this market is not always easy for the Made in Italy brand. "It's true that Americans love Italian quality, but it's also true that Giorgio Armani's restaurant on Fifth Avenue doesn't work and it's almost always empty and the Prada store in Soho is only somewhat successful." The problems are common to all and to overcome them "we need to play by the local business rules" that consider "fashion shows the equivalent of business cards" whilst "the strongest draw for advertising is in the glossy magazines and the opinion columns," especially if they're written by fashion celebrities like Anna Wintour, editor-in-chief of Vogue, "who is a law unto herself." In 1988 Gucci realized it when Wintour "met Tom Ford and launched him as a designer helping us to rise out of the crisis." The firing of Alessandra Facchinetti is also an exemplary case because Wintour "really didn't like her." The CFO often meets the New York despot-queen of Fashion and he describes her as "cold and stand-offish," but admits, however, that "one of her articles is worth more than a TV ad," because people who buy luxury products "trust specialized magazines more than TV." Then there are nightclubs "where it's important to be seen with the products worn by the stars." The most popular locales are still the rooftop bars, the top floors with stunning views of the city: like the Boom Boom Room on the top floor of the Standard Hotel in the Meatpacking District, "that's still the trendiest neighborhood," or 230 on Fifth Avenue at the corner with 26th Street. Fashion shows, glossy magazines and nightclubs are the mainstay of the fashion business, what's new is e-commerce, online sales of luxury products. "It's a real boom," he confirms, "equal to 8-9 percent of the 2010 earnings which were close to a billion dollars" and it's interesting to note how "people buying online often live close to our stores, and because of the crisis they are ashamed of coming in to buy in the store." Proof is in the fact that "when it comes time to wrap their purchases, more and more in-store buyers want a bag without our logo printed on the front."

The oil man from Third Avenue

The manager, who headed the Mobil energy company and spear-headed the merger with Exxon creating one of the biggest oil giants, works on the nineteenth floor of building 805 on Third Avenue. Lucio Noto, born in 1938, is a Sicilian from Brooklyn. His parents left the island at the end of the eighteen hundreds, after they got married they went to live in Bensonhurst, Brooklyn, and his father supported the family with his job as a presser who made headway in the Garment District in Manhattan and eventually became leader of one of the biggest unions. In 1945 his father, originally from Noto, decided to leave Brooklyn and gamble the family future on the suburbs: they got into the car and crossed the Washington Bridge over the Hudson for the first time, and arrived in Englewood Cliffs New Jersey, where they bought a Victorian house with a garden where Lucio Noto spent his adolescence, commuting to Manhattan, to attend Regis, a Jesuit High School. The big adjustment to life in the suburbs – destined to become cradle of the postwar American boom – was followed by another drastic change: Noto graduated in Physics from the University of Notre Dame, but he didn't have any intention of starting a career in that field and so he went to Cornell University. In 1962, he graduated from the Business School and went in a completely different direction: the new energy company, Mobil. He started to work in that same year, earning 625 dollars a month. He expressed a desire to work abroad for the company and his request was immediately accepted, and so his career in the company with operations spanning from Eastern Africa to New Zealand took off. It was the beginning of a career marked by such levels of success and earnings that it represents the fulfillment of the American dream. In 1966 he was in Genoa, in 1967 in Palermo and in 1968 in Tokyo, where he earned Mobil an important share of the local market. In 1973 in was back in Italy, in Rome, as vice-president of Mobil Oil Italiana and six years later he was in Saudi Arabia to launch refineries and petrochemical plants. In Tokyo he studied Japanese, in Genoa he studied Italian (to purge his Sicilian dialect that made it difficult for others to understand him), and Saudi Arabia transformed him into the interlocutor of many Middle Eastern leaders. In 1986, the CEO Allen Murray brought him back to New

York to manage global planning and this marked the beginning of his ascension through the ranks within the company that led him in 1989, as head of the financial sector, to seal the merger agreement with Exxon and to become the new CEO in 1994. He was CEO until 2001, when retirement for him meant founding Midstream Partners, as well as adding some important appointments on the Boards of IBM and Philip Morris, leadership roles in banking in the Arab world, an advisory position at Mitsubishi, and a host of clients, awards and profits. It was no surprise in 1994 when David Rockefeller proposed him as Chairman of the Board for the United States and Italy of which he is still an active member because "I love to go to Italy often, at least once a year, close to Florence or Sicily so my five children and their families can visit it."

But Noto's true passion is the world of crude oil, that he knows inside out and that he has seen evolve over the last fifty years. "The revolution began with the setting up of national companies like the ones in Saudi Arabia or Abu Dhabi, and then technological innovations followed that made achievements that once were unimaginable, possible, like the closing of a very deep underwater leak on the seafloor by British Petroleum in the Gulf of Mexico." What "hasn't changed" is "the fact that it is an industry where the capital-factor prevails over the human factor, because while extensive resources are required to run the company, it only takes three hundred people to operate a refinery or twenty team members for a giant oil tanker whose load is worth billions of dollars." This lack of balance "is one of the weak points of the crude oil industry because by employing so few people, politically we are weak and bring few votes." But that doesn't mean that the scenario playing out "the end of crude oil" that some experts have proposed is at all convincing to him. On the contrary, he says "there still isn't a substitute for crude and natural gas, and in the next twenty years massive amounts will be needed to support global growth." As for the possibility of the development of green energy, from solar to wind and electric batteries, Noto is very skeptical: "The only true alternative is nuclear energy, the other forms of energy aren't practical and they won't be for many years to come." It doesn't mean that we can't "choose a green economy," "but that we must do it in the right way," which means "increasing the efficiency of energy consumption," changing the habits of residents, "beginning with turning off the lights when offices close in the evening to travelling in lighter SUVs capable of consuming less." This is why he believes that in the short term the United States "will not be able to give up crude but will be able to consume less of it," reducing the cost of dependence on hostile or unstable nations like Hugo Chavez's Venezuela or regimes in the Persian Gulf. Lucio Noto speaks as an American CEO, he identifies the interests of the American nation and sees a more perilous danger on the horizon: "a war for control of planetary resources, not so much crude oil but mineral resources, and "China" could be the country to set if off because "it is very aggressive on this front." Russia, instead, "is pursuing its own national strategy intended to increase Europe's dependence on its gas and oil reserves, and it's obvious that that's what it's doing." And in this perspective of the future where does Italy stand? Noto answers recalling years past. "When I was in Italy Ciriaco De Mita, who used to oversee the department of energy before he became head of the government, used to call me and ask me not to raise gas prices so people wouldn't complain about the government" and because at the time there were no reserves due to low gas prices he wanted to be certain that we would insure supplies to his constituents. This episode underlines how "in Italy there has never been a real energy policy because political fears have always had the upper hand," but that doesn't take away from the fact that ENI "is a large international company, that diversifies its energy supplies, and invests also in liquid gas and looks to the future." The weakness of ENI "is one that we Americans feel too" which is the fact that our business isn't sexy, the best engineers and technicians choose other fields and the biggest companies must depend on external contractors, encountering very high risks." Noto speaks loud and clear and his lean physique confirms the image of a no-frills, practical and down-to-earth manager. He is also very clear about his bond to Sicily: "I am proud to be Sicilian; my homeland has been the victim of seven invasions one after the other and each time it rose up stronger than before, we know how to stave off every adversity, and we always rise again. We know how to stand on our own two feet."

Berlusconi, Sophia Loren, and 434 ships

At the entrance, the autographed photographs of Silvio Berlusconi welcome anyone who visits Captain Nicola Arena, the American CEO of the Mediterranean Shipping Company (MSC), which is an international colossus of maritime commerce valued at an annual 12 billion dollars. It boasts a fleet of 423 container ships plus 11 cruise ships, all based in the port of Genoa, eight of which have been inaugurated by Sophia Loren. Arena was born in Messina in 1940, he grew up in Genoa, he is an ex-officer of Italia di Navigazione and since 1988 he has been CEO of the company now known as MSC USA. He is proud to be head of "the business in North America with the greatest number of Italian employees in one company." There are more than 300 of them, graduates in Engineering, Law, Economics and Computer Science–out of a total of 1,100 employees–who constitute the back bone of the second largest container transportation company to and from the United States, second only to the Danish Maersk Line." Anyone who thinks that the Europeans are losers in the globalization market must come visit MSC," Arena says, sitting between a painting of Christopher Columbus and a photograph of Mother Teresa of Calcutta on the twenty-sixth floor of a skyscraper on 37th Street that has a view of the Empire State Building. It was from this window that he saw the Twin Towers collapse on September 11, 2001 after they had been struck by Al Qaeda's kamikaze planes. "We immediately thought about the safety of our many employees living in New York," he recounts, "but right afterwards I feared for MEC USA that at the time was centered in Manhattan, I thought that we could be destroyed and lose everything." That's why he decided to flee to Warren, in New Jersey to build a computer operations center from scratch "capable of running everything for us if someone decided to drop an atomic bomb on Manhattan." The other operations centers for MSC are in Geneva, where the headquarters run by the founder Gianluigi Aponte are located, and in Singapore. Because it is a company built on the transportation of containers "collaboration with the authorities to prevent terrorist attacks is part of the daily routine for us." There isn't a security agency in the United States that doesn't have some form of contact with MSC and with all of the other shipping companies. This is one of the new strategies adopted by Homeland Security to avoid the risk of large-scale attacks–like the shipping of an atomic device inside a container. Captain Arena is a veteran of maritime transportation and also of the development of transoceanic trade, "not only with Europe but also with Asia." The fact that American companies trail the Europeans and Asians in this sector is "an aspect that many people in France and in Italy ignore" but it suggests that "it's wrong to presume that globalization penalizes the Old World." Arena believes that "the transportation of containers to every corner of the world, requiring 16 transactions for each shipment, is an impressive operation that requires care, logistics and technology along with creativity, all aspects that Europeans, and most especially, Italians, know how to synchronize." He is self-confident, proud of the results he has achieved, grateful for the trust that Aponte continues to place in him, and married to the daughter of an old Chilean wine-producing family that attributes the strength of the national economy to the reforms carried out by Augusto Pinochet. Captain Arena is one of the members of the *Azzurri nel Mondo* Association who meets Silvio Berlusconi whenever he comes to New York. "When he can, he meets us and we talk about everything, he's a political leader with vision, he is very connected to the United States and his competence in business is extraordinary," Arena confirms, adding that "his daughter Eleonora comes to our office sometimes to chat about her work plans and her travels." Arena says that he has been "impressed by some Italian political exponents like Sandro Bondi and Valentino Valentini," the Premier's international political advisor. But the invitation to attend Berlusconi's speech before Congress in June of 2006 and the two photographs with the inscription "to my friend Nicola" attest to a certain level of personal connection also.

The fact that he has been a New York resident for more than forty years and that he heads an American company with a strong Italian presence makes Arena a citizen of Manhattan who always has Genoa and Messina on his mind. He has come up with his own theory about the problems that limit economic development in Italy. "If you want to discover the difference between New York and Rome, you must look at the difference between Messina and Genoa," he states, recalling that "when I went to request a birth certificate at the Registry office in Messina many years ago a *spicciafac-cende* (a facilitator) met me and demanded 500 lire in exchange for the document, acting as if he was the sole and exclusive owner of the entire establishment." These things don't happen in Genoa and everything works much better though "we must recognize that, compared to New York, Genoa has a long way to go…"

The research cashier

Whether it's a hospital, from Mount Sinai to Beit Israel, or a labora-tory in one of the universities in New York, researchers in the field of medicine know that they need grants to develop ideas and innova-tions. These grants are conferred every year by Antonio Scarpa who lives and works at 6701 Rockledge Drive in Bethesda Maryland, in an open plan office not much different from where his colleagues work. He's a doctor who was born in Padua in 1942 and who grew up in Venice, and he oversees the annual distribution of scientific research funds for the Scientific Review. The total amount is a stag-gering number and it gives a clear idea of how much the US invests in the health of its more that 300 million citizens: 20,206,478,808 dollars. Since the Spring of 2005, "Tony" Scarpa has had a respon-sibility that's unique in the world: he's on top of the pyramid of independent commissions assigned the task, by the NIH (National Institute of health), of deciding which medical research projects to fund, in the United States and around the world. Every laboratory on the planet, every researcher and every university, can apply to the Center if it is convinced that it has a study, a result, or even just a hunch that it could prolong or protect life. "It is a responsibility that keeps me awake at night," Scarpa admits, "because it's a ques-tion of deciding which discoveries to gamble on, which diseases to combat, and, ultimately, which patients to cure." Scarpa speaks in a low voice, he presents himself with a blend of caution and de-termination without which it would be impossible to oversee 500 commissions, each one with between five and fifty members.

The criterion that he follows is to favor the most innovative 'proposals,' though he admits that this is not always easy because, even among the scientists of human body, "nowadays they tend to favor conservatism": to follow routes that have already been tried and seeking out minor improvements rather than gambling on unexplored paths. "Science and research are very competitive in the United States, " he says, "and making a selection is an enormous responsibility." Scarpa travels all the time: a conference in Prague, then a five-day tour in Australia, then returning to Washington for an Italy-USA conference on biotechnology." If you ask him which direction medical research is taking, he replies with an analysis of the health of Americans in the XXI century: "The situation has changed, in the past, heart and liver diseases were the top priority but nowadays it's obesity." The urgency comes from the impact that public health has on the federal coffers: 17 percent of GDP. Managing the support apparatus for medical research funded by the United States means assessing tens of thousands of requests for funding that are assigned to the totally independent commissions. The decisions are sent back to Scarpa's desk and the money is sent to its destination. Of the more than 20 billion dollars a year, 19.9 billion stay in America and 284 million are distributed around the world. The first foreign countries on top of the list are the UK, Canada, Australia, South Africa, Denmark, Israel, Holland and Sweden. Italy is in ninth place with 7,132 million dollars: 1.2 million more than Ghana. Antonio Scarpa comes from a family of surgeons, he was educated in Italy, he studied at universities in Holland and Israel, and came to America in 1971 (to the University of Pennsylvania). He loves his country of origin but is quick to admit that many things aren't right on the research front: "Because all funding depends on the government, those who are employed stay on indefinitely and the distribution of resources isn't competitive." Scarpa knows the phenomenon of brain drain from Italy well and he interprets from a perspective that's midway between science and life experience: "In Italy, there's the security of the permanent job, here everything is uncertain, competition prevails, and you always have to fight. It requires enormous sacrifices but it's good for scientific research because progress doesn't depend on any government." The American model is tough, but it guarantees results. Who are the most feared rivals? "The Asians, beginning with China," because "they study here, then they go back and they are creating a completely new model, that is, however, similar to ours."

Curing is a team job

At 160 East Thirty-Fourth Street, all you have to do is say "Silvia" and they'll bring you to her. The entrance to the Langone Medical Center of New York University can be described as a hybrid between a sea port and a sitting room: it's crowded from morning to night, but every particular is well tended to. The clothing of the secretaries, the language of the switchboard operators, the color of the couches, the neatness of the tables, and the fact that everybody, both patients and doctors, speaks in a low voice, make you feel at home whether you're here, in one of the bastions of the fight against cancer, by chance or by necessity. On the ground floor, in front of the elevators, beyond a door with frosted glass, there's the ward where Silvia Formenti works and practically lives. She's a medical oncologist and a radiotherapist who's the chair of the Department of Radiation Oncology and is in charge of breast cancer research at NYU.

Silvia is from Milan and she has a lean physique. Her computer screen is dotted with icons that indicate the frontlines of the most advanced research, like the work of a team of more than 160 people that she coordinates 24 hours a day. "My work is team work, I'm a Chair and at the same time I'm responsible for research as well as budgeting and patient care," she explains, "and that means always being at the cutting-edge on different fronts, from laboratory research to patient care, from publications to the management of both human and financial resources. She is directing one of the four most important clinics in New York in the fight against cancer, in constant competition for four-year funding from the NIH. Her method is to "find consensus between her collaborators" in a team that includes doctors, researchers, radiotherapist technicians, nurses, computer specialists, databank managers and a myriad of other employees. She got her degree in Medicine in Milan and from the beginning she had a passion for oncology. She cut her teeth in California where she arrived in 1982 at twenty-seven years of age. She began at the University of Southern California where she worked in the laboratory, in cancer immunology, on a scholarship from the CNR (Italian National Research Council). After this important experience she decided to stay and become an American doctor in the County Hospital of Los Angeles, on the frontlines of the Aids epidemic that had just begun at that time. "It was a tough period, I was working the nightshift every 48 hours, five or six girls would come in every night with bad pneumonia, they often died that same night, in respiratory arrest," she recounts, admitting that the impact of "a disease that at the time was partly underestimated by the Reagan administration" led her to "learn how to intubate and resuscitate" people who were dying, something "I had never done in Italy." In Los Angeles she married a TV producer who brought her to the world of Hollywood, she had three children and went to live in Santa Monica, where she commuted every day to the oncology clinic at the university. The jump to New York came in the year 2000. She wanted to bring her children to Manhattan –one of the reasons being that she wanted them to study Italian–and the offer from NYU gave her the opportunity to build a new department and at the same time continue her research on breast cancer. Silvia and her group were the first to identify the role of the immune system in the response of tumors to radiotherapy and, to show, with a series of fundamental experiments, how radiotherapy can be used to help the immune response against tumors. At the same time, in a completely different field, Silvia designed and developed the first inclined radiation bed that allows patients to receive breast radiation while completely excluding the heart and the lungs from the field of radiation.

But for her, New York opened the doors to a world in which "patients have more anxiety compared to those in California where they often tend to deny the ills they suffer." Perhaps it is because of the "contrast between the sun and the wide-open spaces of California and life immersed in the metropolis of New York," but Silvia Formenti has found new challenges that she confronts with Franco Muggia at her side, the Italian oncologist who was her mentor also in Los Angeles. The most important thing is "to work as a team" and "to concentrate yourself on improvement and excellence, while at the same time you worry about avoiding any errors, because in our work consequences can be very serious."

She is optimistic about the future of basic cancer research because "here in America the potential is extraordinary," whilst she is skeptical about the persistent difference "between what happens in the lab and in the clinic," where the funding of pharmaceutical companies dominates, "without them, nobody has the resources to support clinical research in the fight against cancer." The disconnect concerns the high cost of clinical research and the endless series of regulations. Furthermore, when the development of a new cure threatens the survival of existing or emerging drugs that have resulted from the allocation of large funds by the pharmaceutical companies, the obstacles become insurmountable.

But has the cancer death-rate decreased? In response to the query, Silvia Formenti, who always looks her interlocutor in the eye, moves her fingers slightly, and answers showing the statistics related to the deaths that occurred between 1970 and 2003 on her computer screen: the numbers caused by cardiovascular diseases are in constant decline, but in the case of cancer the line stays straight. "The situation hasn't changed today, in Italy and in America." That doesn't mean that there hasn't been progress, but the progress made isn't reflected in "the number of cancer deaths but rather in the fact that people with tumors are living longer. For example, if a seventy-four year old man discovers that he has lung cancer he doesn't die at seventy five as would have happened in the past, but he can reach seventy seven, seventy eight or even eighty, often with a good quality of life." In short, people live longer but don't die less. Citing studies, analyses and research from memory, Formenti broadens the horizon on what's happening to the health of humanity that, "perhaps because of globalization that creates a wider circulation of genes, registers an increase in the average age a little everywhere, not only where medicine is advanced like in America or Europe, but also in poorer countries." The most striking case for her is Japan "where in 2020 there will be a small percentage of women who will reach one hundred and twenty years of age, a realty that wasn't even thinkable when I was a child." Longer life-expectancy is the most compelling challenge for medicine, according to Formenti. She explains it thus: "today we live in a more diluted way, we are young for longer, thirty-year olds become forty-year olds and fifty-year olds become sixty-year olds, but the most difficult period is from seventy onwards when you notice a progressive decrease in cognitive abilities, and this is precisely where neuroscience can gather the most important results": helping the old to age better.

When she speaks about future challenges her eyes shine, though the language she uses remains anchored to scientific terms and the use of few adjectives.

Apart from research, what counts in the doctor-patient relationship is "the ability of the doctor to project hope in any situation," a type of "positivity" capable of sparking the same reaction in the patient. The perception that the doctor is involved, worried but optimistic, changes the patient's quality of life because he no longer feels alone in his battle." "It often happens that I meet wonderful people with horrible illnesses," she confirms, "and if they have a doctor who is positive and involved, their experience with the disease can be drastically changed. They reacquire space to breathe." This interaction doesn't always occur because it requires both an innate tendency towards empathy in the doctor as well as the medical knowledge to encourage and facilitate it. Silvia tries to transmit this to her residents and fellows, leading by example. "It's a legacy that I learned in California, when I worked with a hematologist named Alexandra Levine and we treated the Aids patients together. I learned from her that we can be different types of doctors, just as scientific and rigorous, but at the same time more involved and closer to our patients."

She loves America "because it gave me a new dimension and helped me overcome prejudice based on appearances and other preconceived ideas that I grew up with," but she often goes back to Italy, where "I still encounter the reality of those who say that 'you can't do this' or ask me 'why on earth are you doing this?'" "In America, nobody says these things because the impulse is to move towards ideas, challenges and originality," and she adds regretfully that "the innate originality of Italians" suffers because of such "immobility." She believes that at the bottom of this national flaw is "the individualism that reigns in the Italian scientific community where often the best and the brightest are submerged in feuds, competing for small pockets of space or influence, considering it an insult to have to move from Livorno to Pavia." It's the exact opposite of the combination of "personal mobility" and "team work" that in New York and Los Angeles brought her to observe how "working in a team means being willing to make sacrifices, like completing grant applications, or writing papers with various authors, where you have two published sentences in the end and somebody else has ten."

The other pivot of "protestant culture that asserts itself in academia in America" is the discipline of "protocol," a method–both of operating and of conducting treatments–that is the result of continually updated studies and that everybody follows as if it were a sacred text. "Protocol is very rigid, but it makes it possible to run an office, a laboratory or an operating theater even in a high-stress situation," she confirms, confessing that during her frequent trips to Italy she has often had to deal with "people who speak about doctors as if they were wizards." A magical and idealized vision of medicine prevents a proper data evaluation. Not to mention when she has to explain how the Healthcare system in the United States works because "there are people who idealize treatment in Cuba and maintain that in America anyone who doesn't have private health insurance risks being left to die on the street." The answer that she has for such criticism is articulate and to the point: "They ignore that public healthcare exists in America, it guarantees free treatment to anyone who is younger than eighteen, older than sixty five, or has a minimum annual income of under 16 thousand dollars," without counting "the existence of hospitals like Bellevue or the County Hospital of New York where emergency rooms have the facilities and capacity such that if Lady Di had been hospitalized there after her accident by the Seine, she would never have died. These Emergency Room facilities cannot refuse anybody care or prioritize those who can pay over those who cannot. And it doesn't end there: "It is difficult for Italians to understand the American mentality, where everyone has the right to work and is responsible for the pursuit of their own happiness," as the Constitution states. "The concept of this individual responsibility is very deep and it explains why society expects a family that has started to earn an income to automatically subscribe to a health insurance policy: if it chooses not to do it must accept the consequences of the public hospitals, with long lines and fewer services." She is critical about America's future yet optimistic, and she doesn't believe much in the scenarios of decline. She still considers it the most successful example of democracy. To explain it she tells a story about her daughter, a student at Berkeley: "her roommate was born in

China, she came to California when she was five or six, and she won a scholarship, based on her grades, that covers the entire tuition costs of the school of Medicine. And yet, she's the same girl who eats the leftover food that her parents, street sellers of kebabs, bring her every evening. In what other country could it happen that in just one generation there's progression from poverty to a graduation from Berkeley?"

Theoretical physics from Lenin to Goldman Sachs

At 4 Washington Place, on the fifth floor of the Department of Physics at NYU, Massimo Porrati teaches. His lessons on quantum gravity shape students who are courted by financial giants like Goldman Sachs. Pinstriped suit, gold cufflinks, a learned vocabulary, a passion for vintage prints and a Bolshevik poster on the wall, Porrati receives people in his office at 525, where he loves to look over at Broadway because "I came to live in New York because I love big cities, where there's a vast offering of everything, but it's also possible to live with a level of privacy similar to what the British countryside has to offer." Born in Genoa in 1961, Porrati is one of the dozens of Italian scientists and researchers who meet in New York at the ISSNAF, the Italian Scientists and Scholars of North America Foundation created by Giorgio Einaudi–the former science officer at the Embassy in Washington–to transform the brain drain phenomenon into a bridge of knowledge and investment between the two countries. To understand the importance of the phenomenon you just need to look at a study edited by Riccardo Lattanzi for the ISSNAF itself: in 2008 there were 3,272 Italian researchers and professors in American universities, an increase of 4% over the two preceding years, with a total number, compared to other European countries, that was lower only than Germany and France.

Porrati comes from the Scuola Normale Superiore di Pisa, where he studied with Luciano Girardello, a professor from the University of Milan, and took an interest in Theoretical High Energy Physics and in String Theory applied to Quantum Field Theory, and in Gravitation. He graduated in 1984, and a year later he was at CERN (the European Organization for Nuclear Research) with Sergio Ferrara, one of the permanent members and intellectual leaders in the theoretical division, and he followed him to the University of California at Los Angeles, and then went on to Berkeley. Italy offered him important opportunities and he went back and worked there successfully at the beginning of the Nineties, but then in 1992 he heeded the call back to the "big city" and since 1992 he has been an Associate Professor at NYU, where in 1996 he received a professorship and tenure in 1998. Porrati is a physicist who deals with string theory applied to quantum field theory, the core model used for understanding the physics of elementary particles since the Thirties and that was very successful in the postwar period when the problems linked to electrodynamics were solved starting in 1948. Now he is working on the study of the "energy spectrum that we will test in the coming years," along with what he confesses is "the biggest problem of quantum gravity: we don't know what questions to ask, not to mind what the answers to give."

"I'm interested in what the theory of quantum gravity can tell us," he explains, "especially about its aspects related to cosmology and string theory." The fact that he is the most talked-about theoretical physicist in the city doesn't bother him too much, and he explains that "both here and in Italy, the work is very similar, and at the Ph.D. level you begin with students and end with collaborators." But what he hastens to add is that "in America, there are more job opportunities for theoretical physicists because there are other career paths outside the world of academia, like the one that leads to highly skilled jobs such as investment banking in New York." That's exactly how it is. "Many students begin by studying theoretical physics and then they decide that they want to stay in New York and so they go to work on Wall Street," he says, noting the fact that "the knowledge of physics that they acquire is useful to the big financial institutions because on Wall Street they're not just looking for people with technical knowledge in the field, but for people who know how to think." Thus Wall Street is interested in the "most important thing that we teach" which is "how to think." Here are some examples: "We teach how to think to solve problems, like when you are faced with a difficult problem that has many variables. How do you go about confronting it? Do you solve the model in its entirety or do you break it down to better approach it? Or "when you are faced with a difficult question for which you don't have the answer, how do you avoid embarrassment?" Half of the students he's had work on Wall Street and they were hired after interviews where they were asked questions of logic to see if they knew how to find the answers. Porrati shapes this young generation with "the questions that we've been asking ourselves since Albert Einstein," like "what is quantum gravity?"

One of the victories of physics in recent years that most excites him is the fact that we can now see relics of the Big Bang. "Up until the Nineties we saw the Universe as a uniform reflection of the Big Bang, now instead, we have a detailed map of the Universe as it appeared a few thousand years after the Big Bang. To explain this map, it's natural to hypothesize that what we call the Universe is only a minuscule part of a whole that is at least 10^{80} times bigger (10 with 80 zeros)" he explains with a flash of enthusiasm in his eyes. What incites curiosity is the fact that "whilst our Universe is a cold Universe, meaning it is composed of galaxies, there are regions in the Universe that continue to expand and this poses fundamental questions, for example, how typical is the Universe in which we live." Or in other words, are we destined to debate Copernicus' Axiom again which states that "we're not in a specific point in the Universe and what we see around us isn't so rare." Theory aside, Porrati is very interested in the Obama administration's stake on the development of alternative energy. "Physics can play a major role in optimizing the resources that we have and in the development of new sources of energy and even just in the analysis of the inherent problems in energy sources," he states, giving the example of the "pot of hot water on the stove that wastes a colossal amount of energy to reach boiling point" whereas, "heating it using a heat engine would require a fifth of the energy." Porrati is one of the representatives of the Italian school of physics which is famous in the field of high energy elementary particles and was created by Enrico Fermi and his group. Fermi was the first tenured professor of theoretical physics in Italy and his school continued in the postwar period and still survives to this day, it is respected at Harvard and Princeton where many professors and postgraduates Italian, many from the Scuola Normale di Pisa. "Despite the problems that afflict the Italian university system, Fermi's legacy lives on thanks to people like

Raul Gatto whose name is not as familiar as Fermi's but who nevertheless shaped an entire generation of theoretical physicists," he confirms, clearly troubled though by the fact that "Science culture in Italy is not highly regarded, partly because the greatest Italian philosopher in the last century, Benedetto Croce, influenced the intellectual disciplines favoring the historical-philosophical stream. The intellectual value of the scientific branch is therefore not appreciated enough." Among the negative consequences of this Italian system is the dearth of academics in government: "We don't have instances like that of Steven Chu, the Stanford professor and Nobel laureate that Obama nominated as minister for Energy" or "Tsung-Dao Lee, the great postwar theoretical physicist who played a vital role of contact between the United States and Communist China." A certain level of attention to the origins of international communism can be seen in the Soviet era poster standing in Porrati's office. It shows a young Lenin with a line from Mayakovski. He brushes it off saying: "It belongs to a friend, I actually wanted to put up a poster of the first five-year plan where you see Stalin and two other Soviet leaders, a soldier and a farmer, with '2+2=5' written above the image: it aptly describes the work of a theoretical physicist."

Lidia's four stars

She is very particular about the place settings at her tables: knives and forks are placed far apart and inclined slightly inwards. For her, the set table is like a color palette: she can do whatever she likes with it. She places (or has somebody else place) glasses, plates, bread, napkins, bottles and dishes according to a scheme that constantly innovates the meal, accompanying a sequence of different foods without ever distracting the diner too much. I had the opportunity to eat in the company of Lidia Bastianich in Del Posto, her most recent New York restaurant that opened in 2005 with an investment of more than three million dollars. There I had a front-row seat to observe a woman-manager (bolstered by her 50 million TV viewers) who is passionate about food and capable of describing the Bavarian goulash prepared for Benedict XVI, of discussing how the flavors of Italian dishes in America have evolved, and of explaining the secret to her success, the "strength of her family." The different dishes that were brought to the table gave substance to, and often reinforced, what she was saying.

The *New York Times* calls her "The Queen of Italian cuisine" and gave Del Posto four stars – the first Italian restaurant to achieve such a prestigious recognition since Parioli Romanissimo (no longer in business) in 1974–because it exemplifies the combination of quality and style. Quality is guaranteed by Mario Batali, the chef who is her partner in various restaurants and whom the Times' food critic Frank Bruno described as follows: "The risotto with red beets could put pasta out of business. It could keep (the restaurant) going strong for another quarter century." Style resides in the sixty-four year old Istrian woman's tradition of growing her own vegetables with her elderly mother Erminia in the garden of her house in Queens, in her frequent travels around Italy in search of inspiration and innovation, in her direction of an impressive editorial-TV empire, and in her ability to find time, despite everything, to spend most evenings watching over the tables of Felidia, her restaurant on 58th Street on the Upper East Side where her success began, success that brought her prominence in a metropolis where Italian restaurants abound and competition is fierce.

None of this would have been possible without the drive that stems from the fact that she is a refugee. In 1947 she was born into the Matticchio (Motika) family of Pola which at the end of World War II became Yugoslav territory. Her father Vittorio, who saw no future for them under Tito's communist regime, sent her to Italy with her mother and aunt when she was eleven years old. The Yugoslav police allowed the family to leave on the condition that Vittorio stayed in Pola as a hostage where he would await the return of his family members, but as soon as night fell he too fled, risking his life to get to Trieste. The family joined other Istrian and Dalmatian refugees at the San Sabbia rice mill –a former nazi internment camp – and they survived on Erminia's work as a cook and Vittorio's job as a driver. With the help of some American Catholic charity organizations they were able to buy tickets to New York where they went to live in Astoria, Queens. Lidia worked fulltime as a waitress, she met Felice Bastianich, and they married in 1966 and had two children, Joseph and Tanya. Family cohesion is the secret to

Lidia's method because each family member has his/her own role in the business that now extends beyond the boundaries of New York, stretching from Philadelphia to Kansas City. She opened two restaurants in Queens with Felice and then, in 1981, she opened Felidia (a combination of their names Felice and Lidia), whilst Joseph, a Wall Street trader, inaugurated Becco with Batali in the Theatre District and Esca on 43rd Street. Tanya, instead, who graduated in Art History, manages Lidia's Esperienze Italiane that are organized trips for Americans who want to immerse themselves in the origins of Italian food products. Tanya's husband, Corrado Manuali, is the lawyer who carefully assists Lidia in a variety of roles: from book-signing marathons for the fans who wait on long line in bookstores (she has written 6 best sellers), to the promotion of new sauces in supermarkets, from the debut of Lidia pasta for the Midwestern markets, to the negotiating of all contracts for her TV shows that has led to her own production of *Lidia's' Family Table*. The show boasts 50 million viewers across the entire United States and from time to time she invites members of the four generations of the Bastianich family on to speak about food. Sitting at one of the tables at Del Posto, the restaurant on 10th Avenue at the edge of the Meatpacking District that was established by her son Joseph along with Mario Batali and assigned to the American chef Mark Ladner, Lidia reiterates: "What distinguishes me from the competition and what explains how I'm capable of continued growth across different fronts is the fact that I have delegated roles to my children."

Her personal drive is evident in the care with which she positions the silverware on the table (course after course) and in the attention that she demands of her employees as they prepare the food, but to understand her idea of cooking you must taste a plate of spaghetti with fish and jalapeño. First of all, Lidia believes in "Italian products," in traditional flavors and in brands "that Italy should protect to avoid imitation," and she considers Italian cuisine "different" from Italian-American cuisine which is "another thing entirely" because it's "the product of the poor immigrants who when they arrived, cooked what they had by remembering the dishes from home and preparing them with what was locally available." That's how we can explain "the abundance of peppers" like chicken parmesan or pasta with meatballs that generated a new tradition." The American influence has modified Italian dishes for over a century, but now "we are in a new phase" thanks to the arrival, over the last twenty years, in America and especially in New York, of real Italian cuisine, with the opening of numerous restaurants "where you can eat today just like you would in Rome, Naples, Palermo or Milan." These are restaurants like Sirio Maccioni's Le Cirque where Gianni Agnelli used to love to eat Paillard, Tony May's San Domenico (today it's known as SD26), Da Silvano on Avenue of the Americas, Paolo della Puppa's Via Quadronno and Antica Bottega del Vino, Teodora on 57ᵗʰ Street and Barbetta, the Piedmontese place in the Theater District owned by Laura Maioglio, daughter of the antifascist forced to leave Italy during the last war and wife of the winner of the Nobel prize for Medicine, Günter Blobel. Felidia was one of the protagonists of this shift, but now Lidia is taking a new path with Del Posto, presenting traditional Italian dishes infused with American flavors. It's the exact opposite of Italian-American cuisine, because here Italian dishes aren't suffocated but rather enhanced by local ingredients: pasta that's cooked al dente and topped with spicy jalapeño creates a particular flavor, as does gazpacho served in little cups dipped in powdered capers, or steak that's been "aged for 130 days"–just the way cowboys of the West like it–served like a cut of beef. "These dishes show that Italian cuisine can maintain its own traditions, enriching them with new tastes from other traditions." The words of the four-star Queen.

The food merchant

When you step over the threshold at 200 Fifth Avenue, you enter into a new dimension of Italian food in Manhattan. Within a 7,000 sq. m. space there are 14 restaurants set among meat, fish, cheese, pasta and vegetable markets with twenty chefs and 400 employees that offer New Yorkers the option to sit and eat (there is seating for 600) the very same DOC products (products that have a controlled designation of origin) that are on sale at dozens of counters and shelves. The combination, within one space, of the real-life feel of the typical Italian town square market with haute cuisine grew out of an understanding between Oscar Farinetti, creator of Eataly, Lidia Bastianich, the undisputed Queen of Italian food in America, Chef Mario Batali, owner of some of the most popular restaurants in the Big Apple, and two young former Wall Street managers, Alex and Adam Saper, who chose to turn their backs on high finance after visiting Eataly in Turin. Joe Bastianich, Lidia's son who's an associate of Farinetti, the Sapers and Batali, is the owner of the catering section and he sums up the gamble that they all took together: "To offer both the table and the product in the same space in an effort to innovate food culture in New York and move beyond the reliance on prepared foods." At the end of the nineteenth century, Italian immigrants brought a culinary tradition to America that had to bow down to compromise with local products, and from the Eighties New York has gradually rediscovered the original Made In Italy flavors, Eataly now wants to take a giant leap forward, launching the best of traditional Italian products where Fifth Avenue meets Broadway.

You just have to cross the threshold, right in front of the Flatiron Building, to understand what it's all about. On the left there's Caffé Lavazza, then there's the Gelateria, then desserts and pastries, all the way to the square where mozzarella is made by hand, and where you can decide which area to go to next: meat, fish pasta or vegetables. It's a route that not only maps out Italian food, but also Italian identity and history, with 320 posters on the philosophy of Eataly–that owes much to Carlo Petrini's Slow Food–starting from the premise that neither the client nor the seller is always right. To reinforce the impression of being in Italy, there are corners where Unicredit has Italian ATMs that permit the withdrawal of dollars, there are La Stampa" iPads and a big screen "that allow customers to be constantly updated on what's happening around the world, Alpitour offers the possibility to go visit the places that produce the items on sale and Lidia Bastianich offers her very popular cooking lessons on American cable TV. Farinetti who is busy taking care of the last few details of this enormous project explains: "After Turin and Tokyo we are opening in New York because this is the capital of the world, with 8 million residents, and 45 million tourists a year, 500 thousand of whom are Italian." The intention is "to offer New Yorkers a place where they can find the best quality Italian foods and offer Italians a place where they can feel at home even though they're on the other side of the Atlantic." The whole thing is topped with a "beer restaurant" that has breathtaking views of the sky-scrapers of Midtown, 1,000 sq.m. of basement level kitchens and a wine cellar, near the 23rd Street entrance, all within a space that is impressive in size, even for a metropolis that is used to beating records.

Farinetti is a fifty-five year old who defines himself as a "XXI century merchant" and it's his approach to food that is behind the whole project. This approach is founded on the "apparent conflict between the informal setting and the prestigiousness of the products, between having pride in one's traditions and presenting oneself ironically, between the cunning of a business of undeniable financial success and honesty in dealing with the customer." Farinetti manages to be more of a New Yorker than the New Yorkers themselves: one of the signs explains that in every single product there is "50 percent less salt" which is twice the reduction that Michael Bloomberg demands of restaurants."

Every morning the first to shop at the stalls will be the chefs purchasing the products that they'll prepare for their customers, and so setting in motion a buying-consuming cycle in motion that will continue until late into the evening in the place that the architect Carlo Pignone–who also designed Eataly in Turin–created by adapting the neoclassical stucco and marble of the original Toys Building in New York to the needs of the Made in Italy city of flavors.

A few blocks to the south, Farinetti's office is located in a loft where, together with Joe Bastianich and the Saper brothers, he's focuses on a horizon that unites New York, Turin, Bra, Barolo, Novello and Alba (the founder of Eataly's native place) and represents the fusion of the global market and the localities that drive it. From these rooms, Farinetti coordinates the network of top-secret operations that made his arrival on Fifth Avenue possible: beginning with the Montana farms that six years ago imported the sperm of a Piedmontese cattle breed so they could produce rare cross-breeds on site, an effort he undertook because of regulations that make it impossible to import meat into the United States.

The Arts

The writer from Ocean City

Waistcoat, tie, scarf and hat all in order, Gay Talese is the most successful Italian-American writer in the United States. He lives in an elegant building on 61st Street on the Upper East Side with his wife Nan Ahern, a veteran of New York-based publishing who, among other things, edited three of Oriana Fallaci's books. They got married in the Campidoglio in the summer of 1959 when Talese was sent to Rome by the New York Times to follow Federico Fellini who was filming *La Dolce Vita* there. "That Summer, the heart of international cinema beat in Rome," he recounts, "Fellini, Visconti, Rossellini and Sergio Leone were all in Via Veneto. It was like living during the Renaissance at the time of Michelangelo and Leonardo da Vinci." The photograph of the wedding in Campidoglio sits on a shelf where no books have been placed, between the living room and the kitchen. Talese takes it in his hand and tells the story of that day: "We had been together for two years and I decided that the time had come, I called Nan and when she arrived we went to the Campidoglio. Both of us are catholic but we decided not to get married in church because we didn't want to assent to the rules imposed by the Vatican."

For Talese, who was born in 1932, being the son of a family from the South counts more than his catholic faith. His father and mother both came from Maida in Calabria, they arrived in New

York via different paths but met and became a family in Brooklyn. "The vast majority of Italian immigrants in America come from the South as a result of the disintegration of southern society after Italian Unification," Talese says, sitting in his living room with a glass of cognac. It's a topic that he has studied intensely and to which he has dedicated an autobiographical book *Unto the Sons*, published by Random House in 1992, that came out in Italy with the title *Ai figli dei figli*: "The south had a very structured society, the big cities were Palermo and Naples, it had an aristocracy and a peasant class and all people, both rich and poor, had their place, had their social circle, and could lead their own lives with the hopes of progressing up the social ladder." The jewel of this pre-Unification south "was Naples which had been a true capital city for 400 years, from the time when Columbus discovered America." All of this was swept away by unification: traditions, social hierarchies, ways of life, livelihoods." "It caused an enormous upheaval and it pushed many people to immigrate to America, including my father Joseph." The result of this social disintegration was that "those who came to America brought a parochial identity with them." The southern immigrants "didn't feel Italian nor did they feel Campanian, Sicilian, Calabrese, or Apulian because they identified themselves only with their towns and villages of origin." In the case of Talese's parents, "they lived in Brooklyn in a world that was divided between those who came from Catanzaro, Cosenza or Reggio Calabria." It was a very limited geography, that excluded all identification with Italy and also hampered contact with America. "Italians immigrated to and were born in big built-up areas like Boston, Brooklyn and Philadelphia that were hybrid realities because the territory was American but the people spoke a myriad of dialects from the Kingdom of the Two Sicilies." Talese's parents left this world when his father was told, for health reasons, to go live near the ocean. They chose Ocean City in New Jersey where Joseph Talese, who was a tailor by profession, opened a clothing store right in the center of town. The Talese Township Shop became quickly popular as the place where men and women could buy better quality clothes. "My father was an excellent tailor and my mother was very good at socializing with the customers." The Taleses were the only Italian family in Ocean City and living in this environment meant that Gay grew up "in a world where only English was spoken." "That was my first piece of good fortune" he adds, explaining that "the second was growing up in a clothing store where I used to go every afternoon up until I was seventeen" because "I listened to discussions with the clients and to the care with which my mother treated each one of them, it all expressed a different world that I tried to understand." Talese is convinced that "because of this experience I became a good journalist and a successful writer" creating, also, the New Journalism style– the use of narrative techniques to describe news events. His most cited article is *Frank Sinatra has a cold*, but Talese is just as attached to his descriptions of Dean Martin and Joe DiMaggio. "I owe my good fortune to the English language and to what I learned in that store in Ocean City, the result of my parents' choice to leave Brooklyn" turning their backs on a past that imprisoned them. But that's not all of it, because "the store was at street level and along with the many storerooms our home was also on the first floor, and we ate there together every evening." In Talese's recollections, "the difference between the ground floor and the first floor" is imprinted on his mind because "while in the morning my father dressed the Mayor and the most important local businessmen, in the evening when he spoke with us he expressed very different sentiments." It was because of World War II, which at that time had been going on for a while, America saw Italy as an ally of its enemies and two of Talese's brothers had enlisted in Mussolini's army. The model tailor felt torn between the two countries and at times this tension surfaced, "as happened when America bombarded the Abbey of Monte Cassino, my father went on a rampage" and destroyed all the toy airplanes that his son had collected. That doesn't change the fact, the journalist-writer observes, that "thousands of Italian Americans served in the allied army that freed Italy from Nazi Fascism" creating, with their sacrifices, "a bond in blood between the immigrants and the United States that hadn't existed up until then." Thus the world conflict proved to be "a catalyst for the integration of Italian Americans" and it resulted in "moving them towards the Republican Party and distancing them from the Democrats for whom they had voted since they first arrived in America." For Talese, this conservative shift of the immigrants "also has another explanation in the strong opposition of Italians against an all-powerful government that invades the lives of the people." It's also a consequence of the opposition against the intrusiveness of the unified State that overturned the South" and today leads "most Italian Americans to support the need for small government," that is also the traditional platform of the Republicans.

What torments Talese is the fact that this integration "opened the doors of the business world to Italian Americans, but this didn't occur in literature or in journalism." You just have to read any Italian newspaper "to notice that journalists of Italian origin are few and far between," whilst in the genre of fiction the only other well-known name is Don DeLillo, another New Yorker. It's for this reason too that Talese feels that, at over sixty eight years of age, his was a unique story "made possible by his parents' store in Ocean City."

The bull of Manhattan

The 3,200 kg bronze bull in Bowling Green Park in the Financial District represents the prosperity of Wall Street and it was sculpted by Arturo Di Modica, a Sicilian from Vittoria born in 1941. The bull was sculpted in his workshop-home at 54 Crosby Street that he literally built with his own hands. Di Modica has sculpted since, as an adolescent, he used to go to the workshop of the master cart maker in his town, where he worked with olive wood, helping to shape the characters of the Sicilian puppets. His father didn't like his passion for carving and one day flung a chair at him. After that, still an adolescent and with a few liras in his pocket, Di Modica left Vittoria for Florence where he stayed for twelve years, he studied, he perfected his craft and in the end he clashed with the interests of the galleries that wanted to dictate to him what he had to produce and how to exhibit it. In 1971, when he got the opportunity to put on a show in New York he crossed the ocean on a voyage that changed his whole life. In Manhattan he found an art world where "sculptors create and are free to exhibit." It was the possibility of being independent that pushed him to stay. His first house was at 127 Grand Street but his challenge was to build himself a new house from scratch, one that could also function as a workshop. He found the piece of land on Crosby Street (which is now part of Soho), he erected a fence and began to build. He found, carried and assembled everything by himself: lime, beams and bricks. He worked by night in his undershirt. He raised the building floor by floor. He bought four jacks for armored tanks to support the roof that he raised every night a few centimeters. Then with a few Hispanic workers he finished the job, digging out two floors underground. In this environment, built by himself from nothing, he decided that he wanted to "help New York" when in the fall of 1987 the market crash swept over Wall Street and hurled the metropolis into its worst nightmare. "I thought of the bull because it's the symbol of prosperity, I worked sparing no costs, it took everything I had to purchase the materials." Until the night of December 15th that year when he brought the giant bull by crane and placed it right in front of the entrance to the New York Stock Exchange. It was a way of spurring the markets to pick up again, the city to rise again. But the following day the metropolis was taken by surprise and the tabloids put the mysterious bull on the front page. Richard Grasso, however, the Italian American who was President of the New York Stock Exchange in 1988, didn't much appreciate the exploit and he ordered the bull be moved, and it vanished out of sight. Di Modica didn't give up, he went in search of his artifact, which wasn't too easy to hide, scouring the city until he found it in a police warehouse in Queens. He had to pay a heavy fine to redeem it but he paid what was due and got back to business. "The arm wrestle with Grasso was tough," he remembers, "he wanted at all costs for me to sculpt a bear too because in the world of finance it symbolizes the downward markets, but I didn't want to do it, what was important for me was prosperity." A compromise was reached when Bowling Green was chosen as the new location for the bull, and it still stands there today where its tail is caressed by tourists who want to be photographed beside it, on top of it and under it, because they're convinced it will bring them good luck. For Di Modica, it marked the beginning of the bull phase: there are five copies of the original which were recently bought by the British philanthropist Joe Lewis, then he sculpted others (different in color and in positioning of the hooves) for the Shanghai Expo, and now he's working on a third set destined for Vladimir Putin's Moscow. "New York, Shanghai and Moscow form a triangle of prosperity that must also be a triangle of peace" he states, identifying in his bulls a strong symbolic element that is "capable of uniting the world."

The other value in which Di Modica believes is "the memory of the past as a source of wealth for Sicily." This is the reason why, whenever he can, he returns to Vittoria to work on the "project of my dreams": two giant bronze horses, both 30 meters high, destined to form one sculpture in the Ippari Valley through which the eponymous river flows. In the belly of each horse there will be a history museum, one about Ragusa and the other dedicated to Vittoria. "Sicily is dying, Third world countries are stealing our jobs and well-being," he says explaining the motivation that drives him, "the only way to save it is by attracting tourism and by reevaluating our history which is our wealth." When the horses will be in place in the valley beside the river, Di Modica plans on organizing "big displays of naval battles between vessels that will be identical to those of the ancient Roman and Greece," so that "my valley will attract people from all over the world, allowing it to be reborn." This is why he buys land so that he will have enough space for his horses, he funds his international art school, he builds structures, and he sculpts. With this same passion he builds bronze doors in Hong Kong, fountains in Kuala Lumpur and bulls in Shanghai. "I work in Asia, I live in New York and I love my native Sicily" he repeats gesturing as he sits at a table at Cipriani on West Broadway. He designed the restaurant himself and helped start it up fifteen years ago, making, with his own hands, the iron stools benches and tables that are still part of the decor. The place with yellow curtains at 376 West Broadway is "my second home" and his friendship with the owner Giuseppe Cipriani is "very close." When he's not working at his new house at 253 Church Street, he spends his time here, drinking only tea. He sold the building on Crosby Street a few years ago after a very ambitious project fell through: he had invested 1.2 million dollars to create a pub on the underground levels of the house where the artists of Manhattan could meet, exhibit their work and speak to the public informally, building objects of all sizes and types to decorate the different spaces. But at the 11th hour City hall denied him the permit to set up shop "and you know what I did then? I told them they were animals and went home, I closed myself inside and I destroyed everything that I had built with my own hands, everything." His passion was just as intense in the destruction as it had been in the construction. And now, at just over seventy years of age, he lives commuting back and forth between Church Street and the foundries of Wyoming where the new bulls of the XXI century are being created.

The recipe for an Oscar

Both he and Robert De Niro share the fact that they have African American wives and mulatto children. They spent last Christmas together, discussing Bernardo Bertolucci's films and the overlapping of values and identities between America and Italy. This is only one aspect of life in New York for Antonio Monda who was born in Velletri in 1962, but it allows us to catch a glimpse of the personality and passion of the only Italian capable of bringing together and facilitating a dialogue between directors, actors, writers and celebrities (in Manhattan just as in Capri) that come from the two worlds that he inhabits. The "New York Times Book Review" devoted an article to him because Philip Roth had met Al Pacino, Salman Rushdie had met Roberto Saviano and Renzo Piano had dined with Meryl Streep, all at his home. Sitting on the couch in the living room of his Upper West Side apartment he explains, "I like to put a variety of accomplished people together." He recalls the lessons he learned from his father Dante who, he says, "used to say to me, evoking a Chinese proverb, if you give me one thing and I give you another in return at the end of the exchange each of us will have one thing, but if you give me an idea and I give you an idea in the end we both will have two ideas." Antonio Monda believes in the exchange of ideas, in learning from one another, and he likes to speak of sophisticated topics in a casual way, merging profundity and levity. It's a style that puts those who are surrounded by fame at ease, and it's a style that he adopts also at New York University where he has been teaching for seventeen years and has had tenure since 2003. He explains "in class I have a very anti-academic approach because I believe very strongly in the value of conversation." He reiterates the fact that the festival that he organizes every year in Capri with Davide Azzolini where Italian and American writers come together is called "Conversations" because "we take important issues such as human rights, identity and memory and lay them out in a way that makes them understandable to everyone."

At the Lincoln Center at the beginning of every Summer, Monda organizes the Italian Film Festival "Open Roads" that is now in its eleventh year. The Festival has presented 120 films altogether, about thirty of which, thanks to this platform, have been distributed also in the United States. He is one of the architects of the Italian Film Festival in Rome, organizing big events with celebrities such as Al Pacino, Francis Ford Coppola, the Coen Brothers and Meryl Streep. He considers America "an adoptive mother who is very strict but who keeps her promises," where "you'll rarely be led on, "and in the seventeen years that he has spent here "there has never been a dull moment, not even in the difficult times, and there has never been a lack of transparency."

The ability to facilitate a dialogue between Italy and the United States takes place along different lines but always follows the same script. At university, in his course titled *Hollywood Authors*, he confronts the relationship between art and industry and discusses, with his students, the opportunity that actors have of "making a living" by positioning themselves between the producers and the market. The actors and directors that he invites to speak to his students are the same Coen Brothers, David Lynch and Spike Lee, who then go to lunch at his place, participate in the festivals that he organizes, whom he interviews for the *Repubblica*, writes about in his books, and presents in his retrospectives. In the end, Monda manages to create a relationship of trust that allows him to become one of them. That's why he can look at Italian cinema objectively. "The situation is really bad because there are only three or four directors of an international caliber, Paolo Sorrentino is first among them but there are also Matteo Garrone, Paolo Virzì and Emanuele Crialese. The tragedy is that a solid industry hasn't been built around them." He identifies the reason for this deficiency in the fact that "at a time of difficulty our cinema survived by financing itself through television, and that produced negative consequences because on the one hand it altered the mode of expression of film because on TV there must be careful use of nudity, violence and long shots, and on the other it created an industry that survives on external funding and doesn't seek out its own." It's this stranglehold that, "in the space of twenty-five years, destroyed the Italian film industry that was internationally prominent at the time of *Dolce Vita.*" The result is that "Americans identify the image of Italy and its cinema with feel-good, outdated, and simplified tales "and that's why *Nuovo Cinema Paradiso, Il Postino* and *Life is Beautiful* (all movies set in the past with child protagonists and beautiful sets) were big hits. "People don't like" the Italy of today with its torments and contradictions, as displayed in Gomorra, for example "and films such as this only reach a niche audience." In short, to be successful in the American market, Italian cinema must fall back on old constructs because the Italy of today doesn't interest the general public." That's why "the only two directors that have an international career are Gabriele Muccino, who makes movies with Will Smith, and Paolo Sorrentino, who is filming with Sean Penn in Ireland and New York." This framework explains the difficult path that our films have to make to get to the Oscars, and what makes it even more difficult is the fact that producers find it hard to do what's necessary to get publicity like "investing resources and lobbying."

"To be successful on the road to the Oscars you have to talk, convince, send DVDs and brochures, rally together the maximum amount of resources," he explains, bemoaning the fact that "few Italian companies actually do this" and "there are even those who confront the challenge without American distributors and find themselves up against impossible odds." That's why "the golden age dates back to when Miramax released *Nuovo Cinema Paradiso, Il postino* and *La vita è bella,* whilst in recent years films like *Gomorra* haven't even received Oscar nominations. To reverse the trend Monda suggests "taking a leap of courage, investment and vision." The example that comes to him is that of the "monumental and controversial" Dino De Laurentiis, "who completely reinvented himself in America" because when he got to Hollywood he achieved success by "getting Sydney Pollack, the best director at the time and Robert Redford, the best actor, for *Three Days of the Condor*, and then he recruited Al Pacino for *Serpico.*" The strength of De Laurentiis lay in the fact that he "played in America by American rules" demanding the best without making excuses or looking for shortcuts."

And the American cinema? "After a down-turn it's now starting to come back, but there have been significant changes because
the digital boom caused the demise of DVD and videocassette sales
and this has led to upheaval within the big Hollywood production
companies because they don't have a tangible product to put on the
market that can drive advertising." "A great deal of damage has"
also "been dealt by piracy." The way out is "high technology" that
James Cameron used, for example, when he made Avatar," because
a film like this must be seen on the big screen, a pirated version
loses so much, it's not the same thing if you watch it on a computer
or an iPhone." As for themes, "war films are on the decline, The
Hurt Locker is the only exception that was a winner at the Oscars
in 2010, because unlike what happened in Vietnam, conflicts today
are still ongoing and people react to them in a different way." There
has been "a return to other styles as we can see in the Coen brothers' decision to make Westerns." What strikes him most is the fact
that "young actors, like Ann Hathaway and Jake Gyllenhaal who
are in their twenties and thirties dominate the box office, and that
confirms the cynicism of Hollywood; as soon as talented actors get
older they are promptly replaced."

Besides cinema and culture, Monda's other passions are his
faith and his wife Jacquie. His faith is evident in how he defines
himself as a "Roman Apostolic Catholic." He doesn't like to pros-
elytize but he tries "to live out his faith through his actions." "The
Pope is my Pope, I go to mass on Sunday, I pray in the morning
and in the evening because that's my one true home." This is why
he doesn't put too much stock in the rest because "faith allows me
to detach myself from what I do, which is a source of strength because if you give too much importance to material things you risk
going under." Jacquie is Catholic too. She comes from an upper
middle-class protestant family from Jamaica and her grandfather
was a reverend. They got married in 1991, on the 499th anniversary
of the discovery of America, and have three children. Jacquie is the
one who prepares Italian and Jamaican dishes and she has invented
a cooking style that makes the Monda home a unique feature of the
New York City melting pot. With this diverse and contradictory
background, Monda reflects on what the protagonists of these Italian and American "conversations" seek: "Both want to controvert

the stereotypes of the other. Tthe American celebrity doesn't want Italy to be presented just in the most convenient way but wants a presentation that's' fresh, energetic and different, just as the Italian isn't happy with a vision of America as a crude and violent place, home to gunslingers and cowboys." He thinks of recent examples. "When Jonathan Frazer came to Capri he told me that he wanted to know Naples so he could discover if it really was just a city of Camorra and garbage, just as Roberto Saviano asked me to introduce him to Nathan Englander so he could explore a possible common denominator between the son of Russian immigrants who was born on Long Island and residents of Casale del Principe."

On the stage

Bribestown went on stage a few years ago in Manhattan, in an avant-garde theater on the Lower East Side. With tales of "bustarelle"(bribes)–the Italian version of the word was always used–and references to the "good Judge Di Pietro," the play by Mario Fratti tells the story of one of the people investigated by Tangentopoli who, persecuted by an endless array of arrest warrants, decides to leave everything behind and take refuge in a marble chapel near the tomb of Ezra Pound on an island in the Lagoon where the Venetian Cemetery is located. The corrupt politician explains to the audience how his life up to that moment has been: they weren't bribes but "unavoidable compromises" so that roads and buildings could be built and contracts awarded; he feels no remorse because that's "how things were done"; and he is satisfied with what has been done for "his Country and society." The New York audience listens with great curiosity to an actual theorization of Tangentopoli: "The more money I have, the more goods I buy, the more production I drive, the more jobs I create," the character–played by Dave DeChristopher–states, adding "and I've always spent a lot." In the funeral chapel decorated with a red couch and an antique table, the corrupt politician begins his new life with the help of the cemetery caretaker, a young ex-musician who secured the job after the politician put in a good work for him. The caretaker is devoted to him and he becomes an efficient personal secretary:

he takes care of keeping the chapel-home neat and tidy, he gets rid of any busybodies who approach the cemetery, he keeps him up-to-date on any trials going on and, most importantly, he ensures the daily arrival of his many young lovers by prompt Laguna taxi. The subtitle of the play is *Erotic Adventures in Venice* because the corrupt politician, though he is living a forced exile on the island, doesn't renounce his compulsion towards vice, beginning with women and sex. The place, however, isn't very appropriate for romantic adventures and so the young ex-musician takes on the task of redesigning the layout of the island and uncovering, among the headstones and memorial slabs, caves and gorges that are suitable for salacious encounters. The whole setup is so successful that the politician, besides satisfying his own sexual desires with various fantasies and adventures, has the caretaker transform the cemetery into a place for sexual encounters offering a service to the whole lagoon, with a "guest" registry and different pricing "depending on the tomb," encounters set in underground grottos being more costly than those under the starry skies. The comings and goings of clients and prostitutes display the business savvy of the disgraced politician and the initiative of the young caretaker who negotiate a contract together and then hire the children of a couple that is buried in the mausoleum. They offer them a substantial sum for playing the roles of "ghosts" that lurk around the couples who want to be observed during their encounters. As part of this new business, photographs are provided for a fee to interested clients. The irreverent and erotic play that went on stage at La MaMa on the Lower East Side of Manhattan, at different points in the dialogue provokingly summons characters of note from the Italian public arena like "Mr. C" and "Mr B."

What makes *Bribestown* unique is Fratti's touch of irreverence and unpredictability. The playwright was born in L'Aquila and came to New York in 1963, and since then has lived in the same apartment on 55th Street. It's an apartment on two levels with a terrace perched among the skyscrapers of Midtown with a view of the City Center (once the Syrian Mosque), where Fratti lives surrounded by books, posters, awards and mementos from his successful and prosperous life on the stage. His most popular show was *Nine*, a musical that he staged in 1982 based on Federico Fellini's *8 ½* that earned him five Tony Awards and totaled 729 shows on Broadway (not counting revivals). Fratti, who was born in 1927, believes in unpredictability as a recipe for success in Manhattan's Theater District. "To write a script that works, you need to have a story in mind and to know right from the start how it's going to end," he states, "with a plot twist at the end, if possible, that the audience won't forget." Within the many works that he has penned there is a range of dramatic and unexpected twists: from the young woman who accepts the advances of an older man and has an affair with him and then asks him to marry her mother who is older and not quite as beautiful, to the elderly woman who lies to her friends telling them that her son is dead just so that she can join an association for people with suicidal tendencies, but then she has to appeal to her son, who is actually alive and well, to help her out of a predicament she has gotten herself into because of all her lies. "Theatre is structure, it requires a complex framework," he states, "it begins with the idea of a story, the end is added and then everything in between is assembled." He is a theatre professor at Columbia and Hunter College and he discusses four masters with his students, "Pirandello for the mask that each of us wears, Bertolt Brecht for the political struggle, Arthur Miller for greed, and Tennessee Williams for poetry." Williams actually lived in the house opposite Fratti's, they used to write looking at each other from the window, "then one day he died after choking on the cap of a bottle he had just finished drinking." He names the theatre greats to stimulate the young students and convince them to take a chance on the theatre because "in America you can work in the theatre and be rewarded with success, here newcomers can put on a show Off Broadway with just 20-25 thousand dollars" and "this is the best place in the world for musicals." And what about Italy? "It's a country where producers prefer the works of foreigners as opposed to Italian writers because of laws that favor such choices" and as a result "nobody is familiar with our authors." As proof he shows a photocopied page with the names of 39 Italian playwrights "that I distribute all the time to show how Italian theatre still exist and is alive and vibrant, despite the fact that it hasn't found the right channels to express itself." His other bitter disappointment surfaces when he talks about "Italian Americans who go to the theater much less frequently to see shows that relate to them than African Americans or Jews do with their respective productions," and "this distance between the Italians of New York and the theater" can be explained, to his mind, "by the fact that the fathers and grandfathers of today's immigrants were farmers and not intellectuals" and therefore "they prefer to watch TV rather than go to the theater." As it comes time to take leave, at the door Fratti glances at the portrait photograph of Katharine Hepburn providing his guest an unexpected finale: "she desired me, courted me, wanted to be with me... but she was ten years older than me and I turned her down."

A star in the Oak Room

To honor her grandfather and highlight her Italian heritage, Lady Gaga chooses the Oak Room of the Plaza Hotel with a view of Central Park. The reason for the gathering is the passing of Giuseppe Germanotta at eighty-eight years of age after suffering from Parkinson's disease for many years. His granddaughter Stefani, together with her grandmother Angeline, walks into one of the rooms that's most frequented by New York VIPs. Only a post on Twitter precedes her: "A perfect Manhattan for a perfect person, *I love you* Giuseppe." She chose this place because her grandparents used to bring her here when she was little. They would spend the money they had set aside so she could live the life of a queen for a few hours. It's a window into her humble beginnings in New Jersey, where her father and mother (Cynthia Bissett, originally from France), constituted what Lady Gaga describes as "a lower middleclass family." Compared to the sacrifices made at home, the Oak Room with its antique mirrors, large chandeliers, wood paneling, and waiters in livery, was a triple jump forward, a way of showing that they believed in a brighter future. Lady Gaga, born as Stefani Joanne Angelina Germanotta in 1986, starts by saying, "I have many happy childhood memories of this room." She speaks of the "determination" and the "energy" that she inherited from the old Italian Americans, and the drive that the immigrants brought with them when they came to America at the beginning of the century. She attributes her meteoric ascent in the world of show business (even to the point of overshadowing Madonna) to this very same drive. On this occasion, Lady Gaga comes to the Oak Room dressed in a way that amplifies the success that the queen of pop has achieved: she is a cave woman dressed in furs, adorned with pieces of costume jewelry held together by fishing wire, and a long blond wig runs down the length of her body that is mostly uncovered. She sings all the songs that evoke nostalgia for her grandfather, founder of her family, like *Someone to Watch over Me, Ev'ry Time We Say Goodbye* and *The Very Thought of You*. She impulsively steps over the line between personal sadness and the burlesque style that has made her a star, and after remembering her grandfather and addressing her grandmother, she screams into the microphone that she has "ingested enough tequila to cross over the border faster than Speedy Gonzales." Then turning to the orchestra, she asks the musicians to "do what you're supposed to do without getting distracted by looking at my behind."

Giuseppe Germanotta, known as Joseph, was born in Jersey City on the other side of the Hudson, opposite Manhattan's Financial District, and up until World War II he moved across the Garden State for temporary jobs to places like Elizabeth and Montville where, at the time, mostly Italian Americans lived. After going to fight in Europe, he set up a company as a "self-taught businessman" and Lady Gaga states that this was a source of great inspiration for her. Her grandfather's funeral took place at Saint Pius X in Montville, the church to which she is most connected and to which she donated most of the offerings made after his death. She describes the bond she had with him as follows: "It's true, I don't often speak about my private life, but I was really close to him and when he was sick I cried every day and while I was on tour in Nottingham, in England, I sang *Speechless* for him." Lady Gaga attended the funeral at the Church of Saint Pius wearing very conventional clothing, for once - a black suit with a skirt below her knee and a veil over her head- and she was accompanied by her father Joseph and her sister Natali. They then went to the burial at the Catholic cemetery of Gate Heaven in East Hanover, though the real farewell to Giuseppe actually took place in the Oak Room at a later date.

The Broadway dancers

Our appointment is at Café Luxemburg on 70th Street and Broadway at 5:30 pm. For the Broadway ballerinas it's like being at home because this is one of the places where they take refuge after their shows end late at night. Vanessa Van Vranken comes in wearing a black leather jacket, and Kristin Piro wears a light-colored shawl around her shoulders. Vanessa is very open, Mediterranean, she laughs and gestures all the time and she's 5'7" whilst Kristin, instead, has an American reserve about her, her eyes are always focused on the ground and she's over 7 inches taller. They are inseparable friends and their friendship developed as they danced on the stages of Broadway. Though Vanessa's last name is Dutch, her mother's maiden name is Lecoco and she comes from a family in New Orleans with origins in Palermo. Vanessa has traveled across America playing various roles in the dance troupe of the *Chicago* musical. Kristin Piro grew up in New Jersey in a Neapolitan family, she became a dancer because of *Saturday Night Live* and *West Side Story* and now she's in the cast of *Catch Me if You Can* that debuted at the beginning of 2010 bringing the plot of the film with Leonardo DiCaprio (a box office hit) to Broadway. As can often happen with people who manage to let friendship prevail over rivalry on Broadway, the lives of the two dancers are deeply intertwined. Vanessa is a red-head, she is now thirty three, she has had many boyfriends, and she says that her best season on the stage is coming to an end, and this is why she has decided to return to Louisiana to invest the savings she has accumulated in the family business. Kristin is a brunette, she is twenty five, and the critics consider her "a rising star of musicals," she has only had a few boyfriends, and with a slight smile she says: "I don't know what to expect in the years ahead." Both eat very little: they share a tuna salad and don't drink any alcohol. Their rigid diet is a fact of life for those who start to dance as children and choose to do it as professionals when they reach the ages of sixteen and seventeen. They met in Tampa, Florida, during the show *Chicago* and then their friendship took off in New York where they now live close to the Lincoln Center. But how do you get to be a dancer on Broadway? Kristin replies: "By being passionate as long as you have high endurance because you

have to face countless auditions and physical endurance is fundamental." "The toughest moment is when you are rejected," Vanessa
adds, "because you're the one putting yourself on the line, it's your
body, you're the one singing and dancing, the 'no' that you receive
is directed exclusively at you and no one else." Determination is
necessary to get a start in camps like "Theatre Camp," the major
step forward is when they become members of the union, Actors'
Equity Association, because from that point on "all you have to do
to find an audition is to check their website." That's exactly how it
works. Now they start to talk over one another: "On the site there's
a list of auditions, they state whether they want dancers or ballerinas, you go and wait for the result and they tell you right away
whether you are accepted or not." Being hired for Broadway musicals means earning about 1,600 dollars a week for both the period of
rehearsals and the actual show, and getting into a company "where
you're always together, every day from 10 until 6 in the evening,"
Vanessa says, acknowledging that "love stories abound" but with
one fundamental problem. "There are too many women and too
few men, especially because 9 out of 10 of the men are gay." For
the straight guys "it's a blast," Vanessa adds, because "they sleep
with a different girl every night, men who have other professions
really don't know what they're missing..." But that's where the
relationship between sex and the theatre ends. Kristin rejects the
misconceived idea that it's necessary to be sexy and voluptuous to
be successful: "It's not true at all, having large breasts, as if they're
padded with paper is necessary if that's what the part requires, otherwise the exact opposite is true, what counts isn't your appearance
but how your features match the script." Their Italian heritage is
there but it remains in the background. They speak about it with a
hint of a smile. For Kristin it's "eating with my family." Food signi-
fies "eating macaroni every year before the turkey at Thanksgiving
lunch," while family "means talking with my parents many times
a day while my peers who aren't Italian never do, or rather, when
they speak to their parents it's only to tell them lies." For Vanessa,
Italian food is rum cake, as the *babà* is called in New Orleans. "Being Italian means being honorable, respectful and loyal," Vanessa
adds, emphasizing the importance of the word "loyalty." They've
finished their salad and the two dancers are now talking freely

about their italianness. It's as if they have thawed out. Vanessa says that "my parents are really loud when I bring my boyfriends home, at times that embarrasses me," whilst Kristin remembers that "I learned to love dance when my parents used to do the traditional dances from Naples at home, I was very young but I loved it." Neither of them says much about the controversial show *Jersey Shore*. "What anti-Italian prejudice!" Vanessa observes, "they're just tacky people from New Jersey who buy jewelry and perfume only because they're so close to what they can't actually have, Manhattan." Café Luxemburg is getting crowded, the tables are full and the waiters are under pressure, but there is still time to talk about "what being a star means." Rachel replies: "A star is an actress or an actor who becomes a role model for others, my star is Rachelle Rak, I saw her dance many years ago, she still inspires me, and I would love to be the one to inspire another girl someday."

The smallest theater in the world

A four-floor white building stands at 319 Bowery Street in the East Village of Manhattan; it was the site of the smallest opera theater in the world and the only one in the United States capable of surviving on what it earned from ticket sales. The Amato Opera Theatre was located between a gas station and the Cbgb club that was home to American rock music. It was easy to get in because the little green wooden door beneath the sign "Amato Opera" was always ajar. Crossing the threshold, you entered into what was like an artisan's workshop, with objects of every type scattered all over, a very steep staircase in front, and a little room on the left. The steps led up to the second floor where Irene Kim Freydel offered hot coffee to any visitors, she took care of the accounts with a couple of volunteers, and kept a very taciturn costume designer company. Just another few steps and you were in a loft that housed what remained of the staging equipment that had been used since 1948 when Anthony Amato, a singing teacher, initiated the artistic endeavor. The tenor was born in Minori in the province of Salerno, and he used to love to go back, whenever he could, "to taste the lemons" that grew there. If you wanted to meet "Tony" Amato, you had to go down the stairs, go back to the tiny entrance and go down a very narrow and un-even corridor that led to the basement: this was the theatre hall that measured no more than 25 meters in its widest part. It was just big enough to seat 107 audience members, not one more. The carpen-ters had managed to carve out a little bar at the back of the hall that was decorated with theatre posters: The *Marriage of Figaro, Rigoletto, Madam Butterfly, Falstaff* and many more. I met Amato when he was coming down the stairs from the 7 meter-wide stage, where he was intent on mounting the set for the *Force of Destiny* with Mr. Kim, Irene's husband. He had white hair, dust-covered hands, an open shirt, a beaming smile, and little eyes that were deep blue and dart-ing. "The space is really tight here, the set design is essential and we can't alter it much," he explained, "but it allows us to really show-case the actors, the gestures, the details, the acting, because when a theater is small the audience observes the features of the face more closely, the small movements." When asked how it was possible to run an opera theatre in such a cramped space, Amato replied that it was precisely the fact that it was small that was the secret to the fame it had accomplished: "to be successful you must be small" because that allows you to "maintain high quality, to pay attention to every detail, and not to trivialize or generalize anything."

Amato's adventure began immediately after World War II. He was a young and well-respected singing teacher (his wife Sally was a soprano) and many soldiers who returned from the war came to him, asking to learn something about opera. It was a challenge that consumed him, and Congress gave him a hand to fulfill it by ap-proving the GI Bill, the law that provided financial assistance for the social and professional integration of veterans who found their old jobs taken by women when they returned home. "It's amazing how much singing talent there was in the US Army back then," he remembered, speaking about his first students. Federal assis-tance allowed Anthony, along with his wife who died in 2000, to stage their first production—in the Church of Pompei at the corner of Bleecker Street and Carmine Street—the *Barber of Seville,* followed by *Cavalleria Rusticana* the next week and then by *Pagliacci* the next. New Yorkers loved the singer-soldiers and the performances trav-elled from one corner of Manhattan to the other, from the Kaufman auditorium to the 92nd Street Y Center, until the theater opened its doors at 159 Bleecker Street in 1951. Their new location could house 299 audience members and they staged productions in succession for 50 weeks of the year. Their productions were so popular that the companies did a tour of some New England towns too. In 1959 the establishment closed down but, following a short period as an itinerant company, the Amato Opera Theatre returned to its audience in 1964 with the opening of the building at 319 Bowery Street. "It was donated to me by an opera enthusiast," Amato recounted, "he was a really wonderful old Jewish man who lived right below my studio, he was always listening to our songs and one day he came to me to offer me this little building as a gift, and I accepted."

From then until 2009 "the smallest opera theater in the world," as it is called by New Yorkers, staged at least five operas each season, each one running extended shows for five weeks and rotating a cast of between six and ten different actors. For the young actors of Manhattan, treading the boards of the tiny stage (with space for at most 7 musicians in the pit) meant becoming part of the acting history of America. Tony Amato didn't appreciate compliments very much, and he limited himself to say that his story was just like many others in America. But when you asked him about opera, then he spoke without reserve: "The most important quality of Italy's school of Bel Canto is its spontaneity, but as far as technique is concerned American tenors and sopranos are better. The Germans? I would never direct them, the Germans and opera are two separate things." With just five employees–two permanent and three part-time–Tony Amato managed to balance the theater budget for years despite the low ticket prices–just 23 dollars for a front-row seat, about a fifth of the price on Broadway–because much of the work required to keep the theater going still fell entirely to him. Low prices were Amato's signature, he was always convinced of the importance of teaching, popularizing and making opera accessible to most people: in 1964 a ticket cost 1.80 dollars, in 1975 3-4 dollars and then it stayed at the fixed price of 23 dollars until the theater closed. The last annual budget was around 380 thousand dollars, lagging far behind the Broadway theaters, but the fascination that surrounded it made it one of the symbols of the city. It's no coincidence that from the time of Abe Beame, every mayor has had his photograph taken on those steep steps that every New Yorker, who is passionate about the art of performance, remembers.

The African-Italian director

With one grandmother from Sicily and the other a descendent of slaves, Kym Ragusa has origins in two distant worlds that she tries to draw together somehow through her passion for cinema and writing. Born in Manhattan in 1966, Ragusa has an African-American mother and an Italian father, she grew up immersed in a world marked by the prejudice of her grandmothers who hated each other. She chose to dedicate herself to discovering how her story began, trying to piece together her family mosaic in what seemed an impossible feat. That's how she discovered that her grandfather Luigi and his wife Gilda left Messina for America with their two children in the middle of the nineteen hundreds–including Kym's father–and settled in one of the most poor and ill-famed areas of the Bronx. Her father tried to escape poverty by going to study at Columbia University, close to Harlem, and that's where he met his future wife. They began to go out, they went to work sporadically at the same places just to have some money in their pockets, and they fell in love. But Luigi and Gilda didn't want to hear about it, they disapproved of the sentimental relationship and they forced their son to break it off. Gilda didn't like blacks and Miriam, Kym's maternal grandmother, didn't like Italians because she considered them "poor immigrants," too "low-class" for her daughter. In short, the problem wasn't the difference in skin color but rather the difference in social status and financial means. The opposition of their families was fierce but it didn't prevent Kym's birth that took place shrouded in secrecy. Then the Vietnam War sent her father away and so the little girl grew up with her mother's family. As a consequence, Kym met her paternal grandparents when she was an African-American adolescent, well aware of what the color of her skin signified. It was a surprise for her grandparents because their son had never confessed to having a daughter with the young black girl that he had dated. A twist of faith brought Kym Ragusa to live with her Sicilian grandparents in their house in Maplewood New Jersey, and there she had to attend white schools and to delve into Sicilian culture that she knew very little about. In Maplewood, Kym often found herself in very difficult situations, like, for example, when her grandmother confessed to her that she worried about her white neighbors moving because she was afraid that an African-American family would take their place. This led to an identity crisis for Kym and her decision to dedicate herself to the arts after high school, to concentrate on the theme of interracial relationships. This path led her to make the documentary *Fuori-Outside,* and to write *The Skin Between Us,* an autobiographical book, translated in Italy with the title *La pelle che ci separa,* in which she recounts how difficult it was to define her identity once she discovered such dissimilar roots that were both equally hers. In 1999 she decided to get to the bottom of the problem and she left for Messina, and from there she re-constructed the genesis of the "white voyage" that brought her own paternal grandparents to the Bronx and the birth of an African-American granddaughter, just like her maternal grandparents had the "black voyage" on the ships that brought the slaves from Western Africa in their past. Kym Ragusa now lives in Brooklyn and she says that she feels both African American and Italian "even if the two terms appear to be really disparate."

Carnegie Hall, in search of new voices

At 161 West 56th Street, there's the Stage Entrance to Carnegie Hall, the New York temple of classical music on Seventh Avenue. It was built at the end of the eighteen hundreds like many similar theaters in Europe, and in time it became a veritable foundry of music. Each year it hosts about 800 shows in its three halls thanks to the work of a task force of 200 employees. It has a budget of 90 million dollars that's financed mostly by the public funds guaranteed by the City of New York that owns it. Once you pass through the little brown door, you get to a corridor that has music scores signed by the masters like Ludwig van Beethoven, just up a few steps there's the majestic and at the same time intimate Isaac Stern Auditorium: 2,804 seats that seen from the stage look like an immense sitting room with perfect acoustics. The Music Director of the Opera Orchestra of New York, Alberto Veronesi, directs there. He was born in Milan and his duties include planning the shows, hiring both personnel and the artists, running rehearsals, and "selling tickets" as he puts it himself, because around here "success is measured by sales receipts." Veronesi's orchestra, one of the four in New York, is a 70 piece orchestra with 80 choir members and his challenge is to direct it while increasing ticket sales and at the same time renewing the tradition that distinguishes it, "finding new voices." "Sitting in the stalls of the more intimate Zenken Hall where pianists often perform, he notes: "Opera is going through a crisis because in recent years more space has been given to directors rather than to voices, to the staging rather than to music." The Opera Orchestra of New York is the most appropriate place to invert this tendency because Eve Queler, who founded it in 1971 and directed the orchestra until Veronesi took it over, debuted young artists that later became stars like Renée Fleming, Vivaca Genaux and Deborah Voigt. This is why the Italian *maestro* dedicates so much time to the selection of artists, the master classes, and the rehearsal concerts, in a constant "search for voices." But how do you find a voice? This is how he replies: "Fundamentally a singer must have passion and musicality, but then I always look for four other qualities, the high notes, the intonation and the ability to sing *pianissimo* and *fortissimo* because this is the only way you can reach the greatest level and variety of musical expression." In essence, "to make music at Carnegie Hall you need stars like Placido Domingo but also new voices." As far as opera goes, Veronesi believes in Italian "musical realism" that takes from the *verismo* style from the end of the eighteen hundreds and brings "real events" back to the stage as Nicola Sani did in his opera *Il tempo sospeso del volo* that deals with the murder of Giovanni Falcone: an opera that Veronesi intends to bring to Carnegie Hall. What distinguishes this temple of music–the founding stones of Manhattan are visible in its foundation–is that opera is presented in concert form, concentrating on the voices. Over 80 percent of Veronesi's time is dedicated to conducting, and when we get to the Weill Recital Hall, a flexible space that can take on various dimensions where jazz shows or concerts for children take place, he speaks about "the constant search for the mystery of music" that accompanies him along his path of "color and suggestion" in the city of New York "that after Berlin is the other world capital of music."

The architect of the "New York Times"

Wearing a white shirt and a grey sweater, Renzo Piano, speaking in a low voice, describes his architectural gem as he goes in and out of the glass tower at the corner of 8th Avenue and 41st Street where he built the new "New York Times" building. Looking in from outside he speaks of the lobby that is surrounded by glass and allows you to see in all directions and he explains: "What distinguishes this building is its transparency." The 52-floor building stands in one the busiest corners of Manhattan, it's opposite the Port Authority that sees millions of people and cars pass by every day. The glass tower, recycled metals, and hi-tech inventions, all blend with the surroundings. The architect sums up his building by saying: "From inside you can see outside and from outside you can see inside." He was born in Genoa in 1937, he is an adopted son of Paris and a rightful resident of New York where he adds the new "New York Times" to his other projects: the Morgan Library, the Whitney Museum and the campus of Columbia University that's planned for Harlem. This merging of "the inside and the outside" becomes breathtaking when you get to the fourteenth floor where the cafeteria is located, or to the third floor where you can see the core of the newsroom. The journalists write and eat practically in the city. From their desks, the editors see old advertising signs that date back to the Sixties and invite onlookers to go to the Bahamas or to Bermuda and, if you look down, you see a river of taxis, buses and whatever else inhabits the streets of the metropolis. Inside the building, that Piano planned in 24 months and completed in 37 after going through more than 8,000 drawings, there are no walls or dividers to block your view. The idea of transparency, the backbone of American journalism, is reflected in the entrance where visitors are welcomed by the clicking of old typewriters that comes from 560 little digital screens. On the screens visitors can instantaneously read what the editorial staff is writing. Just get close to the screens and you'll see the signatures of both famous and not so famous journalists, and you'll see passages on Ahmadinejad, Hillary Clinton or Michael Jackson, though the computer that controls the flow of articles is careful to protect tomorrow's breaking news. Attached to the lobby, at the core of the skyscraper, Piano chose to locate a garden with eight birch trees from New Jersey, the only trees of their kind that can be seen in Manhattan. Around them a Japanese garden with green moss transforms the birch trees into a green space that is visible from every corner of Bill Keller's newsroom that is laid out over three floors. On the opposite side of the lobby there's the Times Center, a cluster of rooms with a large auditorium designed to become an agora of both thought and the arts that will host cultural events capable of making the "Gray Lady"–as the newspaper is called–a place where you can see and hear what you'll then read sitting in your armchair. The old site on 43rd Street was one of the most traditional stone buildings dating back to before World War II, this new one displays numerous innovations: from the "double-skin curtain walls" made of 360 thousand ceramic rods that filter sunlight to the adoption of 75% recycled steel ("the amount found in a few hundred Bentleys"), from the bright orange Venetian *marmorino* plaster on the walls of the entrance created using traditional techniques to the most refined security system that is guaranteed by the transparency of the building. The study of building security was one of the steps that defined the genesis of the new building. In 2000, Piano's project beat out his competitors Norman Foster and Frank Gehry, but after the terrorist attacks of September 11, 2001, they considered re-designing the building or even starting again from scratch. At that time the architect was in New York, and on September 14th he was "at the gloomiest birthday dinner that he had ever experienced" with Arthur Sulzberger and Michael Golden, his *New York Times* liaisons on the project, and together they made the decision to forge ahead, without making any modifications, with a decision that merged architecture and philosophy. "The high security comes from the transparency of the building because being able to see allows you to observe, understand what's happening and avert," Piano explains, "it's no coincidence that these days banks don't put their vaults underground anymore." The architect doesn't like to put up barriers and hide. His reasons reveal his particular world view: "I'm for dialogue, tolerance and understanding; because that's the only way we can defeat terrorism. Political solutions and not military ones are necessary, otherwise with the lack of transparency we'll end up in bunkers." That's how the "New York Times" glass tower came to life, interspersed with bright red stairways–"the color that stimulates the imagination"–in which the newsroom is laid out in one environment on three floors. Piano defines this space as the news *bakery*, where the writer has his own computer and desk, but he is immersed in the vast open space that revolves around the birch tree garden, a space that is limited only by the sky. To move to other floors using the elevator you have to pass through white corridors with little digital screens on the walls that show randomly chosen photos from the newspaper archives. "The skyscraper in Turin is the child of this "New York Times" tower, because both blend into the fabric of the city," Piano adds. He suggests that the recent controversy in Italy springs from a "wariness about the future" that he understands, but asks Italians to overcome this fear: "It's not a monster, it's part of the city, from the roof top down to the auditorium, and there's no need to be afraid of it."

The designer of unique pieces

On the fifth floor of the block between Spring Street and Prince Street on Broadway, there's a rectangular studio-workshop interspersed with colorful creations where the designer and architect Gaetano Pesce invents and works. He was born in La Spezia in 1939 into a family with roots in Este, Padua, Venice and Florence; he came to New York in 1981 after living in Helsinki, London and Paris. He travelled a lot between Europe, Asia and America, and he chose to live in Manhattan, and to create in Soho "because New York is a city that's forever in motion, where people work and are always making sacrifices, chasing dreams and projects, whilst anywhere else, from London to Venice, people relax, they're gratified, they don't work on Saturdays and Sundays, and hosting clients is often a burden to them." The "forever in motion" is what distinguishes New York, "that fits the original model of a city, a place where people come for goods and services, always, at any time of the day or night." That's why it's the best place to think and accomplish the "innovative work" that he has dedicated himself to since he created the *Golgotha Chair* in fiberglass and resin for Cassina in 1972; the chair is now on display at MoMA, Museum of Modern Art. In

Osaka in 1993, his Organic Building introduced walls covered with vertical vegetation whilst the series of *Up* armchairs in 1969 is the star, immortalized by a photo on his office wall with Salvador Dalí. "My clients are visionaries,"–he says, sitting in an armchair with a rigid frame and soft back–"and I believe in one-of-a-kind pieces, because off-the-shelf production is passé." He's convinced that "materials have a mood" and in his laboratory he studies them and he models them until he's able to exploit them to create "not a series of objects but many different pieces." What makes this possible is "high technology" that allows me to "enhance Italian creativity" offering the companies that he works for the possibility to "deliver an object that is unique in the world, to every single client." In this idea of "uniqueness" which is possible due to the modeling of materials and substances, Pesce identifies the "answer to the challenge brought to us from China" because "they imitate objects, they produce in high quantity and standardize production, whilst we can respond in the area where they are weak, by creating products that are always unique." Pesce follows a creative path that is his alone, founded on the desire to "follow and understand the processes that are occurring." Here's one example: "75 percent of the planet today isn't educated, there are people who work in an imperfect way and with mid-low levels of education, from this I got the idea about the possibility of creating 'badly made' products, as, for example, the vases with imperfections that become high quality." So I can have an unskilled workforce make "imperfect products," that are all different from one another, that are much cheaper than "perfect products" on the market yet still capable of becoming objects of value. "The future lies in variety," he adds, using another example: "jeans with holes that are all different from one another, that cost 1,500 dollars a pair when you can buy regular jeans for just 50 dollars." What's essential to this relationship between design and creativity is the idea of "democracy founded on variety, and therefore contrary to the esthetic models of the USSR where everything was always the same, forcedly identical." It's "the standard that is totalitarian" just like "the TV is against variety because it forces everybody to see the same program, unlike the computer that in contrast is interactive." This is where his idea of learning comes from. Pesce taught architecture in Paris, Strasburg, São Paulo, Hong Kong, Canton and

New York, and from these experiences he contracted the idea that "schools must force students to think for themselves, to be curious and creative in their research laboratories, and be willing to carry out experiments that could lead to the production of new objects." The Pompidou Center in Paris was like that: "At the beginning it was considered sacrilegious but now we can't do without it." But how do you define a "new object" that everything originates from? "An object that is optimistic, cheerful, sensual, colorful," he replies, "and thus capable of helping us live better." He observes the trends of today with skepticism, beginning with sustainable and environmentally friendly architecture, because he says it makes him feel like he is "surrounded by the conservatism of those who think, and always do, the same things." He uses the New York skyscrapers as an example: they're "all the same, straight-lined, cut out, totalitarian," they don't have "organic shapes" that to his mind could "regenerate the city, imparting a new vitality on it." He is thinking, in particular, about the rebuilding project of the World Trade Center. One by one he shows the designs for the project that he proposed to the city, a project that he still strongly believes in, though his plans were rejected. His design is based on the reconstruction of the Twin Towers destroyed by the Al Qaeda suicide terrorists, but with an important addition: a 27 floor giant heart that joins the towers and houses museums, cultural centers and reflection rooms with a panoramic view of Manhattan. The image of the fire-red heart perched in the New York sky recalls the "I love NYC" logo stamped on the most popular t-shirts in Manhattan, but for Gaetano Pesce what's most important is the architectural revolution that's represented by the success of "recognizable forms" in the structure of the metropolises of the XXI century.

Pesce's thoughts go beyond architecture and city planning because the vision of the importance of "one-of-a-kind pieces" leads him to elaborate the need to "regenerate the democratic system" and meet the need to "showcase the importance of every single citizen," giving him the opportunity to have a say in the activities of political leaders, and moving beyond the phase of "mass political expression" that marked the XX century. To articulate this approach, Pesce begins by picturing a "decentralized government" whose ministers are spread out over the territory, "not all of them in the capital but in the most important cities," as could happen in Italy by "sending the Minister for the Economy to Milan or the Minister for Employment to Turin," according to a plan that he laid out for the first time in 1983. He showed it to Gianni Agnelli who became enthused with it and had it elaborated by the Agnelli Foundation. "Decentralizing political power ultimately means giving the decision-making power back to the citizen-voters"–he adds, sitting in the Veneto restaurant Antonucci, on the Upper East Side– and so why can't we imagine a time when each one of us, let's say once a week, votes by email to renew or deny the trust placed in the political representatives that we elected?" In this way, the relationship between the person who is elected and the voter would be continually renewed "allowing new technologies to increase citizen participation in public life" and thus setting right "the reality of political systems that are progressively less popular because they are run by a group of elected representatives that becomes a caste and can manage power for periods of four or five years without ever having to answer to anybody for what they do." It's the same approach that led him to write to President Giorgio Napolitano, suggesting he alter the location where he delivers his end of year message, "not with a backdrop behind him that expresses prestige and styles of the past that are remote and formal, but a place that is vibrant and represents Italy looking towards the future," that could be "a factory in Brianza, a store where Italian creativity is celebrated, a Made in Italy workshop, a fashion studio or a factory in Modena where the prestigious and legendary Italian cars are built." The overlapping of politics and design becomes clear in the *Sessantuna* project, also known as the 61 tables–a number that recalls 1861, the year of Italian Unification–that Pesce created for Cassina as pieces of the map of the Italian peninsula, each one different from the other and with specific geographical characteristics. This is to highlight the fact that it is the uniqueness of every single difference that can regenerate all nations today.

Reinventing Picasso

On the fifth and sixth floors of 980 Madison Avenue, in front of the Hotel Carlyle, Larry Gagosian has the main office of the largest and richest contemporary art gallery in the world. Valentina Castellani, an elegant, sexy and very resolute woman from Turin, born in 1966, has been his most valued assistant since 2005. On the walls of her office she has two Andy Warhol drawings on display that depict an elegant woman's shoe from 1956, and the symbol of the hammer and sickle that dates back to 1976 when the artist started to draw portraits of Mao following Nixon's trip to China. Castellani states that she "has always had a passion for art," though she came to it by chance: she graduated in Greek archeology in Turin, she could only find part-time work and in 1997 she left Italy for London, "a choice made for love"–she followed the man that she married four years later–that launched her into one of the capitals of contemporary art, where Sotheby's took her on as an intern and then hired her at the department of contemporary art. Sotheby's and Christie's are the two largest auction houses and both have main offices in London and New York; they compete by putting on auctions of art pieces that are catalogued, and the most popular periods of art are modern and contemporary. They have two auctions per year in New York and two in London, and the "expert's" job is to find art pieces for their auctions by convincing collectors to put what they own on sale.

Gagosian competes with both Sotheby's and Christie's because he doesn't have any rivals in contemporary art for the simple fact that he can combine his three galleries in New York,–the one on Madison Avenue plus another two in Chelsea–two in London, one in Los Angeles, Rome, Paris, Athens, and Hong Kong, as well as a little office in Geneva: an empire that's sustained by a top-secret budget estimated to be in the tens of billions. Within this context of competition, Gagosian invited Valentina Castellani to lunch in 2002, and made her an offer that she couldn't refuse in an attempt to steal her away from Sotheby's. The auction house actually did make Valentina a counteroffer, but she "followed her instinct" and changed employer.

Since then she has been one of the six directors of the New York branch, a title that allows her to operate in the two contemporary art markets: the main market that is made up of artists who rely on the gallery to sell their art, and the secondary market made of delicate negotiations with collectors who own works of great value.

To understand what it's all about it suffices to consider that in Gagosian's "main" budget there are artists like Richard Serra and Jeff Koons, whilst in his "secondary" budget the deals that stand out are those sealed with the families of Piero Manzoni and Pablo Picasso that led to ad hoc exhibits. Castellani curated these shows, and became the contact person for the descendants of these great artists. These deals resulted in the first Manzoni retrospective in America in 2009 and it won the Guggenheim award for the best exhibit on display. This victory for the exhibit highlighted changes now occurring that see galleries, armed with more resources, being able to take on more costly initiatives–covering insurance and transportation costs–than the museums. And then there were the two exhibits of Picasso's work from the last years of his life–*Mosqueterros* in New York and *The Mediterranean Years* in London–that revolutionized how critics and collectors see this period. "I work with the Picasso family because we have a relationship with the heirs, they loan us paintings or they have us sell them," Castellani says, describing the web of relatives that the Spanish painter left behind, with four children from three different women. With his first wife Olga Khokhlova he had a son who died in 1975, and that left everything to their daughter Marina and grandchild Bernard. Marie-Thérèse Walter, the seventeen year old girl with whom he had a very romantic love affair when he was forty seven and still married, gave him a daughter named Maya. And then there was Françoise Gilot, with whom he had Claude and Paloma. Each one of them inherited numerous works of art because Picasso died when he was ninety two years old and he had painted up until the last day of his life, leaving about 2000 paintings. Some of the paintings paid the heirs' inheritance tax and also funded the Picasso Museum in Paris. "Each time I deal with them, the fact that they are sensitive and reserved people comes to light, they are very particular because of the important name that they have inherited, but though they all share the desire to appreciate the work of their father, they don't act as a family because they are children of different mothers." The different collections, however, are similar and balance one another because they are made up of batches of paintings that were randomly selected at the reading of the will. "Working with them means always trying to reinvent the artistic message of Picasso," and that comes about at brainstorming sessions in which Castellani can take advantage of a truly expert advisor named John Richardson–eighty-eight years of age, openly gay and connected to people of note like Mick Jagger and the Duke of Windsor–who knew Picasso, became his friend and is now finishing an exceptional biography about him. That's how the idea of the show *Mosqueteros* came about, as a reevaluation of the last twenty years of Picasso's life when he drew musketeers taking inspiration from Goya, Rembrandt and other artists, just as the London exhibit on *The Mediterranean Years* describes the artist who, though he was isolated in the South of France, didn't ignore what was happening in the world of the Sixties–from conceptual art to pop art and minimal art–though he continued to believe in painting above all else. Castellani confirms, "in this way we attained two results at once: we found an interesting critical angle for the works of art, and at the same time we reassessed the market value of some of the pieces that were thought to be worth much less." Her expertise on Picasso can be judged by the other exhibits that are forthcoming.

In the case of Piero Manzoni, the method applied wasn't any different: meetings with family members, a partnership with the most competent expert in the field–Germano Celant–and a reinterpretation of the works of art that surprised critics and attracted buyers.

Inside Gagosian's gallery, there isn't much bureaucracy, the six directors work as a team and each of them manages a few artists. Valentina Castellani has two Italians who reside in New York on her list of "primary market" artists: Francesco Vezzoli, "who wants to transform our gallery on 21st Street into a church," and Rudolf Stingel from Alto Adige who had a show curated by Francesco Bonami in the spring of 2011. Castellani states that "in these relationships, difficulties arise from the fact that the artists dedicate themselves completely to their work, they are sensitive people, managing artist means guiding them in their choices and discussing their projects with them, from a critical point of view and also in terms of the market," she also adds that, in any case, "these are pleasant difficulties to have and through them interesting and constructive relationship are created."

Larry Gagosian is an autodidact, he began selling posters on the beach in Los Angeles and he has become the most important art dealer in the world, who is always on the move and travels in his private plane or helicopter. Being his most valued assistant often means being thrown into a vortex of very high-stakes responsibilities. On one occasion he gave Castellani "carte blanche" and asked her to go to see *Car Crash* by Andy Warhol in Italy, telling her "to get immediate results." As part of a collection, Warhol's *Car Crash* cost tens of millions of dollars. Castellani was there with Gagosian on the phone thousands of miles away. "Stand in front of the painting and decide whether it's worth it or not" he said, abruptly. She bought the painting and it turned out to be an excellent investment, but what Castellani remembers most about the purchase is the feeling she had inside: "Deals worth tens of millions of dollars give you a huge adrenaline rush."

What is worrisome at the moment is the trend that the contemporary art market is taking. Up until 2008 it had reached the limits of pure folly, with pieces selling before they had even been brought to the galleries, this happened with a Koons sculpture that a collector bought for 4 million dollars and three months later sold for exactly 8 million, without ever having actually put his hands on it. Positive changes have come in the form of new buyers who are Russian, Chinese, and sometimes from the Arab world. They possess immense amounts of money and they buy art hoping to be accepted into the circles of the wealthy, "becoming part of a world that aspires to be very glamorous." The financial crisis, after the collapse of Lehman brothers in September 2008, had a negative effect, particularly on young artists because they had enjoyed inflated prices due to the market. Now the remaining collectors buy cautiously, they look for well-known names like Warhol and Koons, they have their feet well on the ground, and they avoid taking risks.

Within this context, Valentina affirms that Italian art "is undervalued." After the war, Piero Manzoni, Lucio Fontana and Alberto Burri commanded a presence as great artists and earned high prices for their pieces, but they never reached the levels of American artists who are supported by a market where the collectors are wealthier and buy mainly the works of their compatriots. As well as this, MoMA, founded in 1929, immediately bought the abstract expressionists, artists like Pollock and De Kooning whose prices are now skyrocketing. "What weakens contemporary Italian art is the financial fragility of the country," Castellani explains, though she also highlights the fact that "Italian art is very well-regarded around the world." "It's true," she adds, "that contemporary artists must leave Italy in order to be appreciated and valued, and it's not a coincidence that Vezzoli and Stigler live and spend most of their time in New York, just like Maurizio Cattelan, because this is the city that offers the greatest exposure." This doesn't mean that there aren't "great artists like Roberto Cuoghi, Diego Perrone and Paola Pivi–who now lives in Alaska–but the fact that they are Italian hasn't been a boon to them." There are beautiful and historical collections in Italy, thanks to the work of gallery owner Gian Enzo Sperone in Turin, who was the first to bring pop art to Italy in the Sixties. Miuccia Prada will open a museum in 2013 and she already has her own foundation, and Patrizia Sandretto opened one of the first museums in Turin many years ago that was entirely dedicated to contemporary art with important pieces by Damien Hirst and Cattelan. This shows that Italians have always collected art and done so tastefully. And they continue to collect.

A pencil for the skyline

Remsen Street is a little street in Brooklyn Heights that leads to the walk with a panoramic view of the Hudson. From left to right your eye moves from the Verrazzano Bridge, Governors Island, Staten Island and the Statue of Liberty, with the cranes of Bayonne and Port Elizabeth in the background, all the way to the skyscrapers of Downtown Manhattan that seem almost close enough to touch, there beyond the waters of the East River. Matteo Pericoli looks at them one by one and he talks about them as if they were his closest relatives. Within the cluster he points out the three "new ones." "The yellow and black one, the tower by Santiago Caltrava in front of the Brooklyn Bridge, and in the distance the top of Building 7, the first one to be rebuilt at Ground Zero." He has memorized the Manhattan skyline because he has drawn it in its entirety, from 1998 to 2001 when Random House published his *Manhattan Unfurled* (translated into Italian by Leonardo Internazionale with the title *Manhattan Svelata*). The book is made up of two drawings, each one is over 11 meters and is a detailed portrait of the island seen from a distance, from the rivers that surround it, one on the west side and the other on the east side, including the Twin Towers that were drawn when they were still standing. "It would have been impossible to erase them, both from the drawing and from the book that had already been printed and was ready for publication in a few weeks," he recalls. Nobody before him had described Manhattan like that, and to do it he had to circumnavigate the island on the ferries, observing it from every possible angle, riding around on his motorcycle and taking hundreds of photos to reconstruct a memory of different images of the same buildings. Thanks to these photos he was able to outline a portrait of the metropolis that he defines as "democratic," because it "includes all of the buildings, not just the most popular ones, and not only the most beautiful ones."

Ten years after the debut of *Manhattan Unfurled* in bookstores, it's still one of the most popular books about New York and on the shelves of Barnes&Noble and Borders it's always placed beside *Manhattan Within–Il cuore di Manhattan* in Bompiani's Italian edition–that describes the city from within, with a 10 meters long drawing of all the buildings that look onto Central Park as seen from the perspective of a person standing in the park. "The best way to see is by taking a step back," Matteo explains–he has lived in New York for thirteen years, and these days he travels back and forth to Turin–"because Manhattan is very egocentric, it envelops you, it blinds you, it overwhelms you with such a passionate love that you must distance yourself from it if you want to be able to describe it and better understand it." That's why he decided to board the Circle Line so he could see it from a distance, "in the stillness of the waters of the river," and came to the conclusion that "there's no perfect vantage point." His work method started with "taking lots of photographs and proceeding through the drawing little by little" working on "just a small section of the skyline at a time." It was the beginning of what he defines as an "ontological study of what's there" in an effort to "grasp a city in its entirety through the perception of its geographical spaces." The mass of photographs that were printed or studied on the computer, sprang from the need to "observe the same building in many dimensions, from different viewpoints, because besides the three traditional dimensions there is also a fourth, the weather." In this respect, for Pericoli, understanding an architectural creation is like understanding a book "because only by spending time flipping through it, reading all of its pages, one by one, can you really understand the meaning that it encompasses. That's how architecture is, it must be experienced from beginning to end." It's an approach to design that's based on the belief that "each line that's traced by the pencil happens for a reason and has its own intrinsic value" that goes beyond "the visual aspect, but is also linked to thought." The analogy between drawing and writing, the idea that every line conceals a particular interpretation and its own thought, makes Pericoli–who was born in 1968–an artist who aims to describe New York "in its entirety, not in small parts, without showing favoritism, going by the perceptions that we all have of what surrounds us."

When the *Manhattan Unfurled* project began, in 1998, Matteo had been in New York for just three years, it was his passion but he never thought it would become a book. He worked on it without thinking about what it would become. "I wasn't even sure whether or not I would be able to finish the skyline on the west side because when I got to 72nd Street I had skyscrapers and perspectives before me that I didn't know how to draw." The turning point came thanks to his motorcycle, "uncommon in the city then, almost as rare as a horse," because it allowed him to move further away, to go into New Jersey and to gather more perspectives. "When I finished the project I was sure that something similar had been done before, but it hadn't and it was that lack of other projects of the type that gave strength to my work." Pericoli sent many letters, he proposed his book to many editors and the only one to reply–after six months–was Paul Goldberger from the "New Yorker, he invited him to visit bringing the massive drawing with him. "That was the first time that I rolled out the whole drawing, just like you would a Torah, and Goldberger was astounded by it, he started to call all the others in the New Yorker offices to come see, like at a market, and each person searched for the corner that was most familiar." This was the moment that opened the doors of American publishing to him and led him to explore the other views of the city, like what can be seen from Central Park or from his apartment windows that he drew in the book *The City Out My Window*. The incentive for this last endeavor dates back to 2004 when Matteo and his wife Holly, originally from New Jersey, left their home on 102nd Street on the Upper West Side to relocate to Queens. Before leaving he decided to "bring the view that we had from our window" with him. "I did the drawing so I could bring the view that corresponded to my perception of the city with me and this morbid attachment that I had to my view made me realize that in actual fact many other people had the same relationship with their windows." This is where the book with the drawings of 63 views of New York springs from, it tries, once again, to see a metropolis "from the inside," a metropolis to which Pericoli confesses he "owes at least 75 percent of myself," especially because it instilled in him the ability "to think independently when faced with any kind of problem. Anyone who arrives in this city must question what he knows because there are always another 50 or 5,000 people who do, think and say what you do, think and say."

The "street dog" of Solita

He was born on the Upper West, he loves Alphabet City, his home is in Solita, and he likes the strong wind that blows off the Hudson because it reminds him that Manhattan is a sea town "where you can get up in the morning and go sailing or boating." Lapo Elkann is a New Yorker who was transplanted to Italy, but as soon as he can he comes back to the city that he describes as follows: "It's made up of villages, each area is its own world, it's not divided between Uptown and Downtown like many people say, because there a thousand different places." He chose to rent a home in Solita–the neighborhood to the south of Little Italy–"because it still has rough edges, it's not polished like the Meatpacking District that's too unnatural, almost completely gentrified now," and he loves the Lower East Side because of Alphabet City "that was once one of the most dangerous areas and now is interspersed with vegetarian and Japanese restaurants, tai chi studios, little bakeries, alternative photographers, underground clubs, all those things that constitute a less conventional America, the real America." There's everything within the geographical confines of Lapo's Manhattan. The Silvano restaurant and the Bar Pitti that are almost next door to one another on Sixth Avenue and owned by two Tuscans who are forever in competition (though sportingly so), just like their respective customers, because "at Silvano's you eat *coach* (more economically) but better than at Pitti where the food is *business class* but where you can always be sure to meet beautiful girls." The MoMA where Paola Antonelli, the curator of Design, introduced the "@". Henry Kissinger's office on Park Avenue where Lapo worked years ago. The Saint Ambroeus café on Madison Avenue for coffee, and Via Quadronno on 73rd Street for cappuccino. Bobo Vieri and Paolo Maldini, both New York commuters just like him. Sirio Maccioni and his "pretty boy" sons, with their Le Cirque restaurant. The new San Domenico, SD 26, in Madison Square Park. Paolo Zampolli, the former owner of the modeling agency ID Models, "who likes everything oversized, big cars and very tall women." Rao's restaurant, "very good, where you find all the mafiosi." The LaVilla twins (Marco and Mauro), Canadian filmmakers, who are working on a 90 minute long documentary about the history of Juventus in a yard on Bank Street. The film, *Black and White Stripes*, recounts the epic deeds of a team that was capable of "uniting a nation" and the twins are dedicating it to the memory of their Neapolitan father Rosindo, a diehard fan of the "Old Lady" who was buried in Montreal wrapped in a black and white flag. Maurizio Marchiori, organizer of the Triennale NYC exhibition space, and friend of Giuseppe Cipriani – in his restaurant on West Broadway "you meet all the Europeans." "The advantage of New York is that nobody here is anybody–he says, eating papaya dressed with lemon and carrot juice at a table at the Standard Hotel–the most famous people in the world live like normal people, you can meet Martin Scorsese at Starbucks without even noticing, talk to a homeless person or a Bengali taxi driver, you are a human being and nothing else, there's no other city in the world that can give you that." This aspect of New York is what his grandfather Gianni Agnelli loved, "when he came here he'd go for walks in Central Park, he'd go to the museums, he'd eat hotdogs on the street and he felt more free." It's a feeling that he too shares today because "in Italy people like me are happy but they live hidden away," whilst here in Manhattan Lapo can drive a white Ferrari convertible down Sixth Avenue and nobody notices, except for a delivery boy on his bicycle who approaches and yells "nice car, in ten years' time I'll have one just like it." This episode sums up "why I feel at home here in New York, there's no jealousy but competition, people want to do better than everybody else, always, but they don't try to knock their neighbors down, just do better than them, that's why when you go to sleep there's always the sensation that you're wasting time. In a European city you live 18 hours a day whilst here in New York 24 hours are never enough, it's like being pumped up on vitamins." Among the New Yorkers that he admires there's Rudy Giuliani, "the mayor who turned the city inside out like a sock with a determination that would be nice to witness in our politicians," then there's Rabbi Arthur Schneier from the Park East Synagogue "because if you want to meet the President of the United States he's the one who can arrange it," and Ivanka Trump, the daughter of billionaire Donald, married to the editor Jared Kushner, whom he describes as "beautiful but fierce, an expert at what she does." His first memory of New York, where both his father Alain and his brother John were born too, is of "when I was very young, I thought the city was gigantic and I always wanted to go there." Today he can say "that it gave me so much, it allowed me to open my eyes to the good as well as the bad, because it can offer you the best and the worst of the world, the best professors in the world, but if you're in a destructive phase of your life, it offers you prostitution and drugs in such quantities that they can kill you." Lapo chose to come to New York after rehab; at that time he lived near Times Square and used to go to the Bar Pitti.

The experiences he has had in the various different "villages of New York," lead him to define himself as "curious about what happens on the streets of the metropolis," a *street dog* who managed to free himself of his "Franco-Italian bourgeois side that tends to make you cling to your habits." And when he's in New York he admits that he feels "the pride of being Italian," he speaks about a

"strong patriotism that comes from within" and he is always thinking up new products for Italia Independent, the brand that began
with a pair of sunglasses that now has more than four hundred
creations and hopes to break into the Brazilian and Asian markets.

The models' guru

Outside his loft on Gramercy Park he has a silver-plated copy of
the Wall Street bull, inside he has the De Chirico paintings that he
grew up with, a digital TV of unusually large dimensions dominates the salon and dozens of photos of Bill Clinton (whom he calls
"my president") cover an entire corner. Paolo Zampolli, born in Milan in 1970, is the most read about Italian in Manhattan on *Page Six*,
the gossip page of the "New York Post" that is circulated all over
America, with articles about his parties on the exclusive city *roofs*,
of birthdays celebrated at the Provocateur, and mostly about his
ability to manage hundreds of the most sought after models in New
York. He earned the title of "modeling guru" in this sector when
he opened the ID Models agency in 1997 managing 1,200 models
throughout the world. "Models need to travel around the world,
they are not bound to one place–he says, sipping champagne, with
one eye constantly on his Blackberry–we had an office in Brazil
where we discovered the models, then we'd send them from Miami
to Berlin, Paris to Milan, always keeping about seventy of them in
New York." For years the business produced financial gains and
contacts in the world of VIPs–from Bill Clinton to the Gulf royals, to
Shimon Peres and Donald Trump–but then "the financial crisis of
2008 changed everything," and the demand for breathtaking models at big events plummeted. It was Trump who advised him to
look into the real-estate business. Zampolli, who before coming to
America in 1994 had sold toys for the family company, followed his
advice but found a formula all his own for getting into the market.
"I realized that models could become the best real-estate brokers."
And that's what he did: he chose "the ones who were most suitable
for the job," and he gave them a portfolio of houses to rent or sell
at high prices. "Being beautiful helps you sell something beautiful," Zampolli affirms, and this is how he scored big with the "pur-

chase of a mansion for 8.6 million dollars that he then resold for 10.1 million." To complete his unconventional style as a broker he put a myriad of marketing tools at the disposition of his models/ sellers: such as boats and helicopters to allow their would-be buyers "observe" apartments and mansions "from the outside." This novel business model is based on the fact that "it's to the model's advantage to try something different in life, she must think of the future when she won't be able to the parade down the catwalk every evening." It's a formula that piqued the attention of TV channels like Msnbc and the BBC, propelling Zampolli into the spotlight because he managed to carve out a cozy niche for himself in a housing market that is still struggling. "There's no doubt that there's a crisis underway and that it has been felt by all, but New York is still the capital of the world. Everybody comes here, people want to live here or stay here for a while, and I can show them some of the most beautiful and captivating properties around," he confirms, specifying that his portfolio depends a lot on the Saudi royal family, first among them being the Abd El-Aziz family, descendants of the founder of the Wahhabi Empire.

Married to Amanda Ungaro whom he describes as the "last of the eight women with whom I've had a bond," Zampolli became a father in 2010, he travels around New York in a Rolls Royce and, whenever he can, goes to dinner at his friend Giuseppe Cipriani's place on West Broadway, the restaurant with little yellow curtains that has a dimly lit club on the second floor frequented by models. In his opinion the city is "always expanding," and he points out the trendiest areas, both for their night life and real-estate, in "West Chelsea, an extension of the Meatpacking District, the Lower East Side and Williamsburg in Brooklyn." For those who ask him to describe himself, he answers by saying: "I'm a warrior who's chasing the dream of playing a part in the creation of a better world." To explain what he means he puts his hand in his pocket and pulls out a light blue passport bearing the United Nations emblem. He got it at the United Nations Association Brazil based in São Paulo that nominated him the Ambassador at Large at the United Nations Building, and assigned him the task that he is most passionate about: "To get the Brazilian government, the energy company Petrobras and the UN to work together so that 54 African nations can produce alternative energy." The first projects that he worked on were in Angola and Mozambique. "I'm convinced that Africa is the new frontier of renewable energy," he states, explaining that "the competitors that I find myself dueling with are the Chinese investors in Africa." At the UN building, he often meets another Italian who works both in real-estate and diplomacy and that's Daniele Bodini who is the permanent representative of San Marino and is considered one of the Italians in New York with the greatest financial success. "He owns 2,000 apartments, he lives in a 20 million dollar house on Fifth Avenue, and spends his weekends with the UN Secretary General. He has made it, whilst I'm just starting out, but, having him as a model to follow is thrilling and stimulating," he states. But there's also the negative example of Raffaello Follieri: he's the young entrepreneur from San Giovanni Rotondo who was sentenced to four and a half years in prison for fraud. "I told him he was doing everything wrong, especially with the overly-extravagant gifts that he was giving to his fiancée and the much too frequent trips on private jets, but he wouldn't listen to me, even when I told him that the FBI was looking to arrest him," he says, bemoaning the fact that "people like him ruin the image of Italians in New York."

The paparazzo from Harlem

There is little love lost between Italians and African Americans in New York. Memories of the riots between racial gangs in Brooklyn and in the Bronx remain, economic tensions between different social classes with opposing political views persist, and there's enduring prejudice–like when some Italians use the derogative term *mulignan* (eggplant) to describe black people that, in return, provokes responses peppered with insults that are just as racist. That's why Gilberto Petrucci's gamble was so unlikely. He's a Roman from Trastevere who was born in 1939, and he opened three Italian restaurants in Harlem, together with his wife Amie of Ethiopian origins, a capable manager who succeeded in convincing the most African-American neighborhood in New York to support a Made in Italy investment. The Gran Piatto d'Oro is at 1429 Fifth Avenue, between 116th and 117th Streets, right in the center of Harlem, and Petrucci is convinced that "the future of New York is here, near the streets named after Martin Luther King and Malcolm X" because "the quality of life is improving, people of every race and origin are coming to live here, there is a great sense of religiosity, the value of the real estate is rising, consumers are spending more than before, and issues related to crime are now behind us."

Gilberto and Amie made the Gran Piatto d'Oro, and their other two nearby restaurants, a meeting place between Italian traditions and the African American community. In their establishments they host events by the neighborhood Rotary clubs, gospel choirs and musicals that celebrate the fight against racial segregation, as in the case of the first African American millionaire Sarah Breedlove. They offer dishes that range from "chicken Sophia Loren," filled with mozzarella and prosciutto, to the "racket," a breaded bone-in cutlet served with tomatoes and arugula.

It is the same cuisine that Petrucci served to his customers at Il Bocconcino until 2002, the restaurant at 168 Sullivan Street that opened in 1980, the year after he came to New York, when he decided to leave Italy and the paparazzo profession that he had helped create. "My first shot was in 1959 at Meo Patacca, that immortalized Princess Soraya and Raimondo Orsini"–he recalls–"I was one of the photographers up front, then we met Federico Fellini in Via Veneto and he chose to depict us in the movie Dolce Vita by the photographer character named Paparazzo, and that's how our profession got its name." Wearing a blue neckerchief under his light-blue shirt, a golden ring, a well-trimmed moustache and with a strong Roman accent, Petrucci recalls those years as "an era when being a photographer meant quality and creativity," unable to conceal the disdain that he holds for "the paparazzi of today, who almost drive over the celebrities that they are after, endangering their lives, not to mention paparazzi like Fabrizio Corona, a real crook who shoots photos just to blackmail people." He defines Rino Barillari as "my disciple" and still has an unbreakable bond with the Eternal City, pursuing the project of "performing a roman chariot race in the Circus Maximus." He spoke about it in person for the first time with Charlton Heston just a few months after the release of the movie Ben Hur in 1959. "I envision it just like a great Capitoline derby, where the 24 districts of Rome each have their own chariot and millions of tourists come from all over the world each year to watch an epic display capable of reviving the splendor of Imperial Rome." It is a dream that brings a sparkle to his eye and he confirms that he "has spoken about it with every single mayor over the last years, with no success." He believes in it because "foreign capital could come pouring in and that could support my city that urgently needs investments to help it rise again." Now over seventy years of age, the ex-paparazzo of Via Veneto, a restaurateur in Harlem, says that "he lives looking towards the future, with a passion for the impossible challenges he has to face." But in his memory there are also tales of the past marked by experiences of New York that have never been expressed. For example, the opening of Il Bocconcino was possible because of the creation of a small partnership with another two people. One of them was "Elena the Greek," wife of Vincent Gigante's ("The Chin") right hand man who took the place of Anthony Salerno as a leader of the Genovese clan in 1981 and became one of the most ferocious bosses in the history of the New York mafia. The failed attempt to murder his rival, the Gambino boss John Gotti, was also attributed to him in 1986. When he speaks about Gigante, Petrucci rubs his chin with a gesture that still evokes the fear of the boss who asserted himself among the members of the Genovese clan and controlled Greenwich Village where Il Bocconcino was located. "The Genovese clan had their club on Sullivan Street," Petrucci recounts, "and their boys used to come eat at our place, Gigante would stop by in the morning to order ten or twenty steaks, specifying that the steaks had to be very thick and juicy because his boys needed a lot of energy to fuel their bodies." One time at dinner, members of the Gambino crime family came and took a table not far from where members of the Genovese clan were sitting. "I was in Rome, Elena called me in a panic, she feared for the worst," Petrucci recounts, "so I told her to keep an eye on them, to let them eat and to update me every five minutes, that's what she did and everything went smoothly. Luckily nobody made a move that sparked a catastrophe." It was the same restaurant that the Hollywood stars he had photographed in Rome frequented: from Barbara Streisand to Sophia Loren and Frank Sinatra. "They came to me because they knew me, or they came by chance and I reminded them of where we had seen each other," he says, showing palpable satisfaction for having been able to trace a direct line between Dolce Vita and his table in the Village. Giulio Andreotti was among his most regular customers, "he always stopped by on the last day of his official trips, often with his wife," but he is careful to add that "he never met with the Genovese clan or other people of that caliber." Antonio Di Pietro instead "used to come eat at our place during the time of Mani Pulite" (the political corruption investigations.) His experience puts him in a position to talk with a certain level of confidence about "New York by night" that, according to him, at the beginning of the XXI century is divided between "places where you eat well and places where there's too much cocaine available." He talks about it sitting at a table with one of his most loyal customers, Bob Guccione Jr, son of the founder of Penthouse magazine who has the same name, who wishes to add: "There are two 'New Yorks by night' that live parallel to one another, one is ephemeral and revolves around the trendiest spots that have an average lifespan of three months and that owe their success to the beautiful women who frequent them, whilst the other is long-standing, constant, founded on the quality of the food that it offers and of the people who go there. They are two different cities, one is fast and the other stands still, that make New York unique, night after night." The ex-paparazzo who came to Harlem feels like he has lived both of them, though at different time in his life.

Yogi "the Great"

He speaks of his father as a man who "only knew hard work," he had expressions and ways of doings things that were borrowed "from the Old County," and he asked his children "to bring money home" to help their big family get by in St. Louis Missouri, where he was born in 1925. Lawrence Peter Berra, known as Yogi, is the champion of baseball champions. A true living legend. When he walks into any room, people always leap to their feet to give him a never ending standing ovation. It happens at the NIAF gala evenings at the Washington Hilton in the capital–where he often receives tributes, honors and awards–as well as in the stands at Giants Stadium in New York. Now over eighty five years of age, Yogi Berra preserves his determination and sarcasm, but he often needs someone to accompany him as he walks with some difficulty. As soon as he gets to the microphone, the brilliant protagonist with his Yogi-isms returns, those bitter sweet sayings with a kernel of truth that made him just as famous as playing baseball did. As in the case of "It ain't over 'til it's over" that he coined on the playing field to inspire his team that became one of the most quoted sayings by political leaders and on sports programs and Sunday morning talk shows. Or "when you come to the fork in the road, take it," to explain how difficulties should be confronted head on, without hesitation, and any choice can bring to the achievement of success. Yogi Berra has been in the Hall of Fame of the most popular sport in America since 1972 because he is one of only four players who has claimed the cherished title of Most Valuable Player of the American League three times, and he is also one of the only six coaches that have won the baseball World Series just as often with teams from the American League as with teams from the National League (the two national championships whose winners face off for the title of World Champions.) For most of his career he wore the Yankees striped shirt: as a catcher between 1946 and 1963, as a coach and manager between 1963 and 1964 and then again from 1976 to 1983. He served the Mets too (also from New York) and the Houston Astros. At the University of Montclair in New Jersey, there's a museum dedicated to his achievements in the stadiums of America. Retracing his life means going deep into the history of Italian immigration. He went to school until fifth grade, he grew up speaking English "broken" by the dialect of the Old Country and as soon as he could, he got into sports: he played soccer on the street with Italian, German and Irish kids, he snuck into gyms to learn boxing, he liked to watch hockey, he kept miles away from basketball because of his Mediterranean stature– 5'8"– and he connected with baseball at the age of fourteen when he was working with his brother Mike in a shoe factory "to bring home the all-important money that my father was always talking about." At the beginning, baseball was just another game like all the others, but then he got a passion for it, he started to leave the factory early to practice in the streets, and with Mike he found a way to train on the American

Legion Ball fields, where he started to play at sixteen. He got it into his head that when he grew up he was going to get to the World Series. Those were the days of the Great Depression, in the Berra household money was tight, and his father pushed him to continue working and this struggle with his family came to an end only at the onset of World War II. When he had just turned eighteen, he enlisted in the US Navy, stationed in the base in Norfolk Virginia, and there too he continued to exude determination. He volunteered for the Amphibious Force though he didn't know what that entailed. He quickly learned: he was put on a small fast boat built of wood and metal that was armed with twelve missiles on each side and five 50 caliber machine guns. Training was tough and when D-Day came, the navy man Berra was on one of the *rocket boats* that General Dwight Eisenhower ordered to stay "not more than three hundred meters from the beach" to hit the first German lines of defense commissioned with the task of blocking the soldiers that aimed at beginning the liberation of Europe. "We began by shooting the first missile, if it hit the target we were to shoot the others, even all at the same time," he recounts, describing war scenes "in which we were always surrounded by smoke" under German fire.

At the end of the war he returned to St. Louis but his family was in such dire need of money that his father was now willing to stake his bets on baseball too, considering that the Yankees were willing to pay the 500 dollars a month that Berra requested. He supposedly got the nickname "Yogi" from a teammate during the interval of a game. The rest is the history of baseball after the war: five years on a team with the inseparable Joe DiMaggio, he was selected as an All Star for fifteen years, he won championships, trophies, earned honors until his last play on May 9th 1965, when he then embarked on a second career as a manager and coach. The New York world of sports teems with Italian names–from the pitcher Tommy Lasorda, to the reporter Sal Paolantonio, from the young tennis player Beatrice Capra to the basketball player Andrea Bargnani–but everyone knows that the only "Great" is Yogi.

Maps of Places

Manhattan

1: East Harlem

Ascione Pharmacy, 2268 1st Avenue and 117th Street.

Gran Piatto d'Oro, restaurant 1429 Fifth Avenue between 116th & 117th Streets.

Morrone Bakery, bakery-pastry shop, 324 Luis Munoz Marin Boulevard.

Our Lady of Mount Carmel, church, 448 Luis Munoz Marin Boulevard.

Patsy's Pizzeria, trattoria-pizzeria, 2287 1st Avenue and 118th Street

Rao's, restaurant, 455 East 114th Street and Pleasant Avenue.

Rex's, ice-cream parlor, 1st Avenue and 118th Street.

2. Upper East Side

Antica Bottega del Vino, restaurant, cafe, wine store, 5 East 59th Street.

Antonucci Cafe, restaurant, 170 East 81st Street.

Bella Blu, restaurant, 967 Lexington Avenue and 70th Street.

Columbus Citizens Foundation, cultural center, 8 East 69th Street.

Felice Wine Bar, restaurant, 1166 1st Avenue and 64th Street.

Felidia, restaurant, 243 East 58th Street.

Gagosian Gallery, art gallery, 980 Madison Avenue between 76th & 77th Streets.

Le Cirque, restaurant, 151 East 58th Street.

Sant Ambroeus, cafe and restaurant, 1000 Madison Avenue and 79th Street.

Via Quadronno, restaurant, cafe, 25 East 73rd Street between Madison & 5th Avenue.

3. UpperWest Side

Café Lab, 201 West 83rd Street.

Café Luxemburg, 200 West 70th Street.

Citarella, grocery store -deli, 2 1 3 5 Broadway and 75th Street.

Grom, ice-cream parlor, 2165 Broadway and 76th Street.

New Pizza Town, pizzeria, 2196 Broadway and 78th Street (Verdi Square).

Salumeria Rosi Parmacotto, deli-snack bar, 283 Amsterdam Avenue (Verdi Square).

4. Midtown

Casa Lever, restaurant, 390 Park Avenue.

De Gustibus Cooking School at Macy's,

226

cooking school and food tasting,
151 West 34th Street.
Giorgio Armani, restaurant, 717 5th
Avenue.
Marea, restaurant, 240 Central Park
South (Columbus Circle).

5. Sutton Place
Teodora, restaurant, 141 East 57th
Street.

6. Theater District
Barbetta, restaurant, 32 1 West 46th
Street.
Becco, restaurant, 355 West 46th
Street.
John D. Calandra Italian American
Institute, City University of New
York, conferences, lectures, library,
25 West 43rd Street.
Esca, 402 West 43rd Street.
Rockefeller Foundation, cultural
center, conference center, 420 5th
Avenue.
Scarpetta, restaurant, 355 West 14th
Street and 9th Avenue.

7. Flatiron District
230 Fifth, restaurant, lounge bar, night
club, 230 Fifth Avenue and West
26th Street, Madison Square.
Eataly, food market, restaurants, ca-
fes, pastry shops, 200 Fifth Avenue.
SD26, restaurant, wine bar & lounge,
19 East 26th Street, Madison
Square Park.

8. Meatpacking District
Boom Boom Room, The Standard
Hotel, lounge bar, 848 Washington
Street.
Del Pasto, restaurant, 85 10th Avenue.

Provocateur, café and night club, 18
9th Avenue.

9. Greenwich Village
Bar Pitti, restaurant, 268 Avenue of
the Americas.
Casa Italiana Zerilli-Marimò, New York
University, exhibits, conferences,
lectures, 24 West 12th Street.
Da Silvano, restaurant, 260 Avenue of
the Americas.
Kestè Pizza e Vino, restaurant-pizzeria,
271 Bleecker Street.
Tiro a Segno of New York, club, 77
MacDougal Street.

10. Noho
Museum of the American Gangster,
80 St Mark's Place.

11. Soho
Cipriani Downtown, 376 West Broad-
way between Spring & Broome
Streets.
Prada, high fashion boutique, 575
Broadway.
Tribeca Grand Hotel, 2 Avenue of the
Americas.

12. East Village
Albert's Hairstylist, owner Alberto
Bonanno, 201 East 16th Street.
Amato Opera Theatre, 319 Bowery.
East Village Visitors Center, guided
tours, 75 East 4th Street.
John's, restaurant, 302 East 12th
Street.

13. Little Italy
Albanese Meats & Poultry, butcher's,
238 Elizabeth Street.
Caffè Napoli, cafe, 191 Hester Street
and Mulberry Street.

Italian American Museum, 155 Mulberry Street.

Matilda, restaurant, 647 East 11th Street.

Most Precious Blood Church, (Feast of San Gennaro), 109 Mulberry Street.

14. Financial District Charging Bull, sculpture by Arturo Di Modica, Bowling Green.

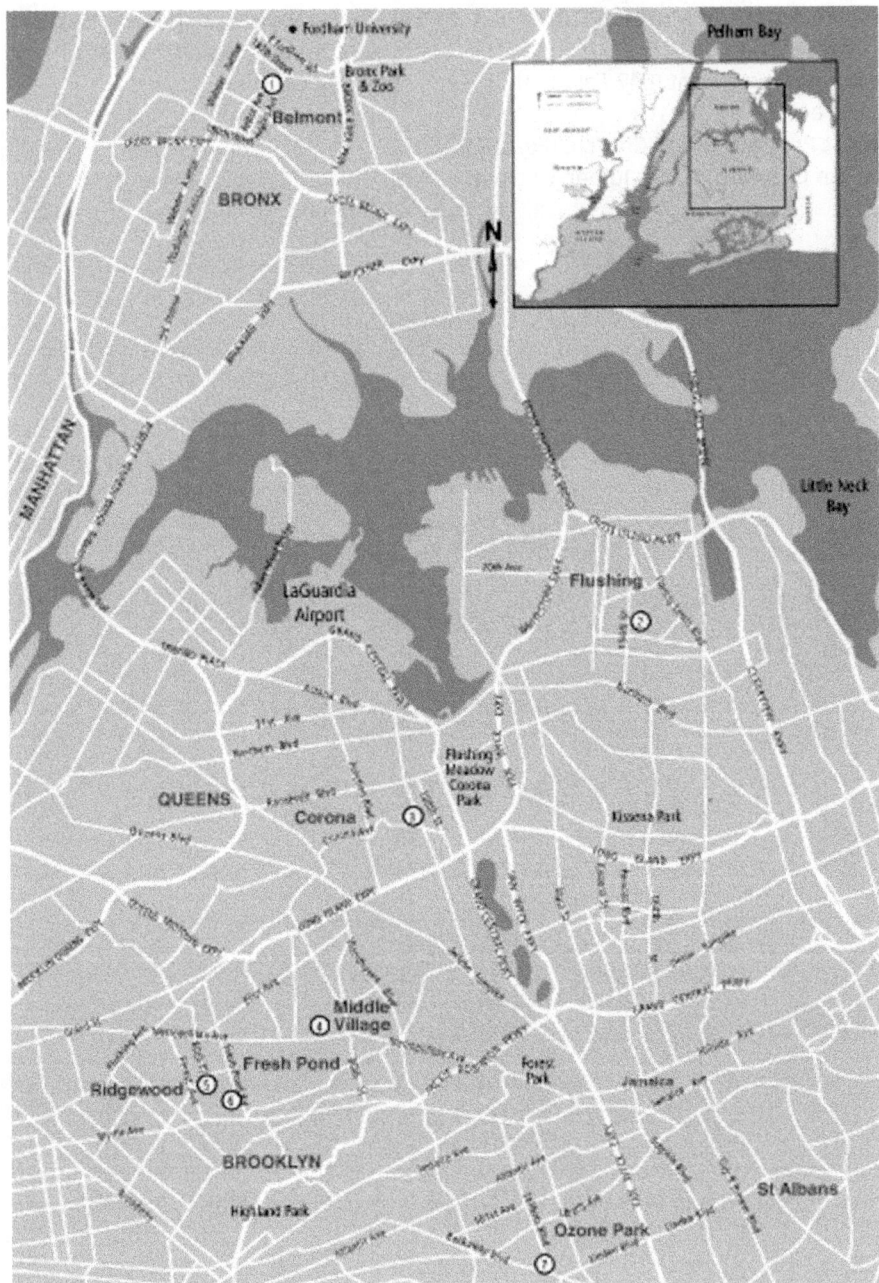

Pelham Bay

• Fordham University

Bronx Park
& Zoo

① Belmont

BRONX

N

Little Neck
Bay

MANHATTAN

LaGuardia
Airport

Flushing

②

71st Ave.

Northern Blvd.

QUEENS

Corona

③

Flushing
Meadow
Corona
Park

Kissena Park

Queens Blvd.

Middle
④ Village

Fresh Pond

Forest
Park

Jamaica

Ridgewood ⑤
⑥

St Albans

BROOKLYN

Highland Park

Ozone Park

⑦

Bronx and Queens

1. Belmont
Addeo Bakery, 2372 Hughes Avenue.
Biancardi's, butcher's, 2350 Arthur
Avenue.
Borgatti's Ravioli & Egg Noodles, 632
East 187th Street.
Casa della Mozzarella, 604 East 187th
Street.
Cosenza's Fish Market, 2354 Arthur
Avenue.
Cuba Cigar, cigars and tobacco, 2384
Hughes Avenue.
El Sureño, snack bar, 2319 Hughes
Avenue.
Gurra Café, restaurant, 2325 Arthur
Avenue.
La Casita Poblana, restaurant, 620 East
186th Street.
Madonia Brothers Bakery, bakery and
pastry shop, 2318 Arthur Avenue.
Mario's, restaurant, 2342 Arthur
Avenue.
Mexico Sports Center, clothing and
sporting goods, 608 Crescent Av-
enue.
Our Lady of Mount Carmel Church,
627 East 187th Street.
Our Saviour's Church, 2317 Washing-
ton Avenue.
Randazzo's Seafood, fish market, 2327
Arthur Avenue.
Retail Market, supermarket and pastry
shop, 2344 Arthur Avenue.

Teitel Brothers, grocery store and deli,
2372 Arthur Avenue.
Zero Otto Nove, trattoria-pizzeria,
2357 Arthur Avenue.

2. Flushìng
St Mel's Church, 2820 154th Street.

3. Corona
The Lemon Ice King of Corona, ice-
cream parlor, 5202 108th Street.
Parkside, restaurant, 107-01 Corona
Avenue.

4. Middle Village
Colombo's, fruit and vegetable market, 7549 Metropolitan Avenue.

5. Ridgewood
L'Aroma del Caffè, cafe, 2235 Greene
Avenue and Forest Avenue.
Our Lady of the Miraculous Medal
Church, 6281 60th Place and
Bleecker Street.

6. Fresh Pond
Valentino's, fruit, vegetables, deli ,and
snack bar, 6664 Fresh Pond Road.

7. Ozone Park
Don Peppe, restaurant, 135-58 Lefferts Boulevard.

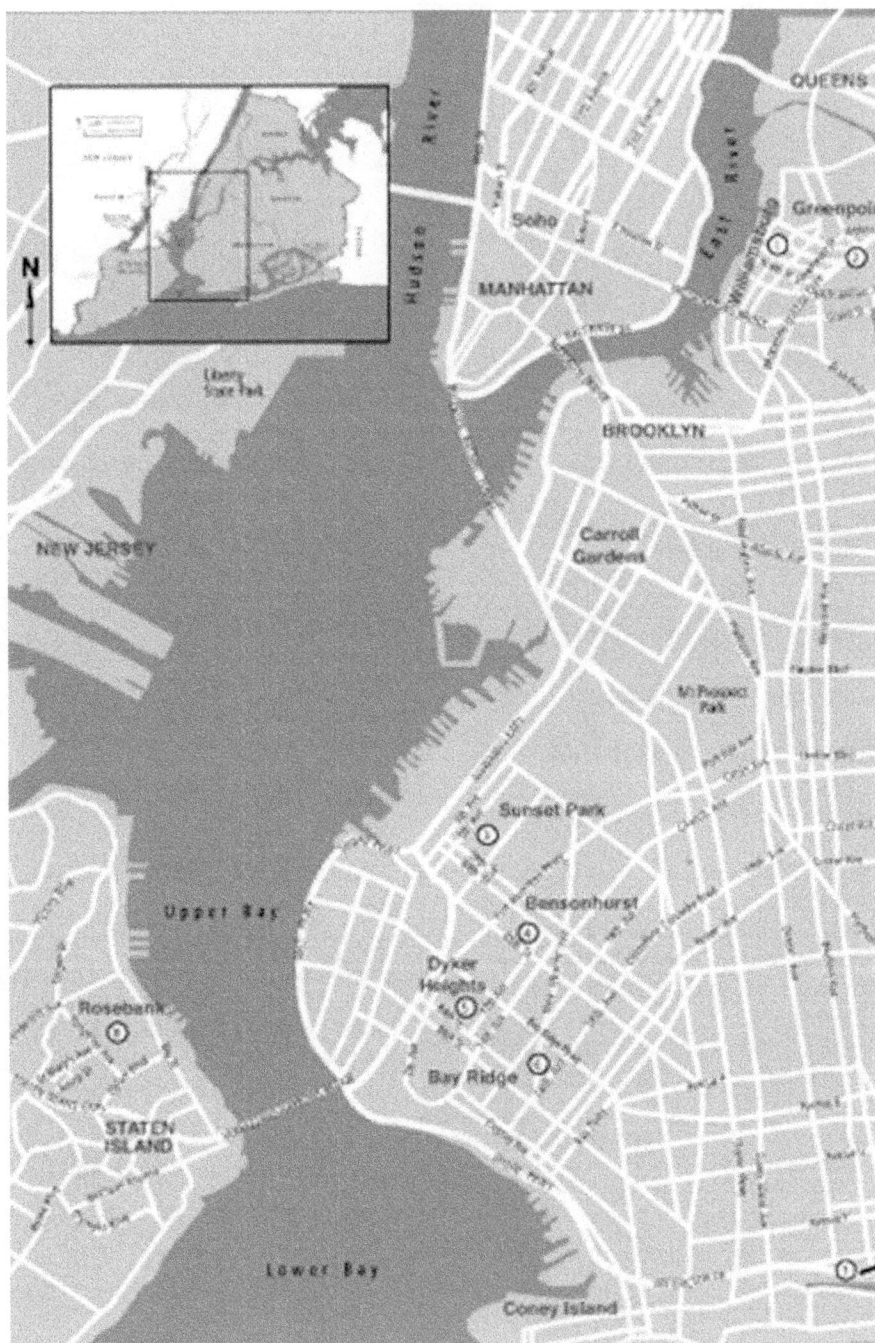

Brooklyn and Staten Island

1. Williamsburg
Bamonte's, restaurant, 32 Withers
  Street.
Our Lady of Mount Carmel Church,
  (Dance of the Giglio), North 8th
  Street and Havemeyer Street.

2. Greenpoint
Fortunato Bros, 289 Manhattan
  Avenue.

3. Sunset Park
Johnny's Pizza, pizzeria, 5806 5th
  Avenue.
Our Lady of Perpetual Help, 526 59th
  Street.
Papa John's Pizza, pizzeria, 5804 5th
  Avenue.
Scotti's Pizza, pizzeria, 5616 5th
  Avenue.

4. Bensonhurst
St Rosalia-Regina Pacis Church, 1230
  65th Street.

5. Dyker Heights
Toyland, neighborhood that's famous
  for its Christmas decorations, 12th
  Avenue/84th Street.

6. Bay Ridge
Caffè Italia, cafe, 6921 18th Avenue
  (Cristoforo Colombo Boulevard).

7. Massapequa
Café Gondola, cafe, 917 N. Broadway
  (not on the map).

8. Rosebank
Garibaldi-Meucci Memorial Museum,
  museum within Antonio Meucci's
  candle factory displaying items
  belonging to the inventor and his
  guest Giuseppe Garibaldi, 420
  Tompkins Avenue.
Grotto of Our Lady of Mount Carmel,
  36 Amity Street.
St Joseph's Church, 171 Saint Mary's
  Avenue.
St Mary's Church, 1101 Bay Street.

Lists of Places and Names

Places of Origin of the Italians of New York

Places of birth, work, or study, or the places of family origin (parents, grandparents etc.) of the people cited in the book.

Agrigento: Maria Bartiromo ("Money Honey"), financial journalist and TV host.

Alba (Cuneo): Oscar Farinetti, entrepreneur.

Alcamo (Trapani): Stella, cook.

Amalfi (Salerno): Nicholas Scoppetta, Assistant District Attorney and ex-Fire Commissioner.

Avellino: Nicholas DiMarzio, Bishop of the Dioceses of Brooklyn-Queens.

Balestrate (Palermo): Antonino Colombo, greengrocer.

Bari: settlement in East Harlem.

Caccamo (Palermo): Joseph Scelsa, academic; Carlo Gambino, mafia boss.

Campobasso: Nicholas DiMarzio, Bishop of the Dioceses of Brooklyn-Queens.

Casale Monferrato (Alessandria): George Pavia, lawyer.

Castellamare del Golfo (Trapani): Francesco Aluzzo, cafe owner;

Santino Battiata, restaurant owner; Carlo Gambino, mafia boss; Gaetano Messina, traffic control officer for Alitalia.

Castelvetrano (Trapani): Joe Bonura, cafe owner.

Catania: Salvo Arena, lawyer.

Corleone: Ronald Marino, priest, vicar of migrants.

Cosenza: Alberto Bonanno, barber.

Cropani (Catanzaro): Gabriella Basile, Italian Studies student at Rutgers University.

Cuneo: Celestino Migliore, Archbishop.

Enemonzo (Udine): Giandomenico (Gianni) Picco, UN official.

Enna: Ronald Marino, priest, vicar of migrants.

Este (Padova): Gaetano Pesce, architect and designer.

Faeto (Foggia): Anthony Julian Tamburri, director of John D. Calandra Italian American Institute.

Fasano (Brindisi): Eugene Nardelli,

New York Court of Appeals Judge.

Firenze: Arturo Di Modica, sculptor; Gaetano Pesce, architect and designer.

Genova George Pavia, lawyer, owner of a law firm; Nicola Arena, capitain, top manager; Massimo Porrati, physicist, university professor; Renzo Piano, architect.

Godrano (Palermo): Vincent Barbacci, ice-cream parlor owner.

L'Aquila: Mario Fratti, playwright, theater professor.

La Spezia: Gaetano Pesce, architect and designer.

Latina: Francesca, undocumented waitress in Manhattan.

Lercara Friddi (Palermo): Charles «Lucky» Luciano (Salvatore Lucania), mafia boss.

Lucca: Edmund Giambastiani, («Admiral G»), Admiral, Vice Chairman of the Joint Chiefs of Staff; Cesare Casella, restaurant owner, owner of a grocery store-deli.

Maida (Catanzaro): Gay Talese, writer.

Melfi (Potenza): George Grasso Jr, First Deputy Commissioner del Dipartimento di polizia.

Merì (Messina): Matilda Raffa Cuomo, charity organization benefactor, wife of Mario e mother of Andrew.

Messina: Antonio Ciappina, journalist; Nicola Arena, captain, top manager; Kym Ragusa, writer and director of documentaries and short films.

Milano: Mariuccia Soncini Zerilli-Marimò, baroness, founder of the Casa Italiana at New York University; Federico Mennella, top manager; Alberto Cribiore, financier and top manager; Silvia Formenti, chair of the Department of Radiation Oncology at the Langone Medical Center at New York University; Alberto Veronesi, orchestra director; Matteo Pericoli, architect, illustrator and author; Paolo Zampoffi, entrepreneur and real-estate broker.

Minori (Salerno): Anthony (Tony) Amato, tenor, singing teacher, theater manager/director.

Montemarciano (Ancona): Edmund Giambastiani, («Admiral G»), Admiral, Vice Chairman of the Joint Chiefs of Staff.

Napoli: Nicholas Scoppetta, Assistant District Attorney and ex-Fire Commissioner; Salvatore De Cicco, store owner; Ciro Silvestri, restaurant owner; Maria Bartiromo, («Money Honey»), financial journalist and TV host; Charles Gasparino, financial journalist and TV host; Federico Mennella, top manager; Kristin Piro, dancer.

Nocera Superiore (Salerno): Mario Cuomo, New York State Governor.

Noci (Bari): Peter Pace, General, Head of the Joint Chiefs of Staff.

Nola (Napoli): Philip (Felice) Manna, entertainer at the Giglio Feast at the Church of Our Lady of Mount Carmel, Brooklyn.

Noto (Siracusa): Lucio Noto, top manager and entrepreneur.

Padova: Antonio Scarpa, doctor, director of the Center for Scientific Review; Gaetano Pesce, architect and designer.

Palermo: Alessandro Fava, grocery store clerk; Vanessa Van Vranken, dancer.

Parma: Giovanni Lanzarotti, chef in a private club.

Partanna (Trapani): Tony Mulè, entertainer for the Italian community in Fresh Pond, Queens.

Pino Torinese (Torino): Alberto Cribiore, financier and top manager.

Pisa: Massimo Porrati, physicist, university professor.

Pola (oggi Pula, Croazia): Linda Matticchio Bastianich, restaurant owner, author of bestselling cookbooks, TV show host.

Polizzi Generosa (Palermo): Moe Albanese, butcher.

Polla (Salerno): settlement in East Harlem.

Prato: Gherardo Guarducci, entrepreneur in the food industry.

Raito (Vietri sul Mare, Salerno): Giovanni Porcelli, retired police sergeant, President of the Columbus Association.

Regalbuto (Enna): Vito Spampinato, retiree, parishioner of Our Lady of the Miraculous Medal, in Queens.

Roma: Silvio Palumbo, financial consultent; Umberto Piperno, rabbi; Gilberto Petrucci, ex-photographer, restaurant owner.

Salerno: Roberto Paciullo, restaurant owner; Nicholas DiMarzio, Bishop of the Dioceses of Brooklyn-Queens.

San Giovanni Rotonda (Foggia): Raffaello Follieri, real-estate broker.

Santa Croce di Magliano (Campobasso): Carl Paladino, businessman, politician.

Santa Margherita di Belice (Agrigento): Filippo Barone, store owner.

Sarno (Salerno): Raymond Odierno, General, Commander of the US Army Joint Forces Command; settlement in East Harlem.

Saviano (Napoli): Fortunato brothers, owners of a pastry shop in Brooklyn.

Senigallia (Ancona): Peter Madonia Jr. manager of the Rockefeller Foundation.

Settefrati (Frosinone): Anthony Julian Tamburri, director of the John D. Calandra Italian American Institute.

Torino: Valentina Castellani, director of a Contemporary Art gallery.

Torre del Greco (Napoli): Franco Zerlenga, americanist.

Torretta (Palermo): Cecilia, elderly resident of the Belmont neighborhood in the Bronx; Battista

Caruso, parishioner of Our Lady of the Miraculous Medal, in Queens.

Tramonti (Salerno): Mario Cuomo, New York State Governor.

Tregiovo in Val di Non (Trento): Fabio Flaim, deacon in the parish of Our Lady of the Miraculous Medal, in Queens.

Trento: Al (Italo) Barozzi, missionary priest, parochial vicar at the Church of St. Mel, in Queens.

Trieste: Umberto Piperno, rabbi.

Velletri (Roma): Antonio Monda, journalist, director, cinema critic and historian, university professor.

Venezia: Antonio Scarpa, doctor, director of the Center for Scientific Review; Gaetano Pesce, architect and designer.

Vittoria (Ragusa): Arturo Di Modica, sculptor.

List of Names

Abd El-Aziz, founder of Wahhabi Kingdom.

Addeo, bakery owners.

Agnelli, Gianni (Giovanni), lawyer, entrepreneur.

Ahem, Nan, editor, wife of Gay Talese.

Ahmadinejad, Mahmud, President of Islamic Republic of Iran.

Albanese, Mary, wife of Vincenzo and mother of Moe.

Albanese, Moe, butcher.

Albanese, Vincenzo, father of Moe.

Albertini, Stefano, director of Casa Italiana Zerilli-Marimò.

Allen, Woody (Allan Stewart Königsberg), director, screen-writer and movie actor.

Aluzzo, Francesco, bar owner.

Amato, Anthony (Tony), tenor, singing teacher and theater man-ager- director.

Amato, Giuliano, Prime Minister and political leader.

Amato, Sally, soprano, wife of Anthony.

Amelio, Gil (Gilbert Frank), com-puter expert, top manager.

Amoroso, police officer who died on 9/11, 2001.

Amoroso, Alex, Italian Studies student at Rutgers University.

Andreotti, Giulio, Prime Minister and political leader.

Andreotti, Lamberto, top manager.

Andretti, Mario, racecar driver.

Andropov, Jurij, Soviet President.

Antonelli, Paola, designer and architect, curator at MoMA.

Antonini, Maurizio, diplomat, XVI.

Aponte, Gianluigi, entrepreneur and shipping company founder.

Aquaro, Vincenzo, UN official, 111.

Arbore, Renzo, showman, singer, musician.

Arcuri, Michael (Mike), politician.

Arena, Nicola, capitan, top man-ager.

Arena, Salvo, lawyer.

Armani, Giorgio, designer and entrepreneur.

Auriana, Lawrence, top manager.

Biancardi, butchers.

Bissett, Cynthia, mother of Lady Gaga.

Bivona, Graziella, radio show host, political activist.

Bizzi, real-estate investors.

Blobel, Günter, Nobel Prize winner for Medicine.

Bloomberg, Michael, New York Mayor.

Bocelli, Andrea, singer.

Bodini, Daniele, realestate agent.

Bonami, Francesco, art critic and curator.

Bonanno, mafia clan.

Bonanno, Alberto, barber.

Bondi, Sandro, politician.

Bongiovanni, Angelo, manager.

Bonolis, Paolo, TV host.

Bonura, Joe, cafe owner.

Bonura, Rita, Office Manager for Fiat Finance North America.

Borgatti, family of pasta makers.

Bossi, Umberto, political leader.

Botte. John, police officer.

Brademas, John, President of New York University.

Brecht, Bertolt (Eugen Berthold), dramatist, theater director and poet.

Breedlove, Sarah, entrepreneur.

Brežnev, Leonid, Soviet President.

Bruni, Frank, journalist, food critic.

Bucchino, Gino, politician.

Burke, Adrian, judge.

Burri, Alberto, painter and sculptor.

Bush, George H.W., President of the United States.

Bush, George W, President of the United States.

Calabresi, Guido, lawyer, university professor.

Calandra, John D., politician.

Calatrava, Santiago, architect.

Calcaterra, Regina, lawyer and politician.

Caltagirone, Gaetano, building contractor.

Calvelli, John, former assistant to the parliamentarian Eliot Engel.

Cameron, James, director, screenwriter e producer.

Campese, Gino, pizzeria owner.

Capeci, Jerry, blogger writer.

Capellino, Emma, maternal grandmother of Admiral Edmund Giambastiani.

Capra, Beatrice, tennis player.

Caputo, President of the Italian Wine and Food Institute.

Carciotto, Orazio, grocery store owner.

Carfagna. Mara, politician.

Caruso, Battista, parishioner of Our Lady of the Miraculous Medal.

Caruso, Enrico, tenor.

Cascio Ferro, Vito, mafia boss.

Casella, Cesare, restaurant owner, owner of grocery store/deli.

Casini, Pierferdinando, political leader.

Castellani, Valentina, director of a Contemporary Art gallery.

Castro, Gregorio, store owner.

Cattelan, Maurizio, artis.

Cavalli, Roberto, designer.

Cecchi, Emilio, writer.

Cecilia, elderly resident of the Belmont neighborhood in the Bronx.

Celant, Germano, art critic and theorist.

Chernenko, Konstantin, Soviet President.

Cuomo, Immacolata, wife of Andrea and mother of Mario.

Cuomo, Mario, Governor of the State of New York.

Cuomo Raffa, Matilda, charity organization benefactor, wife of Mario e mother of Andrew.

D'Alema, Massimo, political leader.

D'Alessio. Gigi (Luigi), singer.

Dalia, Gaspare, parish priest.

Dalí Domenech, Salvador, painter and sculptor.

D'Allara, police officer who died on 9/11, 2001.

D'Amato, Al (Alfonse Marcello), lawyer and politician.

D'Angelo, Nino (Gaetano), singer.

Daniele, Pino, singer and composer.

Dante Alighieri, poet and writer.

Dava, singer.

D'Avanzo, Leo, brother-in-law of Harold Angelo Giuliani and uncle of Rudolph Giuliani.

De Benedetti, Carlo, entrepreneur.

de Blasio, Bill (William), Public Advocate.

De Chirico, Giorgio, painter.

DeChristopher, Dave (David), playwright.

De Cicco, Salvatore, store owner.

de Cuéllar Pérez, Javier, UN Secretary General.

De Kooning, Willem, painter and sculptor.

De Laurentiis, Dino (Agostino), film producer.

DeLillo, Don (Donald Richard), writer.

della Puppa, Paolo, restaurant owner.

Del Piero, Alessandro, soccer player.

Del Vecchio. Industrial company.

De Mistura, Staffan, UN official.

De Mita, Ciriaco, Prime Minister and political leader.

de Niro, Robert, actor, director and producer.

DeSapio, Carmine Gerard, politician.

de Tomassi, Furio, President of the Union of Italian functionaries in international organizations.

DiCaprio, Leonardo, actor, film producer.

Dickens, Charles, writer.

DiLeonardo, Satei, Italian Studies student at Rutgers University.

DiMaggio, Joseph (Joe), baseball player.

DiMarzio, Nicholas, Bishop of the Dioceses of Brooklyn-Queens.

Di Modica, Arturo, sculptor.

DiNapoli, Thomas, State Comptroller.

Dinkins, David, Mayor of New York.

Di Piazza, Tony (Antonio), Vice-president of Comites in New York and Connecticut.

Di Pietro, Antonio, political leader.

Disney Walt, illustrator, comic book author, entertainer, producer of animated films.

Dobbs, Lou, TV host and journalist.

Domingo, Placido, tenor.

Dreshaj, Leonel, Albanian-American entrepreneur.

Dreshaj, Nusha, Kosovo refugee, mother of Leonel.

Drina, store owner from Tirana.

Dubilier, Martin, financier.

Dukakis, Michael, politician.
Einaudi, Giorgio, physicist.
Einstein, Albert, physicist, scientist and thinker.
Elena, known as «the Greek», wife of a gangster.
Elkann, Alain, writer and journalist.
Elkann, John, entrepreneur.
Elkann, Lapo, entrepreneur.
Engel, Eliot, politician.
Englander, Nathan, writer.
Esfandiyari Bakhtiyari, Soraya, Princess.

Fabrizio, Maria, wife of Angelo Grasso and grandmother of George Grasso.
Facchinetti, Alessandra, designer.
Fahd bin Abd El-Aziz al Saud, King of Saudi Arabia.
Faisal Saud Al, Foreign Minister of Saudi Arabia.
Falcone, Giovanni, judge.
Fallaci, Oriana, journalist and writer.
Farinaro, Guido, US Marine who died in Vietnam.
Farinetti, Oscar, entrepreneur.
Fatucci, Don, character in the film The Godfather.
Fauci, Anthony, immunologist.
Fava, Alessandro, grocery store clerk.
Favilli, Giuseppe, diplomay.
Federici, Anthony, restaurant owner.
Fellini, Federico, director and screenwriter.
Fermi, Enrico, physicist, scientist and university professor.
Ferrara, Ciro, soccer player and coach.

Ferrara, Eric, university professor.
Ferrara, Sergio, physicist and university professor.
Ferraro, Geraldine, lawyer and politician.
Ferretti, Dante, designer.
Fiano, Andrea, financial journalist.
Fiano, Edo, Auschwitz survivor, father of Andrea.
Filangieri, Gaetano, Enlightenment philosopher.
Fini, Gianfranco, political leader.
Fiorina, Carly, top manager.
Flaim, Fabio, deacon in the parish of Our Lady of the Miraculous Medal, in Queens.
Fleming, Renée, soprano.
Foley, congressman.
Follieri, Raffaello, real estate agent.
Fontana, Lucio, painter.
Ford, Gerald, President of the United States.
Ford, Tom (Thomas Carlyle), designer.
Formenti, Silvia, chair of the Department of Radiation Oncology at the Langone Medical Center at New York University.
Formigoni, Roberto, politician.
Fortunato, Mario, builder.
Fortunato, Michele, pastry chef.
Fortunato, Salvatore, tailor.
Foster, Norman, architect.
Foxman, Abraham, National Director of the Anti-Defamation League.
Francesca, undocumented waitress in Manhattan.
Franklin, Benjamin, thinker and politician.
Franzen, Jonathan, writer.
Fratti, Mario, playwright, theater professor.

Langone, police officer who died on 9/11, 2001.
Langone, Kenneth, entrepreneur.
Lansky, Meyer, gangster.
Lanzarotti, Giovanni, chef at a private club.
La Russa, Ignazio, politician.
Lasorda, Tommy (Thomas Charles), baseball player.
La Spina, Gabriella, Italian Studies student Rutgers University.
Lattanzi, Riccardo, electrical engineer, researcher.
Laurino, Maria, writer.
La Villa, Marco, director of documentaries and short films.
LaVilla, Mauro, director of documentaries and short films.
Lazio, Rick (Enrico Anthony), lawyer and politician.
Lee, Sandra, TV host.
Lee, Spike (Shelton Jackson), director, screenwriter, actor and producer.
Leke, singer.
Lenin (Vladimir Il'ič Ul'janov), political leader and theorist.
Leonardo da Vinci. Artist and inventor.
Leone XIII (Gioacchino Pecci), Pope.
Leone, Sergio, director and screenwriter.
Lepke, Louis, gangster.
Letterman, David, TV host and producer.
Levine, Alexandra, hematologist.
Lewis, Joe, businessman and philanthropist.
Lincoln, Abraham, President of the United States.
Lindsay John, Mayor of New York.

Lippman, Jonathan, Chief Judge of the State of New York.
LoCicero, John, politician.
Lombrone, family from Toyland (Dyker Heights).
Loren, Sophia (Sofia Scicolone), actrice.
Lovati Cottini, Gianfranco, landowner.
Luciano, Charles «Lucky» (Salvatore Lucania), mafia boss.
Lupo, Ignazio, mafia boss.
Luthman, Lauren, Italian Studies student at Rutgers University.
Lynch, David, director, screenwriter and producer.

Macchiarola, Frank, politician.
Maccioni, Sirio, restuarant owner and entrepreneur.
MacMahon, Lloyd, judge.
Madonia, family of bakers.
Madonia, Benedetto, mafioso.
Madonia, Josephine, wife of Peter Sr and mother of Peter Jr.
Madonia, Mario, father of Peter Sr.
Madonia, Peter Jr, grandson of Mario e son of di Peter Sr, manager of the Rockefeller Foundation.
Madonia, Peter Sr, bakery owner.
Madonna (Louise Veronica Ciccone), singer and showgirl.
Maffei, Dan, politician.
Magnani, Marco, university professor.
Maioglio, Laura, restaurant owner.
Majakovskij, Vladimir, poet and playwright.
Malagodi, Giovanni, political leader.
Malcolm X (Malcolm Little), civil rights activist.

248

Maldini, Paolo, soccer player.
Mameli, Goffredo, patriot and poet.
Mancini-Corleone, Vincent, character in the film The Godfather.
Mandelbaum, Mien, Dante scholar.
Manero, Tony, character of the film Saturday Night Fever.
Manfredi, Nino (Saturnino), actor and director.
Manna, Philip (Felice), entertainer at the Giglio Feast at the Church of Our Lady of Mount Carmel, Brooklyn.
Mantica, Carlo, university professor.
Mantineo, Andrea, journalist and magazine editor.
Manuali, Cortado, lawyer, son-in-law of Lidia Bastianich.
Manzoni, Piero, artist.
Mao Zedong, President of the People's Republic of China.
Maranzano, Salvatore, mafia boss.
Marcantonio, Vito, politician.
Marchionne, Sergio. top manager.
Marchiori, Maurizio, top manager.
Marino, Ronald, priest, vicar of migrant.
Maroni, Roberto, politician.
Martin, Dean (Dino Paul Crocetti), singer and actor.
Massa, Eric, politician.
Masseria, Joseph («Joe the Boss»), mafia boss.
Mastella, Clemente, political leader.
Mattei, Enrico, politician and entrepreneur.
Matticchio (Motika), Erminia, mother of Lidia Bastianich.
Matticchio (Motika) Vittorio, father of Lidia Bastianich.

Maurizio, head waiter in a restaurant.
May Tony (Antonio Magliulo), restaurant owner.
Mazza, police officer who died on 9/11, 2001.
Mazzini, Giuseppe, patriot and political leader.
McCain, John, politician.
McGovern, George, politician.
MeI, saint.
Mennella, Federico, top manager.
Messina, Bianca, daughter of Gaetano.
Messina, Castrenze, father of Gaetano.
Messina, Francesca, wife of Castrenze and mother of Gaetano.
Messina, Gaetano, traffic control officer for Alitalia.
Messina, Isabella, daughter of Gaetano.
Messina, Marco, son of Gaetano.
Meucci, Antonio, scientist and inventor.
Meyer, Gerald, historian.
Michelangelo Buonarroti, painter, sculptor and architect.
Migliore, Celestino, Archbishop.
Milione, Vincenzo, university researcher.
Milito, Diego Alberto, soccer player.
Miller, Arthur, playwright.
Miniaci John Jr, son of a pizzeria owner.
Miniaci, John Sr, pizzeria owner.
Miniaci, Louie, son of a pizzeria owner.
Miriam, grandmother of Kym Ragusa.
Modugno, Domenico, singer.

Molinari, Guy, Borough President of Staten Island.
Monda, Antonio, journalist, director, cinema critic and historian, university professor.
Monda. Dante, father of Antonio.
Monda, Jacquie, wife of Antonio.
Mondale, Walter, politician.
Morandi, Gianni, cantante.
Moratti Brichetto, Letizia, politician and manager.
Morello, Giuseppe, mafia boss.
Morrone, police officer who died on 9/11, 2011.
Moses, Robert, Chairman of the Triborough Bridge and Tunnel Authority.
Mozilo, Angelo, top manager.
Muccino, Gabriele, director and screen writer.
Muggia, Franco, oncologist.
Mulè, Tony, entertainer for the Italian community in Fresh Pond, Queens.
Müller, Gerd, soccer player.
Murray, Allen, top manager.
Mussolini, Benito, political leader.

Napolitano, Giorgio, President.
Nardelli, Eugene, New York Court of Appeals Judge.
Nardelli, Robert Louis (Bob), top manager.
Nardelli, Vito, father of Eugene.
Nigro, Dan (Daniel), Firefighters Chief.
Nixon, Richard M, President of the United States.
Noto, Lucio, top manager and entrepreneur.

Obama, Barack, President of the United States.
Occhetto, Achille, political leader.
O'Connor, John, cardinal.
Odierno, Anthony, son of Raymond.
Odierno, Basilio, grandfather of Raymond.
Odierno, Raymond, General, Commander of the US Army Joint Forces Command.
Orsini, Raimondo, Prince.
Osama bin Laden, leader of Al Qaeda.

Pace, Peter, General, Head of the Joint Chiefs of Staff.
Pacino, Al (Alfredo James), actor, director and producer.
Paciullo, Roberto, restaurant owner.
Padre Pio, see Pio of Pietralcina.
Paladino, Carl, businessman and politician.
Palminteri, Chazz (Calogero Lorenzo Palminteri), actor, director, screenwriter and playwright.
Palmisano, Samuel, top manager.
Palumbo, Silvio, financial consultent.
Panariello, Giorgio, actor and TV host.
Pannella, Marco, political leader.
Paolantonio, Sal, reporter.
Parker, Sarah Jessica, actress.
Pascale, Vincenzo, Italianist and university professor.
Pataki, George, New York State Governor.
Pat, former security guard.
Patrizio, saint.
Pavarotti, Luciano, tenor.

www.ingramcontent.com/pod-product-compliance
Lightning Source LLC
Chambersburg PA
CBHW020658270326
41928CB00005B/184